Union Revitalisation in Advanced Economies

Assessing the Contribution of Union Organising

Edited by Gregor Gall
University of Hertfordshire

palgrave
macmillan

First published 2009 by
PALGRAVE MACMILLAN

Palgrave Macmillan in the UK is an imprint of Macmillan Publishers Limited,
registered in England, company number 785998, of Houndmills, Basingstoke,
Hampshire RG21 6XS.

Palgrave Macmillan in the US is a division of St Martin's Press LLC,
175 Fifth Avenue, New York, NY 10010.

Palgrave Macmillan is the global academic imprint of the above companies
and has companies and representatives throughout the world.

Palgrave® and Macmillan® are registered trademarks in the United States,
the United Kingdom, Europe and other countries.

ISBN-13: 978–0–230–20439–3   hardback

This book is printed on paper suitable for recycling and made from fully
managed and sustained forest sources. Logging, pulping and manufacturing
processes are expected to conform to the environmental regulations of the
country of origin.

A catalogue record for this book is available from the British Library.

A catalogue record for this book is available from the Library of Congress.

10   9   8   7   6   5   4   3   2   1
18 17 16 15 14 13 12 11 10 09

Transferred to Digital Printing in 2010

*Dedicated to Mark Serwotka, general secretary of
the Public and Commercial Services union – probably the
finest union leader of his generation in Britain today*

Contents

List of Tables, Insets and Chart

Notes on Contributors

Andy Danford is Professor of Employment Relations at the Centre for Employment Studies Research, University of the West of England, Bristol. His research interests centre on labour process analysis of new work organisation and trade union renewal. He is the author of *Japanese Management Techniques and British Workers*. Recent co-authored books include *Partnership and the High Performance Workplace* and *New Unions, New Workplaces*.

Ralph Darlington is Professor of Employment Relations at Salford Business School, University of Salford, and the author of *The Dynamics of Workplace Unionism* (1994), *Glorious Summer: class struggle in Britain, 1972* (2001, with Dave Lyddon) and *Syndicalism and the Transition to Communism: an international comparative analysis* (2008). He is currently writing a book on RMT organising and strike mobilisation on the national railway and London underground networks.

Simon de Turberville is a Lecturer in HRM at the University of York. He has published work on the British and Australian closed shop, organising within the NHS and the organising model. His current work explores the role of social theory in industrial relations and, with Vaughan Ellis and James Richards, the labour process within higher education.

Marc Dixon is an Assistant Professor of Sociology at Dartmouth College. He has written on social movement participation, strikes, and labour politics, some of which has appeared in the *American Journal of Sociology*, *Social Forces*, and *Social Problems*. He is currently conducting research on the timing of restrictive labour legislation following the New Deal as well as recent health care reform efforts and coverage outcomes in the American states.

Dr Jack Fiorito is J. Frank Dame Professor of Management, Florida State University and Principal Research Fellow, University of Hertfordshire. His research focuses on employee attitudes, HR policies, and labour unions. He has published numerous journal articles in, *inter alia*, the *Academy of Management Journal*, *Academy of Management Review*, *Journal of Managerial*

Issues, American Journal of Political Science, Journal of Management, Industrial Relations, British Journal of Industrial Relations, Industrial & Labor Relations Review, Journal of Labor Research, and *Labor Studies Journal.* He has also published numerous book chapters, and has co-edited two books, *The State of the Unions* (1991), and the *Sage Handbook of Industrial Relations* (2008). Jack is also the President of the Florida State University Chapter of the United Faculty of Florida, a local union of the Florida Education Association.

Gregor Gall is Research Professor of Industrial Relations and Director of the Centre for Research in Employment Studies at the University of Hertfordshire. His previous work includes two edited volumes on union organising (2003, 2006) and books on postal workers (2003), the labour movement in Scotland (2005), sex workers (2006) and finance workers (2008). He writes regular columns for the *Morning Star, Solidarity* and Guardian's *CommentisFree*. A further edited volume on union organising with Palgrave will be published in 2009.

Paul Goulter was the General Secretary of Finsec, the union for finance sector workers, in New Zealand from 1991 to 1999, General Secretary of the NZCTU from 1999–2003, Director of the ACTU Organising Centre in Sydney, Australia from 2004–2008 and has recently returned to New Zealand to take up the position of General Secretary, New Zealand Education Institute (the union for early childhood, primary teachers and support staff).

Nick McCarthy is a senior national officer with the Public and Commercial Services union (PCS), managing a department that covers 50,000 members across the justice sector of government. He has worked for PCS in this role for three years. Nick started work in 1984 at the BBC and became a lay official with the media union, Broadcasting, Entertainment and Cinematograph and Theatre Union (BECTU), before joining Association of Magisterial Officers (AMO), the union for magistrates' courts staff as Assistant General Secretary in 1996. AMO merged with PCS in 2005. Nick has an MA in industrial relations from Keele University and is studying part-time for a PhD entitled 'Union organising in a recognised environment' at Birkbeck College, University of London.

Miguel Martinez Lucio is Professor of International Human Resource Management and Comparative Industrial Relations at the Manchester Business School, University of Manchester. He works on the question of the changing nature of regulation and the emergence of new forms of regulatory identity and structures. This work includes issues related to management practices and new forms of work organisations. In terms of trade unionism he has researched the challenge unions face in terms of the changing organisational and political environments. His work has focused on the European content and he has evaluated the competing models of change and modernisation within unions. Large aspects of this work have been done in collaboration with trade unions.

Robyn May completed an MSc in Industrial Relations at the London School of Economics in 1999, and worked at its Centre for Economic Performance in 2000 on the 'Future of Unions in Modern Britain' Leverhulme programme. Robyn was Senior Research Fellow at the Industrial Relations Centre, Victoria University of Wellington, New Zealand from 2000–2004 and is now an Industrial Officer with the National Tertiary Education Union in Melbourne, Australia.

Paul Nowak took up post as the TUC's New Unionism Project Director, and subsequently National Organiser, in May 2002. He was one of the first intake of the TUC's 'Organising Academy' in 1998 – and prior to this had been an active member of unions including the GMB, Unison and Communication Workers' Union (CWU). In 2000, he was appointed Regional Secretary of the Northern TUC where he was responsible for the TUC's work in the north east of England and Cumbria. Paul currently leads on the TUC's work to support union efforts on organising and recruitment, which includes the development and delivery of the TUC Organising Academy. He also co-ordinates the TUC's 'Leading Change' training and development programme for senior union officers, and supports the TUC's work on inter-union relations.

Mike Richardson is Senior Lecturer in Industrial Relations at the Centre for Employment Studies Research, University of the West of England, Bristol. His research interests include labour history and contemporary industrial relations. He is the co-author of *Partnership and the High Performance Workplace* and *New Unions, New Workplaces*.

Joseph B. Rose is Professor of Industrial Relations at the DeGroote School of Business at McMaster University. His research has been published in numerous books and academic journals and covers such topics as construction labour relations, trade unions, public sector collective bargaining and dispute resolution. His current research examines the state of public sector unionism.

Mark Stuart is Professor of Human Resource Management and Employment Relations and Director of the Centre for Employment Relations Innovation and Change at the University of Leeds. He has researched and published extensively on employment relations modernisation and partnership, trade union innovation, restructuring and skills and the industrial relations of training. His work has been funded by the European Union and Parliament, the Economic and Social Research Council, the Dept of Business, Enterprise and Regulatory Reform, the International Labour Office, Advisory, Conciliation and Arbitration Service (ACAS), the TUC and a number of individual unions and charities. Current research projects are investigating the union-led learning agenda, trade union modernisation and worker adjustment strategies in the context of globalisation.

Stephanie Tailby is Professor of Employment Relations at the Centre for Employment Studies Research, University of the West of England, Bristol. Her research focuses on workplace partnership, disputes procedures in small firms and employment practices in European healthcare and financial services. She has published articles in a variety of industrial relations journals and is a co-author of *The Realities of Workplace Partnership*.

Martin Upchurch is Professor of International Employment Relations at Middlesex University Business School. His research interests include trade union strategies and comparative industrial relations. Recent co-authored books include *Partnership and the High Performance Workplace* and *New Unions, New Workplaces*.

1
What is to be Done with Union Organising?

Gregor Gall

Introduction

An official fringe meeting at the British Trade Union Congress (TUC) in 2008 was entitled 'Building Stronger Unions: what more can we do to grow?' The press release for the meeting, which saw platform speakers comprising senior employed union officers (EUOs) from three growing unions in Britain (National Association of Schoolmasters and Union of Women Teachers (NASUWT), Public and Commercial Services' Union (PCS) and Union of Shop, Distributive and Allied Workers (USDAW)), the TUC Organising Academy Director and the AFL-CIO Executive Vice-President, lamented that:

> Ten years on from the launch of the TUC Organising Academy, unions find themselves at a crossroads. Over the last decade membership has stabilised, and unions have signed over 3,000 new agreements with employers, but union density is still falling. This [meeting] will ask what more can unions do to grow? How can we put reps and activists at the heart of our organising strategies? How can we step up our organising efforts and reach out to the next generation of union members and activists?

This summation neatly encapsulated the frustrations, dilemmas and challenges facing labour unions[1] in the countries which have experienced the projects of attempted union renewal and revitalisation through union organising (Australia, Britain, Canada, New Zealand, United States) and may yet face those where such projects are at a more nascent stage (Germany, Netherlands). By 2009, more than a decade has passed since the TUC and a number of major unions in

Britain made the move towards union organising.[2] And, similarly, it is much more than a decade ago since many of the large unions and unions' peak organisations in the other aforementioned countries began their moves towards union organising. No matter its limitations and contradictions, union organising represents the most serious and sustained (organic) move by unions and union movements to become masters of their own destinies since the late 1970s with regard to reversing the decline in their fortunes. And yet, on a number of key different indicators, the results and outcomes of union organising have been disappointing to say the least. There is a certain foreboding sense of merely ending up re-arranging the 'deckchairs' on the proverbial Titanic – the 0.1% increase in union density in the US from 2006 to 2007 (US Department of Labor 2008a) being almost the first and only increase in more than 30 years after many years of valiant efforts is a case in point – if the benchmark of returning to former levels of membership and influence of former years in a relatively short to medium time frame is deployed. Even if much less onerous measures and time-scales are used, there is still some dismay at the paucity of progress to date.[3] Given these aspects, it is appropriate for sympathetic parties and observers to now survey the outcomes, assess and explain them as well as to move outside the box of union organising *per se* to examine and analyse what may be necessary in terms of complementing, revising or amending it for the wider projects of union renewal and revitalisation.

This collection of original papers aims to help play a part in making such assessments and analyses. Either union organising will continue or it will not as a result of evaluations from within the respective labour unions and labour union movements about the relative merits and demerits of union organising. What will influence these internal evaluations are assessments and analyses such as those contained in this collection and which act from without. This situation of 'Monte Carlo or bust' – union organising or not – arises because the act of the extent of the focus on union organising by the unions themselves represents such a pivotal point in the existence of contemporary labour unionism. Union organising is just about the only 'game in town' so that its acceptance or rejection becomes a tipping point in itself because of the lack of other credible strategies for renewal and revitalisation. At one level, this is incontestable because union organising is for many, when set against business unionism and union servicing, a refraction of the soul and *raison d'etre* of labour unionism (see Fiorito *et al.* 1991). At many other levels, as will shortly become apparent, the situation is considerably more complex.

Paradoxically and ironically, the simultaneous strength and weakness of union organising is that it is sufficiently conceptually and politically ambiguous and broad that it can be used for both – for want of better terminology – militant and moderate ends (see Kelly 1996). Similarly, it can be used for explicit political ends and ends of 'no politics' (if such a phenomenon could exist) and as just a technique for workplace organising or a strategy of mass collective mobilisation for an entire union. As a result, there are the proverbial 'Heinz 57 varieties' of union organising, and this trait of heterogeneity has become more evident the longer union organising has existed and operated across space and time. Indeed, it is one of the major reasons why discussion of union organising permeates and informs discussion of other strategies for labour unions such as building transnational labour unionism, business unionism, and social partnership at the micro- and macro-levels. They are neither incompatible nor full strategies on their own, with union organising providing a potential foundation for all, particularly when construed as a mere workplace activity. For reasons of this pervasiveness as well as of persuasiveness, it does appear that union organising remains something of the only 'game in town'.

This introduction to the collection seeks to raise, discuss and begin to evaluate the themes and issues that comprise and underlay the phenomenon and dynamics of union organising. Consequently, it does not present a critique as such of the many variants of union organising. Nor does it present a new or preferred version of union organising as the solution to travails and woes of the various houses of labour. What it does hope to do is provide the basis for a future research agenda and, more importantly, some of the intellectual resources needed in order to create robust and grounded theoretically-informed practice – praxis – amongst labour unions themselves.

Thematic overview

In the mounting academic and practitioner evaluation and analysis of union organising, including the contributions to this edited volume, five quasi-distinct approaches have emerged which can be approximated for heuristic purposes as: a) servicing is not unimportant and should not be downplayed; b) union organising is not yet widespread enough to realise its potential or 'make *the* difference'; c) union organising as practiced has been flawed and needs to be corrected to realise its potential; d) union organising as conceptualised, and thus practiced, is misconceived and needs correcting; e) union organising is too narrow in its focus and requires a wider 'political' focus and purpose, whereby social identity formation and collective interest mobilisation are keystones. Many, if not all, of these are, of course, not entirely mutually exclusive of each other.

The first approach emphasises that there is a place for union servicing given that a level of membership passivity is endemic and inevitable and that task specialisation under a (union) division of labour is necessary and desirable. This most easily pertains to legal representation of members, union education or media relations. The second focuses on the quantitative issues of resources, whereby insufficient numbers of unions have invested insufficient vigour and resources into union organising (without there being much questioning of the form of union organising). The conclusions of some of the earlier work of Heery and colleagues (see, for example, Heery *et al.* 2003a) could be placed in this approach. The third stresses that the corruption and watering down of the potency of the model of union organising in implementation – through use alongside, for example, partnership approaches or a 'pick and mix' selective rather than holistic approach – has led to the shortfall in the realisation of its potential. A 'representative' of this approach can be taken to be the work of Bronfenbrenner *et al.* (1998). The fourth argues that the particular version of union organising adopted is off the mark through, for example, a lack of focus on creating self-sustaining workplaces unionism, domination by employed union officers (EUOs), lack of integration with bargaining agendas or lack of integration with sectoral organising strategies. The work of Carter (2000, 2006) maybe taken as illustrative of this type of view. The fifth suggests that union organising lacks a wider social world vision, and is not part of a social vision, that marries together the workplace and extra-workplace concerns of workers in the form of unions as social liberation movements. As such union organising is just not up to the quantitative and qualitative scale of the task at hand of regenerating unions and union movements. Thus, union organising should be subsumed within a more general orientation of mobilising to promote and advance workers' collective interests through union movements acting in the economic, ideological, political and social arenas. An example of this approach can be found in Moody (2007).

Some initial contextualisation is warranted on the manifestations of the five approaches. As the initial zeal of union organising has dissipated because of the emergence of various obstacles – and subsequent reassessment has been made – recognition has been made of the value of the previously denigrated 'servicing' by both practitioners (Wilson

2007) and academics (see, example, Banks and Metzgar 2005). None-theless, the calls and plans for further and greater resources to be afforded to union organising have been made. In Britain, the cases of the TGWU/Unite (TGWU section), GMB and USDAW represent the most obvious cases of unions doing so. But the differences in approaches between these three unions to union organising (see below, and Simms and Holgate 2008) testify to the belief that there is no single 'one true way' on how to construct and implement it. Lastly, and again in Britain, the TUC has tried to move union organising on by promoting its inte-gration with bargaining, environmental and workplace learning agendas, only to find that these attempts have been viewed as not strengthening, but rather diluting, measures by some union activists and EUOs. The most appropriate approach is arguably the re-envisaging of unions as social movements and this will be considered in greater detail below.

Resultant upon these different approaches, various proposals and strategies have been forthcoming. Some argue to stick with union organising but amend it in qualitative and quantitative ways while others argue for a 'revolution' from without. Strategies of social and community unionisms offer, in different hands, examples of proposals of both internal 'reform' and external 'revolution'. But hampering eval-uation of such proposals and strategies is the absence of specifications of what their objectives are in terms of membership gains and union density, membership participation, the numbers of activists, much less stipulations of returning to the power and influence of particular former years, and over what time spans. Without these specifications of intent and expectation, it is difficult to work out and measure whether the different union organising projects, both extant and pro-posed, are credible. For the practitioners themselves, this is a glaring omission. For example, is union organising – when all is said and done – merely a holding exercise as unions wait for more favourable exo-genous developments or is it a means of the internal and external political management of decline?

Managerialism and union organising

One particular but central meta-aspect of assessing union organising that remains still rather underdeveloped in academic and practitioner assessments is whether it, union organising, is appropriate as a 'man-agerial' means to regenerate a 'social movement'. To examine union organising in this way requires making a number of assumptions, namely, that union organising is a managerial means and that the union movement is a social movement, and that the two are largely or wholly incompatible. One can suggest that the dominant conceptual and practiced versions of union organising have constituted – indeed, have been constituted – as managerial, administrative, centralised and top-down responses. The rationale here has been that the union leaderships as organisational leaders can use their unions' limited resources in a targeted manner to achieve certain objectives in efficient and effective ways through the application of employed staff, techniques and specific knowledge. These leaders have recognised that their own extant activist base is too weak or insufficiently strong in qualitative and quantitative terms to bring about the desired change without additional help and resources. Consequently, they have chosen to target these resources and attempt to gain the most efficient and effective expenditure of them. The hope is that these extra resources in terms of EUOS can be a small cog that helps turn, or even create, a bigger, more powerful cog. Such a perspective would scoff at the notion that you can easily or quickly (re)create a vibrant grassroots through being less managerial and technocratic as well as that a vibrant grassroots can be easily or quickly (re)created. With this leadership approach has come bureaucratic and centralised control methods and means of operating to ensure their desired outcomes are achieved and to demonstrate responsibility and accountability in doing so. In essence, faced with organisational decline which is synonymous with a decline, *inter alia*, in activists and activism, union leaderships have used specialist EUOs to lead, direct and implement union organising. Issues of efficiency, effectiveness and managed activism within set parameters have been paramount rather than those of democracy, participation, control and agenda setting with regard to the grassroots members and activists.

The underlying point of critique here revolves around the power structures and ideology in union organising and has several-dimensions; activists cannot be culturally reproduced in this hierarchical and managerially managed way; activism should not be managed by superordinates in this way; activists cannot be substituted for by EUOs; and, that coordination of voluntary labour (of activists) should not be equated with the management of employees. In so doing, the goals of national unions do not necessarily align with those of workplace unionisms over targets and timescales for creating workplace structures or over the ways and means of doing so because the actions of the national union are driven by its organisational concerns rather than workplace concerns. At root here, there is a technocratic view of the way that activism and labour unionism can be created and managed. By contrast, and developing the overall point of the critique, unions and country-based union movements are often held in the former to be part of, and, in the latter comprise, social movements, whose virtue is that their members' and activists' voluntary labour is driven by ideologies of social justice, collective endeavour and democratic participation. Underlying or alongside these views of what union organising and unions should be is the view that any sort of union organising should be centred on a more decentralised, self-determined and self-activity practice (albeit coordinated at the extra-workplace or local level) than has hitherto existed since the late 1970s. 'Participative' rather than 'managerial' or 'professional' labour unionism (Heery and Kelly 1994) is the frame of reference for this analysis and action, and on that basis, union organising is largely inappropriate, particularly where it does not have or is not part of a wider (progressive) social justice vision.

But if unions and union movements are not regarded in reality as being social movements (in part or whole respectively), then the above critique of, and objection, to union organising begins to come undone. Unions may not be viewed as constituent parts of a union social movement because of sectionalist values, because they as organisations are inevitably bureaucratised or because they have become hollowed out in a process of atrophy in the current post-1970s era. To speak of a union 'movement' in the singular implies a coherence and commonality of purpose and values as well as dynamism in action in pursuit of those common goals by voluntary labour (and the direction of employed labour where it is used by activists). In other words, the properties of being a movement implies a significant and tangible sense for the overwhelming body of members of a foremost identity of being part of same social entity that moves in a singular direction to achieve its goals.[4] Union movements may no longer be, and may never have been, 'movements' on this understanding. Unions and union movements are not synonymous. A union movement is more than just the aggregation of unions together, for in addition to the proffered definition of movement, the term 'movement' for unions implies a number of horizontal links at different levels between unions and a loyalty to a higher force. If the contemporary aspiration, existence and activity of unions and union movements are viewed as defective in any substantial way in the terms laid out above – possibly because of continuing dislocation, dissolution and disorganisation allied to membership passivity and so on – then the calculation of what is desirable or feasible – in terms of social movement unionism – must be reconfigured with the result that the union organising *per se* or of the kind critiqued above become serious options (again).[5] So managed activism and bureaucracy may yet, for some, have their places and purposes. This brief discussion of the relationship between a notion of social movement unionism and union organising as managed activism serves to highlight the enforced circularity of the straightjacket of the contemporary period for labour unionism, whereby the goal of achieving what is deemed necessary is stifled by the absence of the requisite social forces, which then, in turn, compels a return to – if not reliance upon – the very practice that is found to be wanting. But this brief discussion also highlights the historical characteristic of indeterminacy and contingency associated with agency, as well as that analysis of 'what is' can seldom be divorced from preference for 'what should be', for the desire to analyse in a certain manner comes with an underlying preference of future *modus operandi*.

Extra-workplace union organising

If it can be accepted that union organising is not and should not be merely about workplace organising in and at the workplace, then challenges and opportunities are opened up for union organising. This is another of the meta-aspects of union organising that still remains relatively under-explored in the academic and practitioner literatures. The tendency to treat union organising as this type of workplace activity arises from the influence of the dominant features of industrial relations systems in Anglo-Saxon countries and the dominant features of labour unionism there, namely, the belief that their focus should be on where their power most obviously resides (that is, the points of production, distribution and exchange), economism, and the separation of economic representation from political representation via labour-type parties. The most obvious counter-responses are those of the approaches of social movement unionism and community unionism for labour unions or, more radically, attempting to recast union movements as social liberation movements. What is common to these proffered proposals is not just to upscale the spatial dimensions and connectivity of union organising but to require that union organising undertakes a form of political organising. The under-explored aspects of these proposals are several. The first concerns the impact of the decomposition of social democracy and decline of the politically organised left since the late 1970s for this reduces the availability of ideologically motivated activists. The second concerns the nature of the recent social movements with regard to their rise and fall as well as their openness to the union movement and vice-versa and the degree of overlap in common purpose. The third relates to the features of social capital *vis-à-vis* understanding how it is created and functions for the purpose of replication inside the unions. The fourth focuses on the conservative nature of Anglo-Saxon labour unionism by comparison to those found at different times in countries like Brazil, South Africa and South Korea, where the point is trying to separate the contextual in order to appreciate the existence of other models of labour unionism (for an earlier discussion of some of these issues, see Gall 2006a). Running through all of these must be a discussion and then assessment of what in the temporal and spatial dimensions are possible and probable, off limits or not, for union revitalisation projects in the five aforementioned different countries.

To take some examples, labour unionism is predicated on intervening in labour markets to modify their outcomes. But in attempting to do this, and necessarily also intervene in product markets and the larger, and more general, 'market' to achieve this in order to more fully defend and advance members' interests, labour unionism needs to operate in other arenas outside the workplace, through other means and in alliance with other social forces. This may concern changing legal regulation, public policy, public values or the centre of political gravity. (For example, recasting labour unionism as a social liberation movement would involve campaigning against the reduction in popular political democracy and the privatisation of society.) In so doing, labour unionism may be said to move from economic to political labour unionism. But however this is attempted or achieved requires utilising and mobilising oppositional ideas and forces. Most obviously, this concerns working with social democrats, socialists, social progressives and so on of the 'old' or the 'new' (in the case of recent social movements and groups) types. Discussion of the key practical tasks, thus, revolves around on what basis and how unions could work in concert with these other milieus. The issues are not just whether agreement could be gained on these tasks but which alliance (with whom) is best suited to achieve the particular stated aims in terms of the human resources that could be brought together and whether a synergy of the whole being more than the sum of the parts is possible. And given the depleted nature of labour unionisms as well as many of the old and new social movements, a balance between caution and ambition would need to be steered. For example, in trying to replicate the Justice for Janitors and the London Citizens (formerly TELCO) campaigning organisations, a hard-headed assessment would try to identity the specific salient social relations in Los Angeles and London in order to find which were peculiar and which were universal (or at least general) so that the prospects of reproduction could be deduced (*cf.* Milkman 2006; Wills 2004a). Put more bluntly: if both Justice for Janitors and the London Citizens are such exemplars, where are all the follow up examples of such success in their respective countries? Without these follow up successes, we cannot talk of two swallows making a summer on this particular strategic front. The same point about transferability and applicability arises in the chapters in this collection concerning the PCS and RMT unions. In the case of the RMT, it organises in the rail sector where, for a number of reasons, there is little labour substitutability and a heavily used monopoly service exists so that the strike weapon is more potent and visible than in many other sectors. The task of assessment is to neither unnecessarily build up a wall of exceptionalism against transferability nor glibly ignore such idiosyncrasies.

Turning to another pertinent issue of this discussion, to what extent do labour unions need a new form of political organisational representation given the transition of western social democratic parties from being leftwing versions to rightwing or neo-liberal versions and the inability of labour unions to influence these parties successfully to the required extent from within or without on their agenda of substantial reform? Other than in a few isolated cases like Germany, labour unions have been unwilling to create new left parties or join with existing left groups to build new alliances. Even in the case of Germany, it is still far from clear whether success in creating such a party is assured, much less whether this party can or will succeed in changing the social, economic and political landscape in favour of labour unionism there. So, overall, the parameters are still confined to being between 'a rock and a hard place' for unions' organs of political representation. The growing (but still minority) want of many labour union activists inside the Fire Brigades' Union (FBU), PCS, RMT and Unison unions in Britain for a new working class leftist party still does not command sufficient requisite social forces for the desire to become a reality. And here, as with much elsewhere in regard of union revitalisation, there is a sense of 'Catch-22' wherein the 'answers' and 'solutions' are in one sense obvious and exist in the abstract – unions need to mobilise members collectively for a more ambitious agenda. But these very same 'answers' and solutions are not so obvious because they do not exist in a manifest way because they remain out of reach in the concrete due to the disconnection between available means and desired ends. Something useful may be learned by considering the writings of long dead, Italian

Marxist, Antonio Gramsci, who enjoined us to conceive of struggles against employers, governments and capitalism in terms of 'wars of position' through a long haul of contesting the cultural and ideological hegemony of the *status quo* by creating anti-hegemonic alliances. Gramsci's writings speak to our epoch of 'down but not out' for organised labour and the necessity of wider conceptions of worker collectivism that are not primarily characterised by economism. In so doing, we can maybe understand better in retrospect what went wrong as well as in prospect, how to make what unions and their supporters want to happen, happen.[6]

Approaching the subject matter from another angle further elucidates the issues at hand. So, if on paper and in practice, labour unionism does not itself possess and cannot generate the sufficient human resources and the critical social weight (on its own or with others) for the creation of any of these types of wider social and political projects at the present time or in the immediate future, are we then left waiting for the exogenous upswing or upsurge in industrial and social struggle of the kind experienced in the 1840s, 1880s, 1910s–1920s, mid to late 1930s and late 1960s–late 1970s periods in western Europe and north America as the best and most viable 'option'? Such a perspective serves to emphasise the definite limits to which the return to agency – that union organising represents – has either *per se* or under late capitalism.[7] Nonetheless, the aforementioned perspective is suggestive of Kondratieff's or long-wave theory when applied to labour relations (see Dunlop 1948: 189–192; Kelly 1998). The problem here is that we are either coming to the end of an exceptionally long (sic) long-wave or we are actually already outside one and there is little evidence of the upswing or upsurge or their pre-figurative stages. Both scenarios could constitute hope and hopelessness, depending on the veracity or otherwise of long-wave theory. But for some observers, either the extension of the current long-wave or the non-appearance of the expected upswing will chime with theses of the decline, fragmentation and end of the working class as social force or political actor. British Marxist historian, Eric Hobsbawm (1981), called this 'The Forward March of Labour Halted'. For some others like Metcalf (2005), it will merely confirm that labour unionism has increasingly become an anachronism as a form of interest representation and that worker dissatisfaction is wildly overstated because HRM is an enlightened management practice. But others, like Darlington (2002) for example, would not doubt respond that simply waiting for the return of, or the next, upswing is defeatist and abstentionist. Whatever the strengths and weaknesses of the contending arguments here, a pervading sense exists of our lack of depth of understanding not so much of why in terms of social relations upswings occur – although that arguably remains true – but of what influence conscious and organised political participants had in creating, furthering and directing the previous upswings. Therein lays the conundrum of understanding the dialectic between voluntarism and determinism, particularly for those who wish to shape or create the future.

Strategy and circumstance

Returning to some issues of a more intermediate nature, amongst unions in the vanguard of the union organising projects in Australia, Britain, Canada, New Zealand, United States, there has been a dawning that attempting to organise workplaces on a one-by-one basis is deficient in a number of respects. These include targeting workplaces in a random manner, providing incentives to individual employers to resist because of the prospect of rising labour costs and so on. The deduction has been made that though it is more demanding of time and resources as well as more risk-laden, targeting all the major employers in a sector at roughly the same time in a coordinated manner allows unions to try to reduce the propensity of employers to resist by taking the labour cost element out of the competition that exists between them and to establish pattern bargaining for the vast majority of the sector. In Britain, and following from the Service Employees' International Union (SEIU) example, the TGWU/Unite (TGWU section) has travelled down this road with some success in the 'white meat' (poultry processing) sector and in aviation (cabin crew) and is trying to do similarly in the 'red meat' (bovine meat processing) sector, cleaning services and in road logistics. The union – which is a large conglomerate general union – consciously decided after weighing up the options (including the value of its existing bases) which sectors to target in a strategic manner. Similar examples can be found with regard to unions in Britain like Community (betting shops) and the CWU (telecommunications) as well as the RMT (rail transport), the NUJ (provincial newspapers) and Connect (telecommunications). However, all these latter examples are not exactly or necessarily what they seem when compared with the TGWU/Unite (TGWU section). Some of the aforementioned unions were compelled more by constraint (associated with weakness) than by choice to target certain sectors while in some cases even being strategic can be mistaken if the 'wrong' sectors are chosen with regard to pre-existing union presence and employer attitudes. In other cases, the targeting of a sector belies a scattergun approach within the sector or where the net is sometimes cast too wide with the effect that resources are dissipated, and often there is more use of strategic planning within companies (like the CWU targeting field engineers rather than all or other staffs within mobile phone companies because of its membership amongst field engineers). The import of this brief discussion is that strategic union organising as a development on from simple union organising (as with HRM becoming strategic HRM) is by no means the magic panacea for, *inter alia*, strategy *per se* does not provide a blueprint and is malleable. Again, the point would seem to be that union organising requires filling out, and this process requires a broadening out of what union organising is. Otherwise, and in the case of the discussion of strategy, strategic union organising can be believed to have a universal but devalued provenance.

While expenditure on union organising has been significant but still underwhelming according to most observers, the same attempts of examination of expenditure and outcome should also be applied to political expenditure. This would encompass general political campaigning as well as affiliations and donations to political parties. In Britain, the sums given over to the Labour Party since 1997 dwarf those spent on union organising. Yet, certainly in the case of Britain, comparative analysis of both expenditures for the purposes of which gives better value has been absent as has been analysis in the same guise of where union organising and political campaigning have been integrated. Again, taking a cue from the experience in Britain, has union organising effected a separation between 'representation-cum-bargaining' and 'organising' which necessarily leads to dislocation and poorer results? Certainly in Britain, there is strong evidence that union organising has compartmentalised 'organising' so that one union hand does not know what the other union hand is doing and vice-versa, cumulatively leading to a lack of integration and thus also a lack of efficiency and effectiveness. Some negotiating officers in the TGWU/Unite (TGWU section) believe this to be the case in their union. This may also be indicative of the idea of union organising not having won over the under-reaches of the cadre of EUOs for a number of reasons in regard of informal, internalised union politics. It may also be indicative of the wish of internal sectional interests to maintain the 'servicing' of their existing members. Such problems as the TGWU/Unite (TGWU section) has experienced through its separation of its organising EUOs from its negotiating EUOs as per above has led the GMB union to attempt to avoid these by building organising into the job specification of each of its EUOs. Yet the pressures of job intensification and firefighting knocking the focus off organising inherent in the GMB approach have to be held in regard of the TGWU's advances with a dedicated team of organising EUOs. There appears to exist both thesis and antithesis but not as yet synthesis here. Alternatively, if there can be no synthesis, this suggests unions need to work out which approach is more suited to which situation (and the variables thereof) and competing versions could be integrated into a more general union organising framework.

Finally in consideration of intermediate issues, in both Britain and the US, where gaining the right to bargain through union recognition has been a prime concern of union organising (as a result of highly decentralised industrial relations systems and derecognition/non-recognition in particular), little attention has been given to the sequential steps of organising and mobilising for bargaining and vice-versa. In other words, union organising does not seem to focus on building bargaining capacity, of which one component would be gaining facility time and resources from employers to support and facilitate this work (and the problem of the *quid pro quos* that might then ensue). It seems almost to be a case of 'gain recognition and then move on' (under the influence of performance targets). In Britain, the TUC attempted to correct this emphasis by changing the focus of some of its Organising Academy courses while 'in fill' organising has become more frequent as a lower cost and less risk laden activity. Yet under these industrial relations systems, this still dominant practice remains precarious because workplace unionism is a weak and fragile phenomenon in the current period if it does not become enmeshed with and supported by other means of union leverage outwith the workplace. Here, unions need to remember that no workplace is an 'island'.

Endpoint: questions arisen

So given that the various country-based projects of union organising have been in existence for a substantial length of time, a somewhat bewildering range of pertinent questions have arisen and should have been raised in the critical mind. Among them are the following. Conceptually and empirically what is union organising, what has been union organising and what should be union organising?; What gains and advancements has union organising delivered or facilitated?; Using the counter or alter-factual method, how much weaker would the union movements be if union organising (and the particular versions of union organising used) had not been practiced? Or has union organising prevented other more credible and effective means of 'union revitalisation' from emerging?; Has union organising been too radical for unions as conservative organisations? Has the context of union organising *vis-à-vis* the pursuit of macro-and micro-social partnership neutered its potential? What is the preferable relationship of social movement unionism and/or community unionism to union organising? Has union organising detracted from 'union servicing' and therefore weakened unions in their existing bases? Are the problems associated with union organising to do with its a inherently flawed conceptualisation as top-down, technocratic, bureaucratically controlled, or are they merely to do with unions not implementing it properly and fully, or are they concerned with there being no one coherent, robust version of union organising? Finally, have some nation-state-based versions of union organising been weaker or stronger than those elsewhere? This collection will touch upon many, but not all, of these questions, and some in more depth than others. It is to be hoped that not only will the answers and responses be compelling and convincing but that the sum of their parts will help provide the basis for a rounded and grounded assessment of union organising, ultimately as a means to guiding successful practice.

Acknowledgements

Thanks are due to John Kelly and Jack Fiorito for their comments in the course of drafting this introduction. As editor of the collection, my thanks go to all the contributors for allowing this edited volume to exist as it does. Particular thanks go to those whose day jobs are not as academics for making the time and effort to make their contributions.

Notes

1 The term 'labour' unionism is used because in the contemporary period the term 'trade' unionism has become inappropriate for most major unions are increasingly general or conglomerate, rather than 'trade' (see Gall (2008: 1) for a brief consideration of the issues).
2 The term union organising is presented as such in order to denote the complexity of the social phenomenon which it is, being a conflation of theory, practice and praxis, from which many variants arise. With that said the term will henceforth be used with affectation.
3 Sitting alongside these calculations, recognition must be given to an acknowledgment that we do not know just how 'bad' or much 'worse' the

situation would have been without union organising (as well as whether union organising may have become an impediment to the emergence and implementation of other strategies of renewal and revitalisation).

4   The dissemination process of union organising in America, Australian and British union movements, heavily characterised by peak organisations from the 'centre' trying to instil into affiliates the new creed but without huge success, is redolent of the absence of there being a singular and coherent union movement in each country. In each case, the peak organisations have little control over those that affiliate to their organisation because affiliates choose not to cede control for political and sectional reasons.

5   But this would not prevent a desire amongst many academics and practitioners for the recreation of an upturn in industrial and social struggles to provide the basis for regeneration whereupon the critique of union organising would emerge again.

6   But even with the aid of Gramscian thinking, it is still relatively easy to see the gap between ideas and practice without being able to build the bridge of critical social mass between them. Appropriate ideas are necessary but far from sufficient from successful social practice.

7   Clawson (2003a) provides one interpretation of the contemporary favourable proximity of challenge and opportunity in the case of the US (as does Milkman (2006) in a different way).

2
Organising and Union Modernisation: Narratives of Renewal in Britain

Miguel Martinez Lucio and Mark Stuart

Introduction

This chapter presents an assessment of the union organising agenda in Britain. It considers the origins and recent developments of organising, and assesses how the union movement has sought to operationalise organising as a tool for revitalisation. The nature and relative efficacy of the concept for union revitalisation has stimulated an extensive academic debate – see for example, the recent exchanges between Carter (2006) and de Turberville (2004, 2007a, and this volume). Whilst there is general consensus on the importance of organising to the reinvigoration of activist networks and self-activity, commentaries on the conceptual ideals and practical realities of organising have been more divided. To what extent, for example, is it to possible to differentiate union organising from 'union servicing'? And how should the respective roles of workplace activists and EUOs be prioritised, and articulated, in relation to the furtherance of organising?

It is not the intention of this chapter to review *in extremis* these finer points of debate, in order to support or reject any supposed nominal model of organising (de Turbeville 2007a). Instead, we seek to tease out an argument along two dimensions, in a framework that is sensitive to both external and internal dynamics and political processes. First, we examine the way in which organising has become contextualised within the specific regulatory dimension of Britain. The tendency has been to give priority to campaigning for union recognition to the relative neglect of wider political perspectives around union identity, purpose and societal status. This has happened despite general acknowledgement in the literature that organising should not be conflated with recruitment. Second, there has been a tendency to isolate the strategic development and capacity of organising within the broad operational imperatives of unions; a process that can, unintentionally, reduce goals and purpose to specific sets of tactics and techniques (and ideal types). We argue that organising should be seen as a template for developing *narratives* that allow unions to focus around new forms of progressive union services and a *shared* repertoire of activities across organisational structures – it has curious internal features and benefits although the external strategic links may not be so clear. We begin with a review of the contemporary development and impact of organising in Britain.

Origins and development of organising in Britain

The 'turn' towards organising became pronounced in Britain from the mid-1990s, in terms of union practice, industrial relations policy and scholarly engagement. At the level of union practice, this was exemplified by the establishment of the TUC 'Organising Academy' in 1998. The Academy was not a loose case of isomorphism: it was explicitly influenced by the development of the US 'organising model' and parallel initiatives both in America and Australia (Heery *et al.* 2000a, 2000b). The TUC Academy takes a small intake of trainees each year, and offers them a year-long training programme in conjunction with a sponsoring union. The aim is to train 'skilled union organisers' in order 'to produce a cadre of 'lead organisers' who can plan and manage organising campaigns and promote the cause of organising across the British union movement' (Heery *et al.* 2000c: 400). The aim is to target companies and build the representative voice of labour, through focusing on the employment interests of workers and day-to-day issues, paying particular attention to new groups of workers and women. Alongside this central initiative, a number of individual unions also started to take a more strategic approach towards building their organising capacity (Heery *et al.* 2003a), such as the TGWU, regardless of their participation in and support (or not) of the Academy (Gall 2003c).

At the broader policy level, the practice of organising has been supported by a changing opportunity structure for unions with the election of Labour governments since 1997. A statutory provision for union recognition was introduced in 2000, within the terms of the *Employment Relations Act 1999* (ERA) (Gall 2007a). Whilst the specific mechanics of the procedure are far from uncontroversial, they provide a 'lever' for organising activity. The 'spirit' of the provisions exhorted the regulations to be used as 'a recourse of last resort' (Gall 2007a: 79), with the emphasis on unions and employers establishing voluntary agreements (Perrett 2007).

Nonetheless, the provisions provide unions with the potential avenue to organise within even hostile environments, using the law to push recalcitrant employers to establish systems of representation and bargaining (Gall 2003c; Wills 2003). Unions have also benefited from a number of state-sponsored funding mechanisms, in relation to labour-management partnership, workplace learning and union modernisation (see Stuart 2009; Stuart *et al.* 2006; Stuart and Martinez Lucio 2005a), although this aspect of strategic 'steering' by the state (Stuart and Martinez Lucio 2008) is given no consideration in relation to the dynamics of union organising.

These developments in policy and practice have led to increased academic interest in the theory, practice and outcomes of organising. This debate is wide-ranging, but is encapsulated in simple terms by three types of work. First, critical, macro-evaluations of developments in organising and union recognition campaigns (see, for example, Heery *et al.* 2003a; Gall 2004, 2007a). Second, detailed qualitative case studies of specific union organising and recognition campaigns (see, for example, Simms 2003; Wills 2003). Kelly's (1998) mobilisation framework is typically taken as the prime conceptual point of departure. Third, analyses that counterpoise organising with other union strategies, initiatives and approaches, such as partnership or servicing, by way of examining the 'credibility' of the 'organising model' (see Carter 2006; de Turberville 2004, 2007a). To some extent, this reflects an explicit point of differentiation advanced by the unions themselves. Thus, the American development of the 'organising model' was presented as a set of more confrontational tactics involving member self-activity, in direct contrast to a model of union servicing. The aim was to direct resources away from servicing to organising, with the stress placed on 'what workers can do for themselves through the union rather what the union as an outside party can do for workers' (Fiorito 2003: 201). This bifurcation is not, as commentators such as Heery (2002) have recognised, unproblematic, as we shall discuss below.

The value of organising is, of course, situated in terms of its potential to renew or revitalise unions and, in the British context, contribute to reversing a period of decline that now stretches for almost 30 years. Whilst its purpose as a union method or tactic is not to focus purely on member recruitment (Heery *et al.* 2000c), as Towers (2003: 187) noted: 'in the end it is, [of course], a numbers game', whether this is measured in terms of more subscription paying members, activists, shop stewards and new recognition agreements or bargaining arrangements. A variety of data sources and indicators can be scrutinised to potentially assess the efficacy of the 'turn' to organising, but statistical data sets in Britain tend to suffer from the same problems as those in the US reported by Fiorito and Jarley (2008) – indeed, if anything, they are even more limited in Britain. More significantly, an obvious caveat needs to be made in terms of the conclusiveness of such data in terms of cause and effect.

Since 1998, some 250 trainees have entered the TUC Organising Academy. According to Heery *et al.* (2000a), the majority of trainees have remained in the union movement. Whilst no data set exists that comprehensively details annual intake by year, the extant data do suggest that trainees have been overwhelmingly drawn from six unions, ISTC/Community, Graphical, Print and Media Union (GPMU) (before merger with Amicus), USDAW, Unison, CWU and PCS.[1] The small union, ISTC/Community, has consistently put trainees through the Academy, and in numbers that belie its size. Unions such as the TGWU have rarely participated in the Academy, preferring to develop their own internal approach. According to Heery *et al.* (2003c: 9), during the first five years of the Academy its trainees: '... targeted more than 1,200 employers, added nearly 40,000 new members and identified nearly 2,000 new activists. They have also established membership at 600 greenfield sites and helped secure or raise the question of recognition for more than 300 bargaining units'.

Internally, Academy Organisers have contributed to the diffusion of organising principles within the overall strategic priorities of sponsoring unions, although the degree of commitment to the specific techniques of the 'organising model' vary by union, and different unions follow different paths of organising (Heery *et al.* 2003a, 2003c). Trainees have been impressively drawn from under-represented groups, such as women and young workers. The Organising Academy has become a permanent feature of the TUC apparatus, although it has recently been subsumed within the apparatus of the new Learning Academy, *union-learn*. It is also evident that the annual intake has declined in recent years – from an average of around 30 a year during its early years to around 20 most recently.

The increased emphasis on organising, coupled with the statutory provisions for union recognition, has contributed to a significant increase in the number of new recognition agreements. Between 1995 and 2005, 3003 new recognition agreements were signed (Gall 2007a). Gall (2007a) estimated that around 1.2m workers were covered by these new agreements. Recognition agreements increased year on year from

1995, culminating in 525 and 685 new agreements in 2000 and 2001 respectively when the ERA provisions were first introduced. Since 2001, the number signed each year has declined (Gall 2007a). Evidently, recognition activity increased during the lead up to the implementation of the ERA provisions, partly due to the impending regulation but also due to purposeful union organising and campaigns and the targeting of voluntary agreements with employers. Since 2001, the landscape has become more hostile. The number of deals gained through the Central Arbitration Committee (CAC) process as a proportion of all new deals has increased and, employer opposition to recognition campaigns has become more pronounced (Gall 2007a).

At an aggregate level, it is evident that the increased organising effort on its own has not reversed the long-term decline of unions. As Table 2.1 reports, density for the UK in 2007 was 28%, around half the high tide

Table 2.1 Union membership in the United Kingdom, 1995–2007(%)

Year	Density of (i)	which		Unions of present in the work-place	which		Employees' pay covered by collective agreement	which	
		Private	Public		Private	Public		Private	Public
1979	55.8								
1990	38.1								
1995	32.4	21.4	61.3						
1996	31.4	20.5	60.7	50.2	35.5	89.7	34.5	21.7	68.8
1997	30.7	19.8	61.2	49.1	34.5	89.5	33.3	20.6	69.1
1998	29.9	19.5	60.4	47.8	33.4	89.4	32.3 (ii)	19.9	68.3
1999	29.7	19.0	59.9	48.4	34.5	87.8	36.1	23.0	72.7
2000	29.8	18.8	60.3	48.9	34.9	87.8	36.4	22.5	74.2
2001	29.3	18.4	59.7	48.2	34.0	88.1	35.5	21.9	72.6
2002	28.8	17.7	59.8	48.0	33.6	88.2	35.2	21.1	73.6
2003	29.3	18.2	59.4	48.4	34.1	87.2	35.5	21.9	72.6
2004	28.8	17.3	58.7	47.6	32.6	86.8	34.7	20.5	71.2
2005	28.6	16.9	58.2	47.7	32.4	86.4	34.9	20.6	70.9
2006	28.3	16.5	58.7	47.0	31.7	86.7	33.3	19.6	69.0
2007	28.0	16.1	59.0	46.6	31.5	86.2	34.6	20.0	72.0

Notes: (i) – Density refers to all employees, excluding members of the armed forces.
(ii) – 'Results for 1998 and earlier were routed differently' (Mercer and Notley 2008: 40). Also, figures from 1998 and earlier are taken from Grainger and Crowther (2007: 36) due to the significant discontinuity in the 2008 published results.
Sources: Waddington (2003) for 1979 and 1990 (which cover GB and not UK), Labour Force Survey for 1995 onwards (Mercer and Notley 2008).

of 1979. In more contemporary terms, decline has continued across nearly all union vectors since 1997, in both the private and public sectors. Density in the private sector is down to just 16.1%, although unions remain present in just under a third of private sector workplaces. An optimistic reading suggests that decline appears to have stabilised during the last ten years. However, there has still been a decline of 9% in aggregate density since 1997 and the 2006 rate recorded the 'largest annual percentage point decline since 1998' (Grainger and Crowther 2007: 2). One positive appears to relate to the level of pay covered by collective agreement. Yet, even here, the significant increases reported between 1998 and 1999 were the result of a statistical recalibration and it is notable that levels have subsequently continued to decline. More significant is the fact that membership has remained stable in the public sector, with a notable rise in 2007 in the numbers covered by collective agreement.

Whilst national aggregate data provide some insights into general levels of unionisation within the economy, they reveal nothing about the impact of organising within specific unions. Since some unions have devoted more attention, and resources, to organising than others, it is reasonable to hypothesise that union fortunes would have varied markedly in recent times. Table 2.2 reports the changing membership levels of the largest unions. The data are based on self-reports to the Certification Office between 1998 and 2007. This period is limited, but corresponds to specific contemporary developments in the policy and practice of organising. With the exception of the retail union, USDAW, and the construction union, Union of Construction, Allied Trades and Technicians (UCATT), private sector unions experienced falls in membership, whilst public sector unions grew. It is accordingly difficult to draw a simple correlation between membership gains and putative organising unions. The TGWU and USDAW, for example, both invested heavily in organising strategies, albeit following different models, with different results. Gains for USDAW were recorded with continued decline for the TGWU. Gall (2007a) argued that it is important to consider the counter-factual that without such efforts membership levels would be lower: certainly there is a high degree of churn in membership in both unions.

More generally, aggregate gains and losses, regardless of organising and new recognition agreements are thus heavily shaped by fluctuations in private and public sector employment. As Gall (2007a: 85) observed, 1.1m jobs were lost in manufacturing between 1997 and 2005, compared to an increase of just over 0.7m jobs in the public sector. The largest percentage increase in membership was reported by the British Medical Association (BMA), the representative body of doctors. The three teachers' unions, Association of Teachers and Lecturers (ATL), NASUWT and National Union of Teachers (NUT), also reported large increases, as did the Royal College of Nursing (RCN) and Public and Commercial Services (PCS) union. The PCS does have membership in the private sector, but the vast majority work in the public sector, with some 80,000 members in the Department for Work and Pensions alone. The largest union in Britain, Unite, was established in 2007 from a merger between the Transport and General Workers' Union (TGWU) and Amicus, and represented the culmination of intense periods of negotiation and merger with a number of different unions (Amalgamated Electrical and Engineering Union (AEEU), Manufacturing, Science and Finance (MSF), GPMU and Unifi). As Table 2.2 shows, nearly all of the affiliate unions now comprising Unite had experienced declines in membership and in some, such as the GPMU, membership decline had been significant. The data above shed insights on the largest unions in Britain. Studies also suggest differential experiences amongst smaller unions. For example, Community's membership has held relatively steady due to organisational mergers rather than its organising activity *per se* (Greer *et al.* 2008), whilst, in contrast, the RMT has seen large increases in membership in recent years as a result of its combative activity (see Darlington, this volume).

Drawing conclusive analytical inferences from such data is far from straightforward. The general conclusion, as in the US (see Dixon and Fiorito, this volume) has been that the turn to organising has not provided the basis for the revitalisation potentially envisaged. It is not always clear whether the problem lies in the nature of organising strategies *per se*, the lack of resourcing or the fact that the challenges facing organised labour are greater than were at first imagined. For example, as shown above, generalisations may be difficult when organising, or specific approaches to organising, have greater impact or saliency in some sectors rather than others. Moreover, the debate on organising has been isolated from a concern with the external and internal context of union strategy (although see Heery and Simms 2008). This is apparent in commentaries that present the 'organising model' as an ideal type strategy or as unambiguously distinct from the servicing model (see Carter 2006). In this sense, there is a curious discourse at play which identifies organising not in terms of what it is but what it is not (see Laclau and Mouffe 1985). It is understood as not servicing – with servicing, in turn, often conflated with business unionism. And

Table 2.2 Membership of trade unions with more than 100,000 members, 1998-2007

	98-99	99-00	00-01	01-02	02-03	03-04	04-05	05-06	06-07	% change~
UNISON	1,272,330	1,272,350	1,272,470	1,272,700	1,289,000	1,301,000	1,310,000	1,317,000	1,343,000	+5.5
Transport and General	881,625	871,512	858,804	848,809	835,351	816,986	806,938	777,325	761,336*	-13.6
AEEU	727,977	727,369	728,211	728,508*	1,061,551 Amicus	935,321*	1,159,755	1,179,655	1,176,594*	
GMB	712,010	694,174	683,860	689,276	703,970	600,106	571,690	575,105	575,892	-19.1
MSF	416,000	404,741	350,974	332,691*						
RCN	320,206	326,610	334,414	344,192	359,739	372,506	382,141	391,347	394,696	+23.3
USDAW	303,060	309,811	310,222	310,337	321,151	331,703	340,201	340,653	341,291	+12.6
CWU	287,732	281,472	284,422	279,679	266,067	258,696	241,849	244,461	238,817	-17.0
NUT	286,503	294,672	286,245	314,174	331,910	324,284	330,709	361,987	368,066	+28.5
NASUWT	250,783	252,021	255,768	253,584	265,219	304,762	327,953	289,930	298,884	+19.2
PCS	245,350	258,278	267,644	281,923	285,582	295,063	311,249	312,725	311,998	+27.2
GPMU	203,229	200,676	200,008	170,279	102,088*					
ATL	168,027	183,144	178,697	186,744	202,585	201,845	195,511	203,241	207,075	+23.2
UCATT	111,804	122,579	114,854	119,993	115,007	110,886	113,280	121,109	128,914	+15.3
BMA	106,864	110,206	111,055	112,872	113,711	128,566	133,160	137,361	138,909	+30.0

Table 2.2 Membership of trade unions with more than 100,000 members, 1998–2007 – *continued*

	98–99	99–00	00–01	01–02	02–03	03–04	04–05	05–06	06–07	% change~
BIFU	106,007	171,249 – Unifi	160,267	154,434	147,607	136,947*				
Prospect					105,480 #	104,755	104,749	102,161	101,532	–3.7
UCU									116,977	
% of all	81.50	82.06	82.24	82.57	84.10	82.33	84.69	83.57	85.27	

Source: Certification Officer *Annual Reports* (1999–2008).
Notes: # Formed through merger of Institute of Professionals, Managers and Specialists (IPMS) and EMA (Engineering Managers' Association)
*All affiliate unions that merged to form Unite. ~ Rounded to one decimal place.

nor is it is about partnership or labour-management co-operation. Given that there is strong evidence that in practice organising and servicing are mutually related (de Turberville 2004, 2007a), with many EUOs committed to historical understandings of servicing (Simms 2007a), the 'what organising is not' perspective can hamper an understanding of the dynamics of organising. A further dualism is presented in terms of the role of local activists versus EUOs, or the organising benefits of grassroots self-mobilisation versus the stymieing bureaucracy of centralised union concerns. By focusing on the internal balance of organising responsibilities important links to the external become sidelined. Campaigns that are successful are often developed both from within the union and its leadership and developed alongside the local community and constituency being engaged with (Milkman 2006). Yet organising is rarely linked to social movement unionism or the socially oriented approach of revitalisation (Turner 2005) or questions around union democracy and identity. We need to now focus on these contexts of organising.

The context of organising in Britain: regulation and identity

The issues raised above suggest a need to try and reappraise the 'organising model' in Britain in relation to the context and nature of such strategic turns. In discussing the need for renewed strategies, Hyman (2007) argued that unions need to review their processes of strategic capacity – a central but often neglected aspect of which is the way in which these strategies unfold through processes of organisational learning and unlearning. However, his concern was that this tends to occur without a re-imagining of the broader purpose and identity of the union movement (see also Hyman 1989). He draws from Kelly (1998) to point out that the framing of workers' perceptions in relation to the problems that afflict them is, quite rightly, a vital dimension of any organisational approach or strategy. But he (Hyman 2007: 207) ventured: 'If [workers] blame employers or governments for their predicament but have no conception of alternative policies, they may protest but are unlikely to prevail'. With hindsight, organising appears to be disconnected from wider concerns. Hence, organising appears to look like a strategy without a mission, purpose or an ideology attached to it – something to do with getting members in a local workplace but not 'building upwards'. How this affects actual outcomes is difficult to say but it means that the problem may not rest with the strategy and tactics of the organisers *per se*, or their academies, but with the overall political and organisational contexts within the unions. Regardless of debates around the new wave of left leaning union leadership since the late 1990s, there has not been extensive political discussion about union identity, politics and purpose.

We, therefore, proceed by looking at the question of organising in terms of a) the impact of the Anglo-Saxon regulatory dimension and how it configures and contextualises the organising agenda, and b) the constraints on organising in terms of the nature of union identity, politics and action. We find that the focus of organising in relation to the state, in terms of recognition and representation, as well as the way mobilisation is understood shapes the character of evolving union strategy in Britain.

What emerges from this examination of organising strategies, and it is an obvious point, is that within Britain organising has been almost entirely linked to recognition campaigns – although there has been a longstanding emphasis on 'in-fill' and more recent activity in the public sector. The development of organising in Britain paralleled a moment of 're-regulation' within British employment relations, prompted by the election of a Labour government in 1997. The emphasis, as many commentators noted, has tended to be on the individual dimension of regulation around workplace related issues (Howells 2006) and highly neo-liberal in intent (Gall 2007a). Nevertheless, there has been legislation on recognition and this has contributed to the organising drive (Gall 2007a). Yet, the content and nature of the recognition laws are well below the standard of legislation that covers most of the older EU countries in terms of workplace elections, union roles, and union representation. It is debatable, therefore, whether these regulations have really developed a platform of support for organised labour (Martinez Lucio and Stuart 2004; Towers 2003). Indeed, some employers, in avoiding unions have used various aspects of the legislation to limit unions (Perrett 2007). In effect, the nature of the contours of regulation and the institutional systems of employment relations – or the lack of those contours as appears to be the case – mediate the processes and outcomes of organising (see Locke and Thelen 1995). This contextual point also mediates the manner in which union identity and policies are framed in relation to organising. The activity (and tactics) of organising is focused on membership and recruitment, and this emphasis is at the expense of other strategies such as, for example, coalition building or social activity which we discuss later.

The debate on organising has drawn heavily from the work of Kelly (1998) on mobilisation theory, but the link with the broader dimensions of the political arena has been engaged with to a lesser extent. Wills and Simms (2004) have tried to expand the debate in terms of the notion of community unionism, but overall the broader context and issue of mobilisation at the level of the state or within society is under played. Heery (2002) used mobilisation theory but sees it as a model or framework for understanding micro-level campaigns on particular recognition-related issues. Hence, the link between political mobilisation and organising is not always a central feature of the discussion – instead, the focus tends to be on the micro-level[2] when in fact engagement with the issue of mobilisation in literature on this topic does have a broader macro level and social perspective as in Kelly's (1988, 1998) work.

Why is the political important? Firstly, it means that the role of other actors and community organisations is not so salient in the calculations surrounding organising campaigns, or at least the analysis thereof. The question of recognition, and particular moments in terms of the interface with employers, continue to configure and mould the nature of union action (as discussed earlier) and the spaces around which union action occurs. Secondly, it means that the political visibility of unions and the way they are understood in social terms are rarely discussed.[3] This is a salient point because unions are joined for a variety of reasons (some instrumental, some related to political and justice oriented issues). Political mobilisation or campaigning can, indeed, raise public perceptions of unions (Kelly 2005) and help connect to organising campaigns. It is also important if organising is to be connected with broader considerations of renewal, which are understood not just in terms of union recognition and action at the workplace, but the role, involvement and, ultimately, power of unions as a social actor within the broader economic, political and social spheres.

How organising is linked into a renewed, mobilisation-based, grassroots view of the union is rarely seen as a legitimate research question or basis for discussion in terms of praxis, limited exceptions aside (see Gall 2006a). As alluded to already, organising is often approached in a technical and bureaucratic manner: a re-engineering of strategies (or tactics) but not, as Hyman (2007) suggested, in terms of social identities. This is in large part something that unions may have little influence over by virtue of the political landscape in Britain or because they think existing worker identities are unproblematic or helpful. The failure – or unwillingness – to generate alternative political roles and missions means that unions are left disconnected from broader social struggles and locked into established political traditions. This is clearly not always so, as in the case of some of the work of the CWU with social movements, but it is curious when we examine the debate on mobilising in Britain that it is very much about the stages, the processes, and the role of traditional actors such as the state, labour and employers who intervene at different stages. Rarely, is it about the content of mobilising and the way social issues in a broader sense engage with those of industrial relations. The relevance of this is that organising is studied in terms of particular industrial relations issues – usually around membership and pay – as poor proxies for union activity. Any discussion on unions must, therefore, take into account the regulatory and political environment as these can, and do, shape the nature of strategy.

From the organising model to an organising narrative: some alternative benefits

This final section deals with the potential for alternative readings of recent developments in unions and offers some informed optimism. We draw our views from many research projects with different unions on issues around community building, vulnerable worker networks, the learning agenda and union modernisation. It focuses on a) the internal organisational and bureaucratic role of organising as a narrative for activism and change, and b) the way organising can be constructed rhetorically *vis-à-vis* other forms of union action and then combined with them at the point of the workplace and, crucially, beyond. In effect, both internally and externally in terms of union structures, we consider how organising can play a broader and more flexible role of creating narratives and templates of action for connecting with the broader renewal of union purpose and roles. That practitioners and not just academics are aware of the environment they exist in and make calculations based on that environment requires recognition. We need to accept that environments – be they political, regulatory, or social – are not exogenous as they too are the outcome of previous political and organisational praxis and legacies. However, in looking at how organising as a strategy or set of tactics has been framed, we must account for the calculations institutional actors and individuals make as a consequence of their views of this environment.

Internal developments and coordination

It is apparent that there have been some curious by-products of organising. These need to be considered to appreciate some of the broader outcomes that have emerged. Much of the debate tends to conclude on the basis of clearly identifiable gains, but outcomes are not always measurable in terms of membership or recognition due to the longer term organisational and cultural benefits which strategies of organising may bring. Organising is, therefore, a significant feature of union renewal, but perhaps in ways that were not anticipated. First, the organising agenda has been a way for the TUC to create a hub for the regeneration of union activists and professionals across unions. One perspective is to see this as a way of bureaucratically controlling the new spaces of organising. However, this is not necessarily the case. It is rather an exercise in bureaucratically re-engineering the 'aging' union movement, through the development of new activists. The aspiration being that these activists become EUOs of the union movement, grounded in the techniques of organising and mobilisation and not just the usual body of knowledge that underpins a career in the union. Such expert knowledge is a fundamental imperative for union renewal in relation to contemporary capitalist developments (Turner 2005).

This project – if it can be called that – of identifying organisers and future lead figures has begun to look increasingly at developing the internal activist base of unions as a source for developing proactive union organisers. In late 2008, the TUC developed the 'Activist Academy'. In the light of difficulties in raising numbers for traditional organising courses, the 'Activist Academy' aims to increase access to organising training of lay activists and representatives (TUC 2008). The aim is to bring activists into organising campaigns by developing training that involves them adopting a recognition or membership drive, for example, that they see through as they study. These projects are likely to be focused on recruitment and more general union campaigns. This intends to reconnect activists with campaigning beyond their workplace. The aspiration is to push activism beyond the workplace, especially as in a more decentralised industrial relations system the sheer pressures of day-to-day issues in workplaces (such as negotiating, grievances and disciplinaries) can pull union activists away from a broader, social role.

The second curious by-product of organising is the political break and cathartic moment it marks in terms of reassessing the prospect of a conciliatory service and business unionism. Thus, organising represents a break, of sorts, with the difficulties of the Thatcherite epoch in terms of union decline and political intervention from the state. Its development marks an important moment of reclaiming the initiative and creating a common purpose for proactive union approaches and agency.

Despite the evident contradictions in practice, the concept of organising marks a turning point in the perceived pessimism and uncertainty of the 1980s and early 1990s. Thus, it acts as a common and shared position amongst a broad range of unions to re-engage membership and the workforce more generally – and in our view, the importance of this 'turn' should not be underestimated.

Third, the move to an organising approach provides an important narrative for renewal. It is a shared repertoire that allows unions, in terms of their leadership cadres and various levels of activists, to focus around new – and perhaps even traditional – concepts and actions. Organising can act as a template that allows the current moment of change in political and social terms to be confronted with a vision of purpose, albeit a limited one at times. In fact, it has created congruence – if only in linguistic and tactical terms – across 'Anglo-Saxon' countries as well as recently in Norway and Germany where the need to encounter the workforce outside the regulatory role of unions and to represent them in new ways is moving further up the union agenda. What is observable here is a referencing back to the basic purpose of union action and the establishment of a common template of action and ideas that can allow for the role of union activists and organisers to be understood within. In political terms, it is easier to buy into the organising agenda regardless of the union being considered. The fact that unions as diverse as USDAW and the TGWU have invested greatly in the organising agenda means that it is not necessarily attached to any political agenda. And, it does not necessarily undermine the establishment of other strategies in terms of learning or partnership (see below) although this convergence brings its own issues as we shall explain.

So what emerge are internal drivers and developments, in terms of organising, that provide it with an internal logic and set of outcomes that can assist union development over time, even if the statistics on longer term effectiveness may not be so clear. In terms of internal relations and contexts, there is a need to complement any discussion about bureaucratic imperatives and organisational narratives with one that considers how organising has developed in relation to other strategies. This is not an insignificant point, because, as we noted above, organising is often cloaked in a discourse that differentiates it from other strategies such as servicing and, to an extent, partnership. Yet, this needs some unpacking, as in practice, unions have been experimenting in recent times with a number of different approaches, and often combining them. Thus, Heery (2002), for example, cautioned against establishing a zero-sum analysis between organising and partnership campaigns and strategies. He showed how conceptually they were the twin faces of a renewed 1990s approach to engage with workers and employers on a more proactive and connected basis. The TUC was very explicit about this. Partnership may be accommodated with organising by having 'portfolio management' and keeping the strategies organised around different functions. Partnership may actually be a strategy developed after recognition and union roles have been established within a firm (Gall 2003c; Heery 2002). Much may depend on the style of partnership being considered and whether it is engaged with on the basis of union independence and negotiated interventionist roles in aspects of the organisation and the firm (Martinez Lucio and Stuart 2005; Stuart and Martinez Lucio 2005a).[4] The reality of organising and mobilising may require a link across different facets of union activities.

Links to broader social developments

Hence, we need to start thinking in terms of how unions have linked this new template of organising into other strategies. We will consider two examples: the learning agenda and community unionism. Both are new terrains that are seen as vital for the revitalisation of unions in terms of debates and reflections – although how they are elaborated remains an issue.

The development of learning strategies and union interest in using them as a vehicle for expanding workplace and social roles is a significant part of the British and European agenda (Stuart 2007), although unions can face an uphill climb as employers do not have a strong record of engagement with such issues in Britain (Stuart 2009). Within Britain, increasing funds have been made available to unions for worker learning and development. The Union Learning Fund (ULF) has allowed unions to engage with the skill and learning requirements of workers and develop innovative projects to support this. Particular initiatives in relation to workplaces and communities (and increasingly black and minority ethnic groups) have been developed by an array of unions. Moreover, the recent statutory rights for the development of Union Learning Representatives (ULRs) have allowed a greater degree of investment in this area: 'Raising awareness and promoting the value of learning; providing information on learning; ... improving access to learning opportunities; [and] monitoring quality of provision' (Whitehall College n.d.). The role of learning centres and learning agreements is a key institutional development. Activity in this area has been significant and, in many unions, is seen as an avenue for organising in itself, with ULRs themselves supported by networks of learning organisers operating beyond the workplace. Since 2000, a network of 20,000 ULRs has been created, representing an important cadre of new union activists. Research has started to explore how ULRs can encourage workers not only into learning, but union membership and activity (Thompson *et al.* 2007; Wallis *et al.* 2005).

A central contribution of the union learning agenda has been to provide a valuable 'new' offer to existing and potential union members (Wood and Moore 2007). This offer has proved particularly useful in connecting with the needs of new waves of migration and immigration. Thus, union-led learning centres (at the workplace and in the community) have acted as focal points for the provision of basic skills training, information and guidance for new labour market entrants. The central tenet of such initiatives is for unions to position themselves around key issues of workforce development, workplace dignity and labour market inclusion. Much of this activity has been underwritten through state funds, be it through the ULF, the new TUC learning academy, union-learn, or focused projects on migrant workers via the Union Modernisation Fund. Naturally, commentators are cautious about the long-term sustainability of such initiatives (McIlroy 2008). Yet the role of learning through learning centres, the provision of basic and work related educational courses and the development of support mechanisms for assisting migrants in terms of having their qualifications recognised is an increasingly apparent feature of union activity (Martinez Lucio *et al.* 2007). The learning dimension can, therefore, act as a link between the organising template and migrant representation. The problem with the learning agenda, however, is that it can be provided in a relatively hierarchical manner, whereby it often is a dimension of union activity that is not systematically connected to broader political or organisational objectives (Martinez Lucio and Perrett 2006). It takes on the form of a service which focuses on a particular aspect of worker needs such as English language training without always being developed further – although clearly the learning agenda has the potential for politicisation.

That said, unions have tended to develop their strategies of engagement around learning in different ways. In some cases, such activity can be relatively isolated, and almost project-centric, but there are good examples emerging where union-learning is becoming a more embedded part of organisational strategy and structure. Thus, for example, in USDAW union learning is intimately connected to the broader organising agenda, whereas for Community the need to support the employability needs of its members in declining sectors, such as steel and textiles, has seen a nascent interest in learning matters quickly redefine the overarching strategy of the union as a (community) 'union for life' (Stuart 2005).

This leads to a second potential hybrid and role for organising, in terms of community unionism. The debate on the community dimension is very well established in the US (Fine 2006; Milkman 2006). In Britain, the recent engagement with this idea has been driven by specific living wage campaigns and a greater engagement with the spatial dimensions of union organising (see Wills 2004a). Union activity requires extra-workplace support, local participation and broader agendas (Simms 2007a; Wills and Simms 2004). Organising campaigns (such as the The East London Community Organisation (TELCO)/London Citizens one) fuse organising with a community and alliance-based approach (Wills 2004a). Given this, we, therefore, see that organising provides techniques, knowledge, and a language for engaging hard to reach or vulnerable communities. As Holgate's (2009) study of TELCO shows, it is curious how the activist skills of local community stakeholders (not necessarily labour unionists) were influenced and informed by US social movement models of activism, and this shaped the manner of mobilisation and engagement with campaigns. This indicates that organising in communities requires skill and expertise that cannot be taken as given. But it also takes us back to the need to ensure that such skills are actively developed, recognised and created within unions where this should not be seen as something peripheral, or as a fad, but as intrinsic to the broadening of union expertise, strategy and, ultimately, identity.

Yet community union initiatives vary greatly from the engaged to the disinterested in terms of unions (Tattersall 2006). Suspicion amongst various parts of the labour movement exist partly because of the way community initiatives and organisations may be seen as competitors – or as in the case of TELCO, more innovative and democratic in various aspects when compared to various unions. Hence, whilst there has been a fanfare of interest in terms of these initiatives concrete examples remain scarce. One explanation lies in the pragmatic nature of much union activity. Community unionism is, thus, often defined by rather instrumental, *ad-hoc* campaigns when there is a clear and pressing need, such as at Gate Gourmet or around high profile migrant communities. The organising agenda appears to have been disconnected from such initiatives as TELCO and other non-recognition-based issues, even if Unison the public services union appears to have maintained a dialogue through a selection of EUOs and union branches (although not without internal tensions and debates between various levels and areas of the union). A curiosity about the community strategy, as well, is that it links with the learning agenda through the use of learning centres and community access to them, although these have rarely been, in turn, linked to each other in strategic terms or through organising discourse and practice. Again, Community has sought to some extent to fuse its recent learning strategy with its commitment to organising, but this is still far from transparent and it is notable that the union is still trying to conceptualise exactly what its model of community unionism involves and means in terms of broader union identity and purpose (Greer *et al.* 2008). Somehow these are all fragments of a series of union renewal programmes.

The failure to combine and construct a systematically broader and more engaged view of organising across various other 'union fronts' is the issue that we would argue needs addressing most. In this sense, organising is, therefore, best seen as a logic – a narrative – that can potentially and productively sustain and tie together different aspects of new forms of union revitalisation. In some cases, this has emerged but this is not generalisable, and has yet to move past nascent even in so-called 'best practice' examples. This failure to connect at the micro-level is exacerbated by the failure to connect at the macro- and political levels (as discussed previously). In effect, the problem is not solely the lack of micro-level and organisational narratives – we have seen that these exist – but the lack of a broader organisational-political narrative with a uniquely novel or engaging view of purpose and change. This is Waterman's (1998) point about the need for such strategies to have a broader social agenda, although again we would argue that such agendas can be constrained by particular environments and contexts as in the case of Anglo-Saxon industrial relations. Whether one agrees with his solution to this lack of a broader social agenda is another issue, yet his point is that new strategies and renewal tactics need an element of social vision and a broader view of participation.

Conclusion: caught in a dilemma

We feel it is ill-advised to make strong conclusions in terms of statistics. Gall (2007a) makes it clear that we do not know what the future would have been without the strategy of organising. There is also a need to move beyond the discussion about whether organising is simply a conscious long-term strategy or simply maneuvering for survival and continuity of roles. Our chapter suggests that such binaries (strategy versus simple adaptation) are not useful because of the different discourses and understandings that pervade the development, and the empirical practice, of something such as organising. The fact that it is the main confederation – the TUC – driving a large part of the agenda does not mean that it is simply a ploy to rediscover a role for itself and create a mere holding strategy in a context of ever larger merged unions with their own organising agendas. Yet, in the British context what appears to emerge is a failure by unions be they activists, officials or leaders to connect organising with a broader political approach and re-invigorated identity. This is in part due to the ongoing hold of 'new realism', but more importantly the legacy of regulation and organisational practices that continues to shape any new strategic development. Organising often occurs within a relative political vacuum. Moreover, the fixation with recognition means that it is not elaborated in terms of long-term campaigning and community- and socially-based strategies. What we see is that internally it has generated outcomes and links for unions in structural and strategic terms, but externally it seems to be disconnected as a strategy. However, it is also unwise to take what is in effect a man-agerialist and empiricist view of union initiatives and de-contextualise them and imbue them with a level of significance which is beyond their capacity. Organising is, therefore, best seen as a logic – a narrative – that can sustain and tie together different aspects of new forms of union revitalisation. It provides a template for engaging with broader community, learning and locally-based strategies regardless of the pit-falls many have pointed to. At a time when the 'basics' of unionism are being forgotten within various quarters – organising as a strategy plays a curious role in reminding activists and engaged individuals about the mobilising habits and practices of unionism.

Returning to Hyman (2007), the need to re-imagine and connect the labour movement into the broader constituencies of the labour market and society requires a series of broader strategic considerations. The changing nature of work and its social dimension must be seen as cen-tral to any discussion, but this has to be linked to a debate about the democratic and inclusive identity and needs of the union as an organ-isation. Strategically reconnecting with 'society', therefore, means rethink-ing the internal structures and forms of unions. It also means linking education, research, and knowledge-based activity in a more strategic manner around political and ideological objectives, according to Hyman. In many ways, organising as a vehicle for reconnecting with workers more dynamically – and of linking current to past activity – has the potential to open a discussion on purpose and identity – and politics – were it not for that fact it has become increasingly technical and narrow in its means and ends.

Notes

This chapter was first presented as a paper at the 2008 *Labor and Employment Relations Association* conference in New Orleans as part of an international symposium called 'Assessing the efficacy of union organising' organised by Gregor Gall.

1 We looked to verify the Academy's annual intake by union through a number of sources. This included the limited data published by the TUC and survey datasets compiled by Ed Heery and, most recently, Mel Simms and Jane Holgate. We acknowledge and thank all those that supplied their personal data.

2 Something that Simms and Holgate's (2008) 'plea' for a more 'political' consideration reinforces with their anarcho-syndicalist framework.

3 As an aside, it is rather perplexing that no systematic study has yet been conducted on the relationship between unions and the 'fourth estate'.

4 This does not mean we are advocating partnership, as some normative, ideal type mutual gains model that does not deliver, but are using Heery's argument to acknowledge that there may be complex relations and hybrids between different strategies. The point is in essence a methodological one, although it has obvious significance for praxis.

3
Goodbye to All That? Assessing the Organising Model

Simon de Turberville

Introduction

The current focus on union agency – which unites proponents and critics of the 'organising' model – contrasts with the traditional analysis of how economic, state and employer influences have contributed to union decline in Britain, North America and Australasia. This shift from the question of 'what is being done to unions?' to 'what should they do about it?' initially appeared to have generated a disarmingly simple answer. Namely, that the dominant regime of union governance, the 'servicing model' (the problem) generated a vicious circle of decline wherein over-centralisation disengaged members from union agendas, reduced their willingness to support union activities and reduced bargaining gains, thus resulting in a falling membership. Consequently, unions should embrace the decentralised 'organising model' (the solution) which, if implemented, could facilitate a virtuous circle of renewal by increasing member participation, generating relevant goals worth supporting, and enforcing better bargaining outcomes, thereby encouraging a rise in membership.

The common-sense reflected within the organising model made it potentially appealing to a range of divergent concerns; for example, union bureaucrats could embrace it as the solution to financial crisis; union radicals could view it as a route to militancy; and finally, pragmatists could simply look back in history to find a myriad of apparent success stories ranging from the birth of the Industrial Workers of the World (IWW or Wobblies) and Congress of Industrial Organizations (CIO) in the US; the historical role of the Organising Committee of Labor Council of New South Wales in Australia (Cooper 2002) or the influence gained by the First Shop Stewards Movement in Britain (Hinton 1973).

Yet 23 years after the birth of the Service Employees International Union's (SEIU) Justice for Janitors (JfJ) organising campaign in 1985 (Jackson 2004), the efficacy of the model appears questionable. Indeed, there is little to suggest that decline of US density from a peak of 35% in 1954 (Graham 2002: 13) was reversed by the creation of the 'Organizing Institute' in 1989, when density was just over 16%, as it continued to fall and by 2006 stood at only 12% (Hirsch and Macpherson 2008: 1). Similarly, Australian density fell from a high of 51% in 1976 (ABS 2000: 1) to 38% in 1994 (ABS 1996: 8), when 'Organising Works' was initiated, to only 20% in 2006 (ABS 2006: 1). Finally, British union density fell from 54% in 1979 (Halsey 1988: 188) to 27% in 1998 when the 'Organising Academy' was founded, to 26% by 2006 (Grainger and Crowther 2007: 13).

Two divergent explanations for this failure to reverse decline emerged in Britain. The first being that the organising model has not been correctly *implemented* (Carter 2000, 2006). The alternative rationale contends that the organising model is a *flawed strategy* (de Turberville 2004, 2007a). This chapter explains key elements of this debate. In so doing it provides an overview of the two frameworks via an assessment of the models' conceptual coherence and 'real-world' application. The upshot of this overview is that union renewal can be predicated on two divergent conditions. On the one hand, if Carter is correct, then renewal is reliant on unions' willingness and ability to put the organising model into practice. It follows that adherence to the model represents the yardstick against which the success of any organising campaign must be judged. Alternatively, my line of reasoning suggests that unions must be strategically adaptive to survive. Consequently, I contend that there is no generic – as opposed to particular – yardstick against which organising success can be gauged.

This chapter is comprised of five parts. Part one questions the status of the organising model by examining Carter's (2000, 2006) belief that it is a discrete union strategy and my (de Turberville 2004, 2007a) contention that it is a nominal construct. Part two undermines Carter's adhocratic (and other potential) definition(s) of the model by exploring the diffusion of meaning within and between organising terminologies (what, for example, are democracy and education and are they of equal import to the model etcetera?). Part three analyses whether the organising model has been distorted during implementation. Contrary to Carter, who defends the model by claiming that it has been distorted by external shocks and union bureaucrats, my approach also locates flaws within the model and contends that the question of distortion is invalid and therefore of no practical relevance. Part four provides an overview of the effects of the organising model within Britain. It finds little evidence that a paradigm shift from servicing to organising has occurred. A further critique of the work of Voss and Sherman (2000) questions their finding that oligarchy has been reversed in unions thus undermining the central tenet of Carter's definition; namely that decision-making can be devolved to members. The chapter concludes that the organising model has been a useful focus for change but that a far more realistic basis for union renewal is one in which the problem/solution dichotomy is recognised as redundant because organising and servicing are mutually dependent aspects of trade unionism that cannot be employed independently of one another.

The status of the organising model: generic yardstick or rough guide?

Carter's *generic* and my *particular* approaches to union organising are rooted in different understandings of how workers interests are generated and realised. Perhaps the most important idea underlying Carter's generic approach is that class (worker/capitalist) and workplace hierarchies (non-managers/managers) generate: 'interests which underpin ... workplace ideologies ... [Consequently], Marxism [aims] ... to abolish the hierarchical control system, the division of labour and private ownership for profit which necessitates them' (Carter 1995: 46). Thereafter, '[u]nder a socialist mode of production, there would be discussion about methods, delegation coordination and collective control' (Carter 1995: 66).

It seems to me that Carter applies this rationale to his treatment of union renewal. For example, within his approach the shared class interests of trade unionists become obscured by the servicing model because their roles become bifurcated between the more active employed union officers (EUOs) who are apt to maintain their elite positions by maintaining a harmonious relationship with capital and an increasingly reliant and thus pliable membership. Three complementary lines of contention follow. First, the servicing model is inherently problematic because it sustains capitalism and should be abolished. Second, by predicating his approach on the existence of material interests, Carter justifies a *goal-orientated* organising model in which present interests are transcended by eradicating union bureaucracy thus (presumably) encouraging unionists to unite against capitalism. Third, it follows, given the stark contrast between hierarchical (servicing) and non-hierarchical (organising) models, that 'there is a *radical difference* between, on the one hand, union orientations that engage members, stimulate activity and develop their confidence (organizing), and those, on the other, that encourage dependency by taking decisions out of the hands of members and vesting them in individuals and officials, whether lay or full-time (servicing)' (Carter 2006: 416 emphasis added). For Carter, the organising model is therefore *the* solution to union decline.

In contrast, my particular approach stems from the idea that drives, or desires, *produce* interests and consciousness. Once created, interests can then attract subsequent drives (such that 'I feel it is in my interests to be a good worker; a trade unionist; a revolutionary etcetera'). People thus reproduce and partially subjugate themselves to pre-established societal patterns during the civil, labour and valorising processes. From this perspective, a rational, Marxist claim such as 'it is in our interests to end class relations' *functions* by assigning us a correct (revolutionary) role[1] thus prescribing how we should relate to one-another (and thereby attempting to bureaucratise us). The consequent risk of *only* basing strategy on existent interests – especially a narrow interpretation of interests such as Carter's – is that this generates a rational basis upon which to subjugate the productive drives of all individuals/groups to a single goal. This privileging of interest-based theory/strategy over practice[2] then shores-up aspects of the past[3] by disregarding the causal and innovatory influence of drives (Deleuze and Guattari 2003a, 2003b; Deleuze 2006). So, drives underpin processes of change as they determine which existent interests members are attracted to and, thus, willing to support whilst allowing participants to creatively contribute to processes of change. This framework is then applied to the subject of union renewal in the following three points. First, an organising model premised on interests effectively subjugates members to bureaucracy (that is, interest-based roles) as much as a servicing model, thus under-mining the rationale for a shift from servicing to organising. Second, the organising model cannot be implemented independently of the servicing model (see also Boxall and Haynes (1997) and Waddington and Kerr (2000)). Indeed, many members want professional advice *and* some level of participation. Consequently, the servicing model pro-vides for a certain level of member activity (upward lines of commun-ication that influence the agenda and legitimate leaderships) and the organising model some degree of inactivity (downward lines of com-munication to plan organising campaigns and activate memberships). The models are therefore interdependent (de Turberville, 2004, 2007a). Finally, (i) members do not have the same interests – some members will have pensions, shares; high levels of control; own their tools/work from home, whilst others will not – and (ii) interests can not predict future desires nor actions (for example, Friedrich Engels had employers' interests but desired Communism). It follows that the starting point for effective organising are the desires of the membership as these predict which interests will be supported. Consequently an interest-based, generic organising model, that is radically different from servicing, is not a credible union renewal strategy.

Configuring the organising model or deconstructing organising models?

Carter (2006) responded to my critique by elaborating a fourfold definition of the organising model based on a supportive leadership, an increase in democracy, a decreasing bureaucracy and an empowered membership. These ideas are reflected in his conviction that 'the role of national and local leaderships in transforming unions is central' (Carter 2006: 422) and that there is 'a need for [union] initiatives to be democratically discussed and agreed, changing demands and expectations of members in the process' (Carter 2006: 418). His goal for organising is made apparent during a critique he makes of Waddington and Kerr's (2000) 'vision of organising. [Apparently this] is still a servicing model, with membership dependency maintained through the delivery of services by lay, rather than full-time, officers' (Carter 2006: 416). In short, Carter's goal is to remove these bureaucratic posts and form an adhocracy. Finally, these initiatives should 'stimulate a movement towards independence and competence in the membership' (Carter 2006: 416). So, for Carter, the organising model is being used when leaderships stimulate participative-forms of democracy that disestablish bureaucracy whilst empowering union members.

Arguably, Carter's definition is flawed because 'if union bureaucracies must be disestablished because they suppress memberships, but this is only achievable once both parties [leaders and members] work in mutuality towards that aim, then it must paradoxically be assumed that those same bureaucracies are predominantly emancipatory, rather than suppressive in nature. It follows that they should not be removed' (de Turberville 2007a: 573). Second, all democracies depend on bureaucratic mechanisms – for example, administrating union-wide democratic procedures that detail who can vote, that relevant literature is distributed and votes collated. Consequently Carter's idea that democracy can be gained whilst dis-establishing bureaucracy is unsound.

Finally, his definition presupposes how members will democratically act, (whereas instead of disestablishing union bureaucracies members could, for example, reconfigure roles, change staff, or alter external relationships).

If it is accepted that Carter's organising model is flawed it could still be assumed that an alternative generic strategy to solve a common servicing problem could be implemented. There are five reasons why such an assumption is mistaken: unions have different servicing orientations; are faced with a diversity of (internal and external) problems that would generate different outcomes from a single model; the purpose of organising has never been agreed; nor is there consent as to how key organising terms relate to each other; and finally, there is not even agreement as to what key terms mean. These issues will now be explored.

First, historical developments indicate that servicing is not equally ingrained on a national basis. For example, a potted overview shows that the genesis of servicing occurred around 1955 in the US (Hurd 1998). Thirty years later the ratio of EUOs to members stood at around 1:1,000 in factory locals and only 1:200 in non-factory locals (Wallihan 1985: 106). Because non-factory locals tended to be responsible for organising, and thus some staff were organisers, high staff to member ratios can only provide an imprecise indication that servicing dominated over organising.[4] Yet it was also the case that unions covering 79% and 82% of private and public sector members raised, on average, less than a third of total revenue from member-based dues (Masters 1997: 93). On balance, it thus seems reasonable to conclude that US unions have been more professionalised (or service-orientated), for longer, and that membership loss has been less of a threat to union survival than in Britain (see below). Indeed, although differential research timing prevents a direct comparison, the increasing pervasiveness of servicing appears to have emerged considerably later – the 1980s – in Britain. It is, therefore, not surprising that the ratio of EUOs to members was far lower at 1:3,229 in the late 1980s (Kelly and Heery 1994: 37) whilst members accounted for a much higher percentage (82%) of income in 1989 (Willman *et al.* 1993: 11). This shorter duration of servicing, lower staffing levels and far greater dependence on members for income and workplace activism, suggests that servicing is significantly less ingrained and member-loss financially a more threatening problem for many British, as compared to US, unions. Finally, the state support which, until recently, was lent to Australian unions has engendered greater centralisation than found in British unions and necessitates quite different renewal strategies in each country (de Turberville 2007c). In short, there tends to be marked national differences in union organisation which suggests that there is not a common servicing problem that could be countered with a generic renewal strategy.

Second, given that unions are faced with a diversity of problems, it is unlikely that they could generate the same outcomes by implementing a generic strategy. For instance, members within a large, heterogeneous public sector union such as Unison are unlikely to have the same level of education and knowledge of other member's jobs, thus, making effective representation and, thus, the potential for devolution more difficult than for somebody within a smaller, craft-style, union such as the British Medical Association (BMA). Similarly, whilst the TGWU had strengthened its commitment to organising (Carter 2006), it is unlikely that its 806,938 members (see below for details of subsequent mergers) would have had 'the same opportunities to participate ... at the same levels and same influence as members of a small homogenous union such as the Welsh Rugby Players' Association' (de Turberville 2007a: 570). Another possible limitation to participation exists in the likelihood that an expanding constituency of members will engender structures of representation to enable prompt decision-making; in short, expansion is likely to place increasing limits on participation. Organising may also be self-limiting to the extent that influxes of non-traditional members, with undeveloped steward's networks, will be highly reliant on EUOs for servicing. Equally, organising can be constrained by external pressures. For example, it is difficult to conceive of devolved decision-making where collective bargaining is centralised (de Turberville 2004). Finally, there is little reason to believe that all organising goals are equally applicable to all unions. A glaring case is that of the public sector union, Unison, which is generally recognised, whereas the Iron and Trades Confederation (ISTC) (now merged, see below) experienced extensive de-recognition and, therefore, viewed recognition as a central organising goal (Gall 2004). So, union size, member heterogeneity, union tradition, and employer strategies, are all likely to undermine a generic organising strategy.

Third, if as advocated by proponents of the organising model, participative democracy should form a central tenet of unionism, then the question of 'what are we here for?' (George Woodcock cited in Taylor 1999: 195) must surely remain open to constant renegotiation to enable grassroots influence to flourish. Put another way, because unions do not have stable, identikit memberships, it is likely that they will never desire (and thus support) a generic goal-based strategy for change. Indeed, the heterogeneous nature of unionism is reflected in the finding that '[t]here is a general understanding that some application of organizing principles to representational work is desirable, [however, f]or some unionists, this implies that internal practices are more democratic; for others, it means there is an emphasis on activities aimed at mobilization and on direct action; and for others... the aim is to involve members in actions that attract coworkers who then join the union' (Fletcher and Hurd 1998: 40). Indeed, one could easily add other goals such as gaining recognition (Bronfenbrenner and Juravich 1998; Gall 2003d) or education (Nissen 2002).

Of course, many such foci are really sub-goals and the real purposes of them are to generate indeterminate gains that reflect the desires of EUOs, stewards and members (such as, recognition will generate partnership, or bargaining gains, or ultimately mobilise workers against management by illuminating injustice). Yet these possibilities only illuminate the fourth problem. Even if it can be agreed that organising is vital for union renewal, little more has been acquiesced to than the idea that some kind of change is necessary. Why? Because the status or relationships between key terminologies still remain unclear. Indeed, a couple of brief examples focusing on education and democracy should demonstrate just how easy it is to translate the organising model into two quite different programs. Within one, democratic debate could facilitate meaningful education, thereby, empowering members with knowledge (Foucault 1991). In this case, organising would be a situated process in which the relevance of education and knowledge vary according to the particular problems being faced, thus, generating localised forms of resistance that can never fully emancipate union members – for new regimes of power and knowledge will always emerge from resistance. An alternative proposition is that education facilitates democratic debate. Democratic agreement encourages convergence between individuals, thus, reducing their alienation from their social nature (Marx 1992). The purpose of organising in this second example is to generate a sense of class which, in Marxist parlance, can act for itself, thus gaining emancipation from exploitative class relations. Theoretical crudeness aside, the point is that the organising model could easily be interpreted into a myriad of alternative viewpoints that ultimately dependent on the ways in which participants desires generate new, or are attracted by existent, interests.

Finally, more complexity can then be introduced by simply asking – what is meant by key but seemingly simple and innocuous terms such as 'education' and 'democracy'? Inset 3.1 interprets key organising model terminology on a continuum of soft to hard. What a brief glance at the inset reveals is that responses to the question posed can potentially be very disparate in nature. Indeed, it is unlikely that a group of stewards, or a branch membership, let alone an entire union, would concur about what any one, let alone all, key organising terms mean. Whilst the ability to perform this exercise suggests that there is some accord regarding the key issues within an organising agenda, it simultaneously demonstrates that the pluralities hypothesised to encourage common support for the organising model (the conservative, pragmatic and radical rationales discussed earlier) could equally engender fervent disagreement regarding its implementation.

In contrast to Carter then, I contend that unions are not experiencing a common servicing problem that could be solved by using a generic organising model. In reality, the organising model is a nominal and quite often problematic concept that is idiosyncratically constructed in the hope of dealing with a plethora of problems.

Inset 3.1   Interpreting key organising terms

Key Terms	Interpretation	
	Soft	Hard
Anti-bureaucratic	Increased Accountability	Adhocracy
Democratic	Rights and duties	Utilitarian
Emancipation	Regulatory	Revolutionary
Mobilizing Focus	Intra Union	Employer/state
Recruiting	Internal	External
Education	Development	Training
Recognition	Partnership	Adversarial Bargaining

Note: This table represents neither an accurate nor exhaustive taxonomy. Rather, its purpose is simply to demonstrate that there are potential variations in the way that key organising terminologies can be interpreted.

Distorting the organising model?

Carter's primary research into organising, which focuses mainly on events within Manufacturing Science and Finance (MSF) (Carter 2000; Carter and Cooper 2002; Carter and Poynter 1999), provides a useful overview of some of the practical difficulties that can be encountered when attempting to implement his model. Carter (2000: 128) himself observed that:

> In the lexicon of the national organisation, organising was good and servicing was bad. But at the level of practice, officers could not

see how the maintenance of this dichotomy was possible ... The general [MSF] strategy of 'Organising Works' was supported but reservations were expressed about the speed and the sensitivity of the changes and the contradictory demands placed upon officers. Examples were given of experienced representatives, who had successfully built workplace organisations, refusing to handle some issues. On occasions, the Regional Officer had received the simple threat that if '[y]ou tell me to do it ... you won't have a Senior Rep in the hospital next week'.

For Carter, the existence of contradictory national policies (partnership and organising), the tension that existed between the dominant servicing and prospective organising approaches, and a pragmatic, as opposed to strategic, approach to change, ultimately provided: 'an example of how even radical ideas become distorted' (Carter 2000: 133). He continued: 'The result has been that the organizing strategy has failed, acknowledged tacitly by the need for ... merger' (Carter and Cooper 2002: 735). My own research within Unison also found that union staff and members could be resistant to change (de Turberville 2007b). I have likewise commented on the implied failure of organising as signalled by the mergers of organising unions such as the ISTC and the Knitwear, Footwear and Apparel Trades union (KFAT) to form Community, and the Graphical, Paper and Media Union (GPMU) merging with Amicus; a union which then further merged with the T&G to form Unite (de Turberville 2007a) – itself now merged with the United Steel Workers (USW) to become the first 'fully functional and registered trade union organisation in the UK, US, Ireland and Canada' (Workers Uniting 2008).

These similarities, however, also obscure significant divergence between the positions taken by Carter and myself. When examining organising from a historical perspective, my central claim was that variations, or approximations, of the organising model were used in the US by the IWW, CIO, United Auto Workers (UAW) and the Steelworkers Organizing Committee (SWOC), and in Britain, by the first and second shop stewards movements. These had generated successes that were unsustainable in the light of state and employer hostility (de Turberville 2004). Carter's central problem with my account was that it gave: 'little significance to the size, scope and importance of rank-and-file initiatives as the basis for the surge of union membership in the 1930s [within the US] ... That organization and militancy subsequently atrophied *was not the responsibility of organizing approaches* as such, but specific historical developments, such as the Second World War and its Cold War aftermath. Militant elements within unions were purged and whole unions expelled from the CIO ... [de Turberville] maintains that any belief that there was "a golden age of organizing" in Britain is equally misguided' (Carter 2006: 417, emphasis added).

My (de Turberville 2007a: 568–569) approach agreed with that of Carter to the extent that 'economic dislocation [generated by shocks such as war] weakened organizing potential [and was therefore] wholly consistent with my contention that the OM [organising model] was often ineffective in the light of state and employer hostility (these being, in part, economically motivated)'. Where the two approaches diverge is that Carter (2006) effectively absolves the model by only blaming failure on context and union bureaucracy – for example, left-wing elements being expelled from the CIO (de Turberville 2004) – whereas my analysis also finds that failures occurred because of four weaknesses within the model.

First, if the organising model really is *the* solution to union decline then its defining features (for Carter these are empowerment via adho-cracy, leadership and democracy) must result in an ability to counter external pressures. Yet, Carter's defence of the model is inconsistent in that he maintains that it is the radical solution to union decline and a prerequisite for political organisation, whilst paradoxically contending that the model failed due to a lack of that same political support which he claims the model generates (de Turberville 2007a). In fairness, my criticism ignores the possibility that broader support could be gen-erated over time and could counter external shocks – though Carter does not discuss this possibility. Second, by locating failure externally and in union hierarchies, Carter enfeebles the influence of union grass-roots agency to the role of victim, thus, treating the empowered members that he claims are generated by his model (after all, they had appar-ently been organised) as being largely incapable of countering resist-ance. Third, there have been significant organising failures which did not occur due to external shocks or bureaucrats. For example, 'Oper-ation Dixie' (1946–53) demonstrated an inability to collectivise groups with disparate ethnic identities in the US. Finally, whilst such organ-ising related failures were occurring, US private sector membership was growing. Indeed, it increased by 14,424,000 and density by almost 29% between 1900 and 1955 (de Turberville 2007a). Similarly, the influence of shop stewards movements on UK growth was partial. The first move-ment had expired by the early 1920s whilst the second 'movement' failed to 'build sustained links even across individual employers' (Terry 1985, cited in McIlroy 1995: 105). It, therefore, stretches credibility to

believe that the growth of 6,351,000 members and density of 33%
between 1933 and 1979 was the result of Carter's organising model
(de Turberville 2007a). So, although there has never been a single organising model whose effectiveness could be gauged over time it remains reasonable to claim that whilst 'broader organizing activities bore fruit those
narrower concerns [more closely] related to... [organising models] tended,
as accepted by Carter, to atrophy' (de Turberville 2007a: 569).

Carter props up his absolution of the organising model (failure due
to external shocks and poor implementation) with the claim that it has
been successfully implemented within the SEIU and in the form of
TELCO/London Citizens. For instance, Carter cites 'a detailed account
of the eventually successful attempts by the ... [SEIU] to organize home
and nursing care workers ... Lopez makes it clear, moreover, that in
cases of failure to organize, the responsibility lies less with the organizing approach, as such, and has more to do with poor planning and
lack of sensitivity in implementation ... Working with Unison [in
Britain ... TELCO] targeted workers in sub-contract companies in three
hospitals and in a two-year period over 400 members were added to
the branches ... The inability to spread the success to other sectors of
the East London community was less to do with the appropriateness of
the model of organizing, or the nature of the potential membership,
and more to do with the reluctance or inability of other unions to
grant sufficient resources or importance to the project' (Carter 2006:
420–421).

If Carter is correct than it is reasonable to expect these instances
of implementation to conform to his radical and adhocratic definition
of the organising model. His definition implies that implementation is
occurring if four conditions hold: the union leadership promotes democracy; the union becomes more democratic; the ultimate goal of this
exercise is to disestablish union bureaucracy; and that these processes
empower members. My examination of change within the SEIU suggests that the answer to these four tests is predominantly negative. For
instance, Andy Stern, the SEIU President, believes that: '[w]orkers want
their lives to be changed. They want strength and a voice, not some
purist, intellectual, historical, mythical democracy...' (Stern cited in
Members for Democracy Archive (2008: 9)). As a result of Stern's limited
concerns for democracy, it is perhaps unsurprising that its practice actually appears to be increasingly threatened within the union. Between
1996 and 2004, 40 Locals or 14% of the union total, were taken into
trusteeship (Early 2004b: 6). Indeed, this undemocratic mechanism has
been credited for exporting the JfJ model (or organising) across the

union (Tait 2005 cited in de Turberville (2007a)). Bureaucratic change within the SEIU also confounds the idea that the union is implementing Carter's model. Figures show that the number of national EUOs employed by the union has grown from 20 in 1984 to roughly 600 at present (Early 2004b: 5); that is, an increase from one EUO per every 26,400 members in 1984 to one per 2,837 members in 2004.[5] Finally, this process of reorganisation has certainly generated gains – membership growth, recognition, bargaining – but do these conform to Carter's model? An objective reply must be, at least, equivocal. Much of the evidence used above comes from self-organised sites, thus, implying that changes within the SEIU are generating a pro-democratic-cum-anti-bureaucratic ethos in many activists. On the other hand, such changes are occurring despite the formal organising approach being employed within the union. Given that any empowerment is fuelled by resistance to a democratically intransigent leadership, a decline in democracy and an increase in bureaucracy it is reasonable to conclude, on balance, that the SEIU have not implemented the organising model as defined by Carter.

The belief that Carter's model has been implemented by TELCO is also problematic. Like the SEIU, TELCO – a predominantly faith-based coalition of community groups and a minority of union branches – can be credited for successfully organising service workers. Their actions, however, differ in three important respects from Carter's model. First, the building of this new coalition tells us little about how to implement Carter's model in mature over-centralised institutions such as unions. Moreover, the relevance of such cases is doubly questionable given that the influence of campaigning and voluntary organisations on union activities has been negligible (Heery 2005). Second, TELCO organised to encourage the integration of communities and workers into the *status quo*. As a result they are simply not attempting to build the class-based interest group envisioned by Carter within his organising model (de Turberville 2007a). Third, TELCO's geographical focus within London must raise questions regarding its general applicability in other locations.

The influence of the organising model and reversal of oligarchy

Finally, it is important to situate the aforementioned cases within the 'bigger picture'. The following section, therefore, provides a brief overview of organising tendencies within British unions and critically analyses the extent to which the reported reversal of Michel's 'iron law of oligarchy' (Voss and Sherman 2000) provides support for the idea that union renewal can occur via devolved unionism.

The most recent summary of union renewal strategies provides tentative signs that many British unions are influenced by the organising model but little to suggest that a wholesale paradigm shift towards Carter's vision is occurring. Organising has become increasingly formalised in many British unions with 17 (59% of TUC membership in the first year) TUC unions having sponsored organisers (Heery *et al.* 2003a: 82). Similarly, trainees reported that in 86% of campaigns they attempt to identify new activists, in 70% they tried to create a workplace committee or branch and, in 88% they encouraged stewards to intensify recruitment activity (Heery *et al.* 2003a: 81). Academy Organisers' campaigns recruited 39,987 new members, 1,800 new activists, and gained (or anticipated) 339 new recognition agreements (Heery *et al.* 2003c: 9). Further optimism is evident in the finding that recruitment and organising has become a more prominent component of EUO's work (Heery 2006). Yet, although unions are increasingly recruiting women, ethnic minorities and atypical workers, recruitment predominantly occurs in workplaces that already recognises unions rather than in greenfield sites – that is, a strategy of consolidation dominates over expansion – and most workers targeted by any one union work in occupations that it has previously organised, thus indicating that union ambitions remain somewhat conservative in nature (Heery *et al.* 2002). Moreover, 'evidence on organizing ... indicates a high degree of variation in practice, even amongst union[s] that have sponsored organizers at the TUC's Academy' and even though 'a "union-building" approach is fairly widespread in the United Kingdom ... it co-exists with a servicing approach' (Heery *et al.* 2002: 2, 4). In a nutshell, evidence shows that a significant proportion of British members are now in unions that are developing mechanisms to support organising related activities, and tentative signs exist that decline is being halted. There is, however, little to suggest that a paradigm shift from servicing to organising is occurring.

It would, therefore, be easy to claim that the tendency for British unions to use a combinatorial approach to organising relegates Carter's radical approach to nothing more than an ideal. Conversely, he could respond, as summarised above, that this finding is merely a symptom of the very problem that his model is designed to counter – namely, the existence of an elite cadre of EUOs who are distorting the radical potential of the model. What remains crucial for Carter's case – though it is noteworthy that he does not make this claim – is that unions must be capable of reversing Michel's law of oligarchy if his model is to have any 'real-world' validity. The remainder of this section explains why such a reversal is unlikely.

Voss and Sherman (2000) detailed the breaking of the iron law of oligarchy in a sample of US locals and this is particularly significant as a similar devolutionary process is required during the implementation of Carter's adhocratic model. Voss and Sherman concluded that the 'iron law' could be broken when three conditions coincided. First, political crisis within union locals generated a mandate for change. Second, this mandate then encouraged a growth of new innovative leaders with experience of activism from outside of the union. Third, support for change was provided by union leaderships. Yet Leach (2005) claimed that Voss and Sherman (2000) provided no evidence of oligarchy being overturned. He reasoned that oligarchy is only reversed when members gain control of decision-making from entrenched elites, but, what Voss and Sherman were interested in was not *who* makes decisions but rather *what is on the agenda*. In their own words, what Voss and Sherman (2000: 316) were 'specifically concerned with how social movements break out of conservatism in goals and tactics. Thus, we defined "revitalized" locals as those that ha[ve] shifted away from servicing current union members to organizing the unorganized and that used unconventional disruptive tactics in these organizing campaigns'. Leach (2005: 320) pointed out that in so doing they conflated oligarchy with bureaucratic conservatism, and it, therefore, became apparent that 'what Voss and Sherman interpret as a reversal of oligarchization is a situation where the leadership (a minority) successfully pushes through a top-down initiative against the active resistance of the membership because it sees the survival of the organization threatened by shrinking membership rolls [not by a crisis of participation]. Far from constituting a refutation of the iron law, this case would seem to represent a quintessential example of oligarchy in action ... *Radicalism is not the opposite of oligarchy, democracy is*' (Leach, 2005: 320, emphasis added).

So, the finding that unions are changing their agendas to cope with contemporary problems remains salient. Yet, more importantly within the context of this chapter, is that without compelling evidence to suggest that unions can devolve decision-making back to members the central goal of Carter's adhocratic organising model remains almost wholly speculative and counter-factual.

Conclusions

This chapter has interrogated the conceptual coherence, and examined evidence for the implementation of, the organising model. It found that the model was not coherent and remained reliant on servicing during implementation. My conclusion is, therefore, that the organising model is not a credible union renewal strategy. Rather, the internal variations and plethora of externally generated problems require unions to be strategically adaptive if they are to reverse decline. More specifically, by examining and extending the debate between Carter and myself, the chapter has shown that a generic organising model, which is radically different from the servicing model, is not a viable conceptual or empirical construct. Instead, the organising model is more realistically viewed as a nominal concept with a broad-based remit which is seemingly capable of attracting the diverse attentions of conservatives, radicals, and pragmatists. This not only indicates the potential appeal of the organising model as a renewal strategy but simultaneously leaves it open to each group's (and individual's) interpretations and (re)configurations of its core terminologies (democracy, education, recruitment etcetera). From this perspective the question of distortion during implementation is invalid – a coherent model does not exist that could be distorted. Moreover, it has been suggested that the changes within the SEIU and TELCO do not, as Carter has claimed, conform to, or support, the viability of his organising model. Nor is there evidence that a reversal of oligarchy – a necessary component of his model – has occurred in unions.

It is undeniable that from Carter's (2006: 421) perspective my line of reasoning offers a 'pessimistic verdict on the ability of unions to become vehicles for membership self-activity and self-determination ... for him [de Turberville] the promise of the organizing model is entirely illusory'. Yet my position is more open than implied by Carter's statement. As contended in my original article (de Turberville 2004), the organising model can attract different interest groups and provides a focus upon which to discuss how a union's procedural/substantive emphasis may be changed via the recombination of the 'two' models. Whilst this assumes an inevitable bureaucratisation of union activity, thus placing constraints on self-determination, the extension of my position detailed above also recognises that drives enable individuals to generate new, or attract them to, existing interests. It follows that self-determination has a central, if constrained, part to play in union reorganisation.

Finally, if one accepts my alternative vision in which organising is recognised alongside servicing as a loose combination of activities and goals that are, to varying degrees, always present in union practice, then the evidence mobilised within this chapter is cautiously optimistic. Exemplar organisations such as the SEIU and TELCO may not be using Carter's model but they do demonstrate how union and coalition agencies can collectivise previously unorganised workers. Moreover, Heery *et al.*'s (2002, 2003a) survey evidence shows that the growing investment of many British unions are beginning to put mechanisms for change into place that show tentative signs of encouraging activism and slowing membership decline. As such, the importance of organising is increasing relative to servicing in some unions. Yet, whilst approximations of the organising model have been, and are again likely to become, comparatively influential within particular national and localised contexts, it is unrealistic to believe that such episodes indicate that a crude shift from a servicing-as-problem to an organising-as-solution dichotomy is occurring. Rather, a more tenable explanation is to view such developments as idiosyncratic combinations of the two models. Ultimately, there is no necessary reason to assume that organising is less of a problem than servicing (or visa versa). What seems important is that unions generate suitable combinations using elements from the 'two' models that remain open to the changing wishes of members. It follows that union renewal is not premised on strategic conformity, but on strategic adaptability.

Notes

1 Unitarist and pluralist frameworks function in a similar fashion by assuming/ engendering roles that function according to shared or sectional interests.

2 It is noteworthy that Marx attempted to avoid being theory-driven by effectively developing a non-systematic corpus of work in response to real-world events (Balibar 1996).

3 For example, the reality of so-called Marxist governance (though not the intent of many Marxists – including Carter) is that it displaced hierarchies based on ownership for hierarchies founded on a 'peoples party' (China, Cuba, North Korea, USSR) as expressed in the joke that 'capitalism is the exploitation of man by man and communism is the exact opposite'. Ironically, the implementation of an organising model such as Carter's would also require a hierarchy that subordinates participative processes to the realisation of his pre-ordained goal of adhocracy (in the members' interests).

4 A comparison in which a high ratio of EUOs per member signals a more ingrained servicing-orientation seems, however, to be justified because a similar variation existed in British workloads (that is, the comparison is not one of apples and pears). For example, 'the time [British EUOs] spent on recruitment

showed a bimodal distribution with a minority of 18 officers ranking it amongst their top three activities, whilst another group of 31 officers ranked it sixth or seventh' (Kelly and Heery 1989: 201).

5   The 1984 figure is an incorrect if roughly accurate guide. It was calculated from Early's (2004b: 5) 1984 EUO statistics and the SEIU's membership in 1979 (Masters 1997: 69). The second figure is correct and was calculated from Early's (2004b: 5) EUO figures and the SEIUs membership of 1,702,639 for 2004 (US Department of Labor 2008b).

4
Union Organising and Partnership in Manufacturing, Finance and Public Services in Britain

Andy Danford, Mike Richardson, Stephanie Tailby and Martin Upchurch

Introduction

More than ten years have now elapsed since the TUC launched its 'New Unionism' project in 1996. As has been well documented, in its early stages 'New Unionism' embodied an attempt to arrest the decline of union membership and influence at work by incorporating certain elements of an aggressive organising approach associated with the North American 'organising model' (Carter 2000, 2006; Heery *et al.* 2000c). In some quarters, early hopes for the potential of the organising model were influenced by the emergence of a distinctive 'union renewal' debate. In an essentially grass roots-based argument, great stress was placed upon the need to democratise union form and hierarchy by locating rank-and-file union activists as core agents in processes both of membership mobilisation at work and democratic practice within union structures and broader community activity (Fairbrother 1996, 2000). Thus, in the context of union decline in the workplace and civil society, looked at through the prism of renewal, the organising model was seen as containing the potential to reverse this decline by shifting the form of unionism to something less concerned with membership recruitment *per se* and more focused on unionism as process. That is, if strong workplace union organisation is to be built and sustained in the longer term, then union activity required re-constructing around principles of member participation at multiple levels. As Carter (2000, 2006) has consistently acknowledged, however, in too many cases the actual adoption of the organising model has been marked by a tendency to de-prioritise the building of grassroots organisation and instead to rely on leadership-driven processes at the centre with an inevitable focus on short-term recruitment.

Considering the pivotal role of union members in the renewal thesis, there has been remarkably little research that attempts to systematically elicit their views on these questions. One notable exception is the work of Lévesque and his colleagues in Canada. Their study of the impact of increasing labour market heterogeneity on union identities surveyed 1500 union members in Quebec (Lévesque *et al.* 2005). Apart from establishing overwhelming endorsement of the necessity of union organising at work, their results showed that, *inter alia*, members who perceive the local union as less democratic are less likely to support traditional, more oppositional union forms compared to those who perceive their unions as more democratic and more responsive to members' views. This highlighted the key processual challenge for union renewal in that member involvement and worker solidarity were not natural, spontaneous phenomena but outcomes of a 'process of socialisation, of repeated efforts to develop alliances and complicities between workers despite the differences that might separate them' (Lévesque *et al.* 2005: 419).

There exists some recent case study research of organising campaigns in the UK that confirms this conclusion. Badigannavar and Kelly's (2005) work on the higher education sector found that where the local union was able to establish more powerful collective action frames by voicing worker concerns and building stronger identification between workers and the union then organising outcomes were more favourable. Similarly, Simms's (2007b) multi-sectoral case studies of organising campaigns in greenfield establishments found that the organising model was more likely to generate success when two conditions obtained. The first was the construction of viable union structures at the workplace. The second was elevating grassroots activists into leading positions alongside employed union officers in co-ordinated multi-site organising campaigns.

These case studies confirm the continuing resonance of the union renewal thesis. That is, organising strategies which attempt to sideline the careful fostering of grassroots organisation and democratic structures in the interests of short-term membership gains are likely at some point to relapse into the long-term expense of servicing and dwindling numbers of disillusioned union recruits. Heery *et al.*'s (2003b) surveys of national union strategy governing new organising processes suggested that many unions have, indeed, come to the policy position of supporting the building of workplace union structures rather than recruitment for its own sake. However, they also found that this pattern was uneven in that support for the organising model increasingly became part of a multi-strand approach, which for other writers, included quite contradictory forms of unionism, the most contentious of which in ideological terms is 'workplace partnership'. The principles of partnership were incorporated into the TUC's 'New Unionism' project in the aftermath of the 1997 general election. The 'new' Labour government provided an important impetus for this development, both materially, through the creation of the Department of Trade and Industry's Partnership Fund and ideologically, with the government's emphasis upon 'modernising' employment relations with a distinctive individualising agenda (Stuart and Martínez Lucio 2005a; Smith and Morton 2001).

The evidence suggests that unions which sign up to partnership relationships with employers do not necessarily enter into a uniform type of power relation. For instance, Kelly (2004: 271) distinguishes between different forms of partnership in terms of variations along a continuum in the balance of power in the employment relationship. Two main contrasting forms are outlined: 'employer-dominant' partnerships characterised by a balance of power in favour of the employer with partnership agendas mostly controlled by employers and characterised by union compliance; and 'labour-parity agreements' marked by a more even balance of power with partnership agendas that reflect the interests of the employer and the union. Writing in a similar vein but adopting a mode of analysis associated with the sociology of risk, Martínez Lucio and Stuart (2005: 808–809) delineate different partnership forms two of which are seen to be more prominent. The first is the transitional form, or 'marriage of convenience' associated with productivity coalitions and aimed at securing mutually agreed short-term objectives. Such partnerships limit the risk of conflict over unreciprocated longer term commitments and expectations. The second is the coerced form of partnership, or 'shotgun wedding'. This is a more elaborate example of Kelly's 'employer-dominant' form in that the management-union relation is marked by coercion and compliance and often designed and sustained by elites within the employer, and sometimes the union too, both detached from grassroots interests.

The extent to which union support for partnership is a reflection of proactive strategy rather than a function of both the power of the employer and the failure or inability of unions to resist the employers' increasingly unitarist interpretation of union recognition is a moot point. Examples of the latter scenario, involving a critical weakening of embryonic union organisation, can be found in a recent volume on union organising campaigns (see Findlay and McKinlay 2003; Gall 2003b; Taylor and Bain 2003). Moreover, current workplace-level studies of partnership have generated little concrete evidence of the 'mutual gain' that we might associate with 'labour parity' or 'marriage of convenience' partnership forms. One recent study by Samuel (2007) argued that partnership can succeed in certain circumstances and notably if management-union relationships at the inter-personal level are propitious. But his case studies are curiously uni-dimensional, focusing solely on consultation processes rather than more concrete indices of union effectiveness under partnership, such as collective bargaining processes, bargaining outcomes, and patterns of union activism at the workplace. Other writers more sympathetic to partnership, such as Oxenbridge and Brown (2004), found that in workplaces where more 'robust' partnership relationships were obtained, positive outcomes were generated in the form of better early warning systems in processes of dispute resolution, union re-positioning in acting as intermediaries to improve management's message and union success in acting as efficient transmission belts for management communications. But it is hard to discern how these can be regarded as an encouragement to autonomous trade unionism and grassroots democracy. Indeed, it is no surprise that Oxenbridge and Brown uncovered a number of problems in this respect, not the least, the distancing of stewards from their members' concerns (for further evidence of this in other partnership contexts, see Danford *et al.* (2003, 2005)).

More critical writers have highlighted also a number of primary concerns related to the employment relationship and the labour process. For instance, Kelly's (2004) review of social partnership agreements in Britain found no evidence that different partnership types compared favourably to non-partnership agreements with respect to wages and conditions settlements or union density. Moreover, the employer-dominant form was more likely to assist employers in labour-cutting processes. And, what of the labour process and job control? Whilst there is insufficient evidence of the impact of workplace partnership on traditions of collective job controls in the unionised sectors, a number of recent research projects have made some progress in this regard. For example, in a series of related articles governing the introduction of teamworking in Britain's steel sector, Bacon and Blyton (2006, 2007) found that conflictual union approaches to bargaining on this issue generated demonstrably more favourable worker outcomes compared to co-operative forms of unionism. More fundamentally, whilst Jenkins's (2006, 2007) multiple case study research into partnership in traditional manufacturing settings discerned nuances in the nature of personal management-union relations, a common thread linking her studies was how workplace unions were forced to forgo the traditions of job control and engage in initiatives which merely facilitated the introduction of company policy on management's terms.

Overall, the pattern of union trajectory in the ten years since the birth of 'New Unionism' seems akin to a position of 'alternative routes to partial failure'. For sure, if we focus solely on membership totals then British unions can be seen to have enjoyed at least some success in stemming the long decline suffered under 18 years of Conservative government. And, notwithstanding the concentration of union members in the public sector, there is no denying a shift in the union membership base towards more women workers and the services industries. Nevertheless, if we look for patterns of progress through the prism of union *process* at work and beyond, then the evidence seems to point to a gradual though persistent erosion of union influence at the point of production and service. For instance, the latest *Workplace Employment Relations Survey* (WERS) results indicate a continuing decline in union membership, recognition, lay representation, joint regulation via collective bargaining and collective action (Kersley *et al.* 2006, see also Gall (2007a)). To augment this debate and provide further insight into the nature of local union processes and dynamics in the highly challenging context of Britain's neo-liberal political economy, this chapter presents longitudinal analysis of the comparative fortunes of different workplace unions (and in one case, non-union employee representation) over a number of years. Some of these have adopted strategies based on oppositional organising approaches whilst others have tended towards more co-operative forms, in some cases, outright partnership. The chapter begins by presenting survey data of the performance of workplace unions with contrasting organising forms in the south and south west England during the immediate aftermath of the launch of 'New Unionism'. This is followed by multiple case study analysis of the fortunes of a variety of workplace unions in six long-established workplaces spread across the manufacturing, finance and public services sectors. Three key research questions are addressed. First, what differences, if any, can be discerned in workplace union performance during the early stages of the development of organising and partnership approaches? Second, to what extent have the contrasting organising and partnership approaches enabled unions to critically engage with the local manifestations of new capital accumulation strategies in the private sector and the drift towards privatisation in public services? And third, to what degree have the strategic positions adopted by workplace unions affected processes of member participation and union democracy at work?

Research data

The data upon which this chapter's analysis is based are drawn from two separate research projects. The first, funded by the Leverhulme Trust, sought to evaluate the TUC's 'New Unionism' project over the period 1998–2000, a time when 'New Unionism' embodied some dimensions of the organising model (see Heery *et al.* 2000a). As we noted above, during this period (in the immediate aftermath of the election of the first 'new' Labour government in 1997), the TUC also began to develop an alternative – and in many respects quite contradictory – organising strategy based on the idea of workplace partnership (TUC 1999). This development enabled us to carry out some rudimentary comparative analysis at a time when both approaches were in the early stages of organisational development. The second project, funded by the Economic and Social Research Council (ESRC)'s *Future of Work* Programme, resulted in a more searching comparative analysis of union strategy during the subsequent period when different organising forms might have been expected to become more embedded. For this, in-depth case study research was completed between 2001–2003 with some additional follow-up interviews between 2005 and 2008.

The first project focused on union activists' experiences of organising in mostly well established workplaces in southwest England where formal union structures existed and a clear potential for in-fill recruiting obtained. This reflected broader trends in union strategy at the time which prioritised better organising and recruitment in workplaces with union recognition over more challenging greenfield sites (Heery *et al.* 2003b). The data comprised a survey of 356 worker representatives in 52 work establishments, a survey of 70 union convenors employed in these work establishments, and semi-structured interviews with over 100 worker representatives and 15 EUOs (for a comprehensive analysis of this material, see Danford *et al.* (2003)). The next section presents some fresh analysis of the questionnaire survey data, comparing the organising and partnership processes in their embryonic phases. The second project focused on the dynamics of workplace partnership (and alternative union strategies) in six organisational case studies. These were located in manufacturing (two aerospace studies), finance (one de-mutualised building society and an insurance firm) and the public sector (one National Health Service (NHS) trust and a large local authority). For this project, a total of 374 management and worker interviews were completed and 2,575 questionnaires collected from managers, manual and non-manual workers. Of the interviews, over

40 were completed with worker representatives, plus in one case in the finance sector, members of a non-union 'Partnership Council'. The second half of this chapter focuses on the interview data with union representatives and HR managers in each of the case studies. (For a more comprehensive analysis of the interviews and worker surveys, see Danford *et al.* (2005) and Upchurch *et al.* (2008)).

Organising and partnership compared: early stages

Our earlier interviews with union convenors and worker representatives enabled us to categorise the form of union organising in each of the workplaces visited. Unions falling into the 'organising' category were those cases where representatives articulated a clear sense of union independence (involving recurrent oppositional stances to management) and where activists met regularly to discuss collective bargaining strategies and membership recruitment campaigns. In many respects these were union forms that emphasised a renewed organising approach by processes of 'stimulating activism and strengthening trade unionism in the workplace in order that workers can resolve their own problems without recourse to external representation' (Heery 2002: 27). The 'co-operative' category comprised active workplace unions that had either maintained a tradition of co-operative bargaining relationships with the employer, or had more recently developed an informal partnership arrangement, or adopted a more formal workplace partnership underpinned by written agreement (for a distinction between these, see Bacon and Samuel (2007), Danford *et al.* (2005: 142–145), Oxenbridge and Brown (2004: 191–192)). In the cases of informal partnership, union representatives described an unwritten but clearly articulated co-operative relationship with management which aimed to secure mutual gain workplace outcomes. In the formal partnership cases, of which there were few, there existed a written agreement adumbrating joint partnership principles and processes. A third category of 'neither' included a variety of workplace union organisations that had not adopted any of the strands of 'New Unionism'. Some of these had fairly healthy membership densities but were often marked by low levels of union activism. Others were clearly weak in term of membership, density and lack of activist presence. In these cases, employed union officers took a more prominent role in initiating recruitment campaigns and servicing existing members.

The quantitative data presented here provide some indication of the comparative effectiveness of the different union forms, albeit in some

Table 4.1   Patterns of organising reported by worker representatives, by sector and union (n = 356)

	Organising (%)	Co-operative (%)	Neither (%)
All	38	28	34
Aerospace	71	12	17
Manufacturing	26	33	41
Insurance	0	50	50
Privatised Utilities	0	70	30
NHS Trusts	26	22	52
Local Government	0	72	28
Universities	0	0	100
AEEU	50	35	15
GMB	29	21	50
MSF	38	19	44

Source: Authors' own data.

cases, at an early stage of their development. We consider in turn, membership and recruitment data, institutional measures of organisational strength, and union influence. Table 4.1 shows the distribution of the three categories based on the reports of worker representatives. Overall, 41% of the representatives surveyed were based in workplaces where facets of the organising model had been adopted, just under a quarter were in workplaces where partnership or co-operative unionism existed and 33% were in workplaces where neither of these conditions were obtained. Use of the organising model was most common in aerospace, a sector that still dominates manufacturing in the southwest region and which is heavily unionised. Partnership approaches were more likely to be found in the small number of privatised utilities and local authorities in the sample. It is also noteworthy that the organising approach was more common in the AEEU and MSF (then both Amicus and now Unite). The AEEU organisational base comprised aerospace and manufacturing, sectors associated with traditional adversarial industrial relations. MSF was notable for the introduction of a grassroots 'Organising Works' campaign at the time of the research.

Our analysis of membership levels and recruitment data highlighted a number of features. The first was that although the scope for in-fill recruiting was greater in workplaces that had not adopted organising model initiatives, the average number of members recruited per workplace was actually higher for the organising unions (Table 4.2). Moreover, and more pertinently, there existed a large gap in membership retention between these organising unions and the two other categories.

Table 4.2   Membership and recruitment data (workplace averages), by organising category, as reported by union convenors (n = 70)

	Size of membership	Membership density	Members recruited previous 12 months	Overall change in workplace membership	Member/rep ratios
All workplaces					
Organising	349	71	22	+17.0	25
Co-operative	295	61	17	+4	34
Neither	147	61	10	–3	44

Source: Authors' own data.

On average, the organising unions achieved a membership increase of 17 at each workplace between the years 1999–2000 compared to an average increase of just four by the co-operative unions and an overall membership loss by the weaker 'neither' group.[1] In the main, this gap could not be attributed to any comparative lack of membership recruitment activity for as Table 4.3 indicates, at the time of the research, there existed a good deal of recruitment campaigning across the different workplaces (around two thirds of establishments) with no significant differences between the three categories. As we shall see in the case study section, grassroots assessment of the utility of the different forms of union activity – and how well they represent member interests – constitutes a more telling factor for assessing this uneven performance in membership retention.

To assess the relative strength of each workplace union organisation we used three different indices. The first measured 'the depth and impor-

Table 4.3   Recruitment activity in previous 12 months, by organising category (n = 70)

	Organising (%)	Co-operative (%)	Neither (%)
Recruitment campaign in past year	69	67	53
Leafleting non-members	50	44	47
Literature targeted at specific groups	53	44	32
Direct postal shot to non-members	6	24	5
Email non-members	3	6	5
Use of recruitment teams	16	18	26
Use of mapping techniques	25	28	21
Social event for non-members	3	6	16

Source: Authors' own data.

tance of representation at the workplace' by collecting data on the number of workers per representative (Cully *et al.* 1999: 193). The 1998 *Workplace Employee Relations Survey* (the latest survey at the time of this first project) showed that this varied directly with size of workplace, averaging 28 members per representative and ranging from 17 in small establishments of 25–49 employees to 53 in larger workplaces of over 500 employees. Comparing this pattern to our three union categories, we found that workplace organisation tended to be significantly stronger for the organising unions compared to unions which followed either the co-operative route or neither of these (Table 4.2). Whilst, as Badigannavar and Kelly (2005) have shown, developing a critical mass of activists is partly a function of the size of the workplace (and the organising unions did tend to be based in the larger workplaces), our interview data showed that the more independent and adversarial orientations adopted by the organising unions the more likely they were to attract the interest of new activists. A similar pattern of difference in organisational strength can be discerned from our other two indicators: the frequency of union representatives' meetings (such as joint shop stewards committees) and of meetings between union representatives and management (Table 4.4). Unions that adopted the organising approach seemed stronger in matters of activist organisation and engagement with management. It was also noteworthy that unions which adopted neither organising nor co-operative strategies looked particularly weak.

Table 4.4 Frequency of workplace meetings, union representatives and management, by organising category (n = 365)

	Organising (%)	Co-operative (%)	Neither (%)
Frequency of union reps meetings			
More than monthly	67	30	20
Monthly	24	43	31
Bi-monthly	4	5	13
Few times per year or never	5	22	36
Frequency of meetings with management			
Weekly	49	48	16
More than monthly	41	23	4
Monthly	10	20	22
Few times per year or never	0	9	58

Source: Authors' own data.

Finally, we evaluated the question of union influence over the regulation of the employment relationship by asking different sets of questions governing the scope of collective bargaining at each workplace and whether certain issues related to employment conditions and work organisation were subject to either negotiation or consultation.

The survey measured the scope of collective bargaining and consultation by asking representatives whether, during the previous three years, they had been involved in discussions over a range of 22 different issues encompassing pay and conditions, restructuring and rationalisation, skills training, discrimination at work, flexible working, maternity and paternity rights, use of non-standard employment contracts and workplace stress. There is insufficient space here to present all of the results but it was noteworthy that the representatives in the co-operative unions were more likely to report greater scope (an average of 9.3 issues) compared to the organising unions (7.3 issues) and the 'neither' group (5 issues).

Table 4.5   Issues subject to negotiation or consultation, by organising category (n = 356)

Issue	Subject to negotiation (%)	Subject to consultation (%)
How pay is decided		
Organising	84	16
Co-operative	71	29
Neither	54	46
How changes to working hours are decided		
Organising	76	24
Co-operative	63	37
Neither	47	53
How redundancy issues are decided		
Organising	51	49
Co-operative	51	49
Neither	33	67
How the introduction of new working practices is decided		
Organising	71	29
Co-operative	63	37
Neither	42	58
How the use of non-permanent staff is decided		
Organising	49	51
Co-operative	33	67
Neither	20	80

Source: Authors' own data.

Perhaps a more robust measure of union power and influence is provided by questions governing joint regulation of terms and conditions. That is, to what extent do union activists exert influence through traditional collective bargaining processes as opposed to weaker forms of consultation and management communication? In this respect, worker representatives were asked whether the five employment issues listed in Table 4.5 were subject to either negotiation or consultation. The results showed that compared to the co-operative union group and weaker 'neither' group, representatives in the organising unions were more likely to report negotiation over four out of the five issues (pay, working hours, new working practices and use of non-permanent staff).

To sum up these initial patterns, our survey data found little evidence to support the argument that co-operative forms of workplace trade unionism, such as the partnership approach, generated more favourable outcomes for either union organisation or level of union influence. In fact, it was those unions that adopted a more oppositional and independent stance, an orientation more associated with the 'organising model', that displayed better records both in recruiting and retaining members and recruiting and organising workplace activists. Equally, if collective bargaining is taken as the central measure of union influence, then the organising approach also seemed the more effective.

Workplace-level case studies: manufacturing, finance and the public sector compared

The second project, based on ESRC project data, focused on the dynamics of union strategy in five employers selected from the original survey research. In addition, a sixth case explored the dynamics of partnership in a non-union firm. Much of the case study work was carried out between 2001 and 2003 but in four cases additional interviews were completed between 2005 and 2008.

Partnership and organising in a high skill manufacturing sector

These two case studies were of union organising patterns in manufacturing plants in the high skill aerospace sector. Both plants (*Airframes* and *JetCo*) employed approximately 4000 workers each with large numbers of designers and skilled shop-floor production workers. There were two main union bargaining groups per plant each dominated by the Amicus union. The majority skilled production workers were represented by Amicus-AEEU; technical staff were represented by Amicus-MSF. Manual union membership density at both plants was virtually 100% whilst non-manual densities for Amicus-MSF were around 80% in recognised areas (which excluded some graduate engineering and commercial departments). At both plants the architecture for collective bargaining and consultation comprised conventional negotiating committees covering pay and conditions plus a number of single site and multi-site consultation committees and works councils.

The development of partnership at each plant requires viewing in the context of the pressure of intense market competition in the sector and management's objective of continuously streamlining labour deployment and cutting costs via processes of organisational restructuring. This restructuring intensified during the late 1990s and followed a similar pattern in both plants. Previously unitary, single site divisions were broken up into a plethora of different business units responsible for specific product families or production processes. Management's objective was to secure improved financial control over every aspect of the business, albeit under the guise of 'managerial decentralization'. In this respect, business unit matrix structures were introduced primarily to reduce costs, particularly labour costs, by securing greater transparency and unit accountability. The specific instruments of labour control took the form of increased labour flexibility, teamworking and the use of outsourcing and agency labour. In both plants, management sought also to recast existing traditions of adversarial industrial relations by developing partnership relationships with the different union bargaining groups. This was seen as an essential pre-cursor to securing a degree of worker compliance with, or even acceptance of, the continuous process of organisational restructuring and rationalisation. Senior managers stressed how partnership should be seen as a psychological process, a battle of 'hearts and minds' that culminated in a permanent re-alignment of trade union priorities towards the companies' new core objectives.

The union responses to this managerial challenge divided into two contrasting camps and both were present in each plant. The manual bargaining group at *Airframes* and non-manual bargaining group at *JetCo* both came to support the partnership approach whilst the non-manual group at *Airframes* and the manual group at *JetCo* each adopted oppositionalist positions. Referring to the themes of our earlier survey analysis, all four bargaining groups displayed strong workplace-level union organisation in terms of recruiting new members and activists and the high frequency of meetings of activists and meetings with management. However, as we illustrate below, the two groups that followed the partnership approach experienced significantly less 'hard' influence over management compared to the two more oppositionalist groups.

The two pro-partnership union groups were led by convenors who, despite displaying differences in the extent of their trust in management, had converted to the idea of partnership on the basis that it was seen to contain the potential for regaining a measure of union influence lost during the Thatcher-Major era. At *Airframes*, the manual union group entered into an informal partnership arrangement with the company in 2000, an arrangement that promised more open and systematic negotiation and consultation on terms and conditions, staffing levels and company strategic issues. At *JetCo*, the non-manual union group signed a formal partnership agreement two years earlier, in 1998. As well as emphasising 'trust and openness' in management-union relations, the agreement authorised the formation of a series of joint working parties to discuss prominent management concerns such as reductions in engineering labour time and use of sub-contract labour.

For both sets of unions, the 'balance sheet' of partnership outcomes, observed over a number of years, was mostly negative. Whilst adopting the discourse of 'mutuality', management actually treated partnership in an instrumental fashion, as a means of legitimating change and securing union approval for employer-dominated agendas. At the same time, workers began criticising their convenors for 'being in management's pockets' and 'sticking their noses up there' as members variously put it. Moreover, a series of deleterious material outcomes generated a growing antipathy towards partnership amongst activists. Labour rationalisation provided one example. Despite voicing commitment to enhancing job security by minimising potential job loss and providing unions advance warning of any threat to staffing levels, both sets of management announced a series of major job losses between 2002 and 2005. These decisions not only took the unions by surprise (denoting an absence of early warning) but no provision was made for the discussion of alternative solutions. The development of the new, 'qualitatively different' partnership relationships seemed to have no impact on the numbers of lost jobs or the redundancy process itself. This lack of managerial trust also impaired the emergence of any meaningful 'employee voice' at the plants. At *Airframes*, for example, a merger with an Italian aerospace multinational required a lengthy process of corporate discussion over a three year period. But our interviews with shop stewards and workers highlighted a widespread feeling that consultation with unions and workers on this issue was minimal. This was despite the implications of the merger for jobs, responsibilities and workloads. Another example was provided at *JetCo*, where management was seen to cynically exploit the introduction of the *Information and Consultation Regulations.* When, in 2005, the company formed a new national Information and Consultation Council leaders of both main bargaining groups took the decision to place less experienced shop stewards on this committee, partly to give them experience but equally, because the new council was perceived as yet another layer of consultation which exacerbated the already excessive demands on senior stewards' time. During our later visits to the plant in 2006, the non-manual convenor described how management attempted to exploit the new forum by engineering a shift in the nature and locale of collective bargaining. Specifically, discussions governing a number of contractual issues that traditionally fell within the remit of plant-level collective bargaining were moved to the new national council and implemented once 'formal consultation' had taken place. These included the use of agency labour, changes to a redundancy agreement and the standardisation of UK conditions.

The two bargaining groups that formally rejected management's overtures to partnership (the manual unions at *JetCo* and the non-manual unions at *Airframes*) did so partly on the basis of distrust of management, partly because partnership was seen as a perverse political development (in the sense that, as one convenor put it, 'you can be with management or you can be with your members but you can't be with both') and partly as a corollary of a distinctive style of leadership. Both groups placed much greater emphasis upon democratic accountability to grassroots members through practices that facilitated grassroots participation and collective discussion. For example, regular plant meetings, group meetings, shop steward patrols, newsletters and emails. And in the case of *JetCo*, many senior activists (including five plant convenors) were members of the union's Broad Left, the Amicus Unity Gazette, and formed part of an oppositionalist political tradition encompassing 'old' labour, the Bennite left and the Socialist Workers' Party (SWP). The union form of these two bargaining groups corresponded, in many respects with the organisational precepts of union renewal.

To what extent did these oppositional stances offer advantages over their partnership counterparts? As far as immediate gains are concerned, there were examples of notable successes. At *Airframes*, for instance, the main union Amicus-MSF proved very successful in recruiting young graduate engineers and scientists (who could be prone to questioning the relevance of trade unionism for their occupation) and then fostering vibrant group activity in the design departments. In one case, groups of new engineering members developed a successful, snowballing campaign around core 'justice at work' issues such as supervisory bullying and forced management to the negotiating table before the campaign was launched with the local media. At *JetCo*, the manual unions more effectively countered the threat of job loss by frustrating management attempts to transfer work to other sites. For example, in 2001, Amicus-AEEU stewards mobilised their members into walking off the job and barricading part of the factory until management withdrew a threat to transfer engine test work to a sister plant in the Midlands. However, this more militant form of union organising did have limitations. Just as Beynon (1984) described the organisational constraints that arose from the grassroots ideology of a 'factory class consciousness', union strategy at *Airframes* and *JetCo* still displayed a plant-based sectionalism that de-prioritised the construction of solidarity links and joint action with other plants in Britain and globally. This stood at odds with the reality of an internationalised aerospace capital which, whilst appearing fragmented at the plant level (through the growth of profit centres and business units), was actually characterised by a more unitary strategic process of global capital mobility through merger processes and systemic international outsourcing.

Union and non-union partnership in financial services

The two financial services workplaces were case studies of a partnership arrangement with a recognised trade union and a non-union 'partners council'. The first of these, *InsuranceCo*, specialised in legal expenses insurance within a large European MNC and employed 500 staff; the second, *FinanceCo*, was a demutualised building society employing 2,700 staff. In both cases, women comprised two thirds of the workforce. At *InsuranceCo*, the union Amicus (and formerly MSF and ASTMS) had been the sole recognised channel for collective consultation and negotiation for three decades. At its height, in 1991, membership density reached 80%; however, by the time of the research in 2002–2003, this had fallen to around 45%. In 1999, management and Amicus signed a partnership agreement that committed the company to providing 'the greatest possible stability of employment and earnings' in return for union co-operation in the implementation of 'measures designed to sustain or increase efficiency or profitability'. In many respects, the workplace union represented one of the weaker 'co-operative' groups analysed in our earlier survey. Despite a number of recruitment campaigns organised by Amicus EUOs, overall membership recruitment performance was poor whilst the frequency of both activists' meetings and meetings with management was relatively low. At *FinanceCo*, a weakly supported staff association had been disbanded in the early 1990s. It was replaced by a Partners Council in 1992, a body comprising elected employee representatives from different departmental constituencies and encompassing all employee grades. In 2001, following abortive attempts by Unifi to recruit members and gain recognition, management put some effort into raising the profile of the Partners' Council and broadening the scope of employee consultation in order to undermine any future Unifi campaigns.

The UK financial services sector has been subject to considerable reorganisation in recent decades, a process of change that has centred on business strategy, corporate structure and work organisation. The underlying pattern is one of a recomposition and concentration of finance capital following waves of mergers in the banking, building society and insurance industries. At the same time, priorities of economies of scale and increasing market share, facilitated by developments in information and communications technologies, have generated a reorganisation of the old boundaries between the main sub-sectors and product types. Indeed, the cross-selling of financial products, driven increasingly at the individual level by sales targets and incentive pay systems are now systemic. These strategic changes coupled with the new customer service ethos have become embodied in new work organisation within profit centre structures. For example, call centre operations and customer-focused teams. Elements of these changes were present in both case studies, more so at *FinanceCo*, a demutualised building society that recently became part of a UK-based banking and financial services group offering a wide range of services in banking, mortgages and insurance. *InsuranceCo* remained in a niche insurance market; nevertheless, its management teams were pursuing a raft of efficiency savings and restructuring performance management systems.

Our research found that the different types of partnership (union and non-union) at the two firms seemed to have little favourable impact upon the 'representation gap' that became a widespread and problematic feature of British industrial relations during the two preceding decades. At *FinanceCo*, whilst many employees acknowledged an increase in the quantity and quality of company communications provided by management and their Partners' Council representatives, few felt that they exerted any direct or indirect influence. Enforced employee quiescence rather than 'employee voice' seemed to be the dominant characteristic of the firm's industrial relations. The Partners' Council was seen by representative and employee alike as lacking the credibility of full union representation since, despite management's intention to treat the Council as a powerful mechanism for representing staff interests it had few sanctions to hold management to its commitment to consult and no sanctions to bring to bear to challenge management decisions. For example, despite different managers' claims that partnership had broadened the scope of consultation, key distributive issues that are central to workers' immediate interests, issues such as pay, conditions and other employee benefits, were excluded from the Partners' Council agenda. During a return visit to the site in 2005, the superficiality of the partnership became further exposed when management decided to sell the branch network and effect job cuts. Council representatives found themselves cut adrift from redundancy discussions when the firm instigated corporate consultations with a union recognised in the company main operations abroad.

At *InsuranceCo*, although our employee attitude survey data suggested higher union influence compared to *FinanceCo*'s Partners' Council, this was mostly delimited to individual processes such as grievance and disciplinary representation. Our interviews with grassroots members also highlighted a problem of partnership 'distancing' in that many felt that their union operated remotely from their needs and interests whilst local union culture and practice provided few opportunities for democratic discussion of workplace problems. Overall, the partnership agreement, and the union's co-operative stance, had not acted to increase employees' direct or indirect influence at work. Neither had the agreement generated any sense of mutuality in material outcomes. Management succeeded in improving efficiency and labour productivity by introducing greater flexibility in working time and task enlargement but improvements to pay and conditions had been modest. For example, in our survey, two thirds of employees reported that their work had intensified over the previous three years; nearly three quarters reported increases in work responsibilities; over a half reported increases in task flexibility; and over a half indicated dissatisfaction with their pay. Perhaps, it was no surprise to discover that by 2008, union membership had nearly halved: from 45% down to 27% (interview with HR manager).

Therefore, both cases of partnership showed little promise in the likelihood of generating mutual gain or, in the case of *InsuranceCo*, concomitant increases in worker support for the union. A panoply of 'soft' human resource management techniques were in place to provide collective 'employee voice', downwards and two-way employee communications, team-based discussions and individual appraisals, and yet employees felt typically a lack of individual involvement in organisational decision-making and only weak collective represent-ation. Within the institutional context of a high pressure commercial environment where employers' prime focus was on improving sales performance and profitability, the two sets of management did not regard partnership as a mode of employee representation that might weaken their prerogatives in any meaningful way. And certainly, for employee representatives, the new partnership processes – in their union and non-union form alike – lacked the means or potential to countervail these prerogatives.

Co-operation in the public sector

Case studies were employed involving the development of partnership at a local authority (*CityCo*) and an NHS Trust; the latter located on two main sites (SiteA and SiteB). These two sites were formerly two independent trusts and merged in 2000 to form one General Hospital Trust (*GHT*). *CityCo* employed around 18,000 manual and non-manual staff, and *GHT* approximately 7,500 direct medical and support staff. The main unions representing workers at *CityCo* were Unison, TGWU (now Unite) and GMB. At *GHT* the Royal College of Nursing (RCN) and Unison were the largest unions. MSF (now Unite) also had an important and active presence in representing laboratory staff. Overall, union membership density in both cases was approximately 50%.

Given the traditional view of the state as a model employer and the willingness of public sector unions to work with rather than against Labour administrations – together with the end of nearly two decades of Conservative governments running public services with privatisation in mind – it was, perhaps, unsurprising that union leaderships in local government and the NHS tended to welcome the development of part-nership working. What they overlooked, or did not envisage, was the potentially negative impact on members' quality of working life of 'new' Labour's drive for greater efficiency and cost effectiveness of public ser-vices. The introduction of both *Best Value* in local government and the modernisation agenda (*agenda for change*) in the NHS provided the instruments to carry through this programme. New systems of financial control together with classic total quality management criteria, such as benchmarking, performance monitoring, training and outsourcing, were employed to cut costs, secure continuous quality improvement, bring about cultural change and, where it was felt necessary, open up the public sector to market forces. To achieve these objectives the government recognised that it would be of great assistance to secure support from the unions. Therefore, partnership principles of co-operation, consultation and union and staff involvement were incorporated into 'new' Labour's public sector modernisation programme.

At *CityCo*, although there were significant clusters of militant shop stewards in some departments, a collaborative relationship existed between the local union leadership and management throughout the 1980s and 1990s when the authority was mostly Labour-controlled. Following Labour's national election victory in 1997, and the introduction of *Best Value* as a replacement for Compulsory Competitive Tendering (CCT), pilot partnership initiatives were launched in some council departments. Local union officials positively engaged with partnership working because they felt that this was the best way to defend their members' interests in the light of the perceived danger, expressed explicitly by one Unison official, that *Best Value* was 'really an outsourcing exercise'. Thus, unions prioritised participation in *Best Value* steering groups and *Best Value* review panel meetings; the latter carrying responsibility of determining whether the provision of local services was best delivered in-house or by an external body. Increasingly, therefore, the union strategy of engaging in partnership was directed towards the fight to keep work in-house. This strategy was regarded as the best way to maintain members' job security despite the fact that to beat external competition unions would risk conceding greater labour flexibility, tighter monitoring of work and increases in workload. The rationale behind this strategy, according to one TGWU official, was that 'if it looks like getting nasty ... there's even more reason to be involved in it, because you could be into some form of damage limitation exercise'.

Partnership at *GHT* first emerged on SiteB in 1997 in the aftermath of a union dispute over the imposition of car-parking charges. In order to rebuild relationships, and provide a platform for sustaining co-operation, a partnership agreement between the unions and management was signed. A new joint union committee (JUC) was established to feed into a joint-site negotiating and consultation committee comprising both staff and management representatives. In addition, a partnership forum was formed comprising all JUC members and Trust executive and operational directors to discuss key strategic issues. While this partnership arrangement had both the support of the management and the majority of the unions, the merger of the two sites presented difficulties for union cohesion in that whilst SiteB unions adopted more co-operative stances with management, at SiteA a longstanding 'confrontational culture' prevailed. According to one Unison official, the adoption of SiteB's approach, following the merger, resulted in tensions because 'on the union side I know that the [SiteA] people felt taken over by the [SiteB] unions.' There was some dissention from MSF activists at SiteA. Here, as our earlier survey had highlighted, in the years preceding the merger MSF had rejected partnership working in favour of assertive workplace activism and the pursuance of an organising approach to union recruitment and membership involvement. This approach had contributed to a significant increase in MSF membership and stood in contrast with a much poorer recruitment performance by the partnership unions at SiteB.

Our case study research in the years following these developments showed that eventual outcomes for workers were mostly negative in both public sector organisations. At *CityCo*, initial union participation in partnership pilot schemes failed to stem extensive labour rationalisation in areas where *Best Value* was introduced, despite the 'success' of keeping these services in-house. For example, the fear expressed by one *CityCo* manager that *Best Value* reviews would culminate 'in downsizing' was borne out in the local taxation division where partnership working was piloted. Staff numbers were cut from 134 before the review to 104.5 full-time equivalent positions in 2002; a further 27.5 staff cuts were planned to meet government targets over the longer term. For remaining staff, changes in work organisation and technology were introduced to assist employees to work more productively and effectively in order to reduce labour input and costs. Our data showed that these types of changes resulted in widespread patterns of work intensification. In light of this experience, the main *CityCo* unions came to distance themselves from formal partnership and reverted to former patterns of corporate-level accommodation mixed with occasional opposition to new council initiatives at departmental level.

At *GHT*, partnership at both sites served to centralise union activity and resources as senior representatives became enmeshed in time-consuming management discussions on operational policy and strategic direction of the newly formed trust. The corollary of this was that the workplace unions became more detached from their grassroots base, particularly organisations such as the RCN which had traditionally displayed a servicing approach to union-member relations. At the same time, managerial concern with budgetary control, compliance with patient throughput targets and cuts in the use of agency labour (with concomitant increases in the labour utilisation of permanent staff) led to widely reported problems of work intensification and workplace stress. From the viewpoint of many grassroots members, their partnership unions looked, at best, irrelevant in these circumstances, and at worst, guilty of collusion in the management of these outcomes. Our questionnaire survey at the time showed that less than 40% of members felt that their union took notice of members' problems; only a quarter felt their union was good at communicating with members; less than 30% felt their union was taken seriously by management; only a fifth felt that their union made a difference to what it was like to work at *GHT*; and less than 40% felt any loyalty to their union.

Overall, the two public sector case studies showed how union engagement in partnership was wholly ineffective in challenging many of the potentially negative processes associated with the imperatives of financial control in the so-called 'modernised' public services. Equally, whilst there remained solid support for union membership and representation amongst many employees, there was little confidence in the efficacy of union representation offered by the partnership union form. Notably, MSF members at *GHT* were an exception. Our data showed that they had greater confidence in their union to deal with members problems, a legacy from MSF's organising approach and more independent local union activism.

Conclusion

Despite the relatively large volume of resources dedicated to union organising campaigns in recent years, very little headway has been made in securing increases in union recognition, membership density and grassroots activism (Gall 2007a; Kerlsey *et al.* 2006). Whilst a number of campaigns have generated some notable successes, unions in Britain have struggled to build sufficient organising momentum in the face of employer opposition, the limited utility of union recognition legislation and an ongoing decline in the quantity of workplace representatives. This is particularly the case in the private sector where the decline in membership density is reaching acute levels. In this context, one might argue that there does seem to be some logic to the proposition that union pragmatism with regard to choice or mix of organising strategies, that is, 'what works' in different organisational contexts, should take precedence over ideological positions governing union form and workplace politics. The same applies to another related argument, that until British unions are able to rebuild workplace structures based on a critical mass of union members and activists then the political choice between co-operative unionism and more aggressive oppositional union forms may constitute a false dichotomy. Whilst, on the face of it, these positions do seem to hold some merit, concrete evidence suggests that strategic decisions governing the form of union activity that should be developed at the workplace level will have considerable implications for the longer term viability of democratic labour unionism. By analysing patterns of union organising in workplaces that are mostly long-established, we have found that union structures designed to support free collective bargaining, union autonomy and union challenges to management tend to be diminished by partnership-based union forms. If such structures are to be sustained in the longer term, they require anchoring on democratic grassroots participation.

To return to our first research question, our initial quantitative survey data and later case studies of workplace union dynamics generated consistent patterns of results pointing to the greater worth of oppositional organising strategies compared to partnership. The survey data also showed, however, that workplace unions which followed either elements of the organising model or more co-operative approaches (such as partnership) both fared better than unions which had adopted neither. In other words, taking up a strategic position was better than doing nothing at all. In the latter case, the lack of union strategy seemed to reflect moribund workplace organisational structures marked by diminished union activism, a consequent reliance on the servicing activity of employed union officers, and relatively low union influence at the workplace. Equally, there existed a number of significant differences in performance between the groups of workplace unions that had adopted either the organising or the partnership approach. The organising unions displayed better records of recruiting members and increasing workplace density. They displayed a greater degree of organisational strength measured in terms of member-representative ratios, the frequency of meetings of union activists and the frequency of meetings between union negotiators and management. As for union influence over pay and conditions, the organising unions tended to score higher when influence was measured on the basis of the range of workplace issues that were subject to negotiation rather than consultation. Thus, despite the argument that co-operative forms of unionism are more likely to generate meaningful employee voice and greater union influence (see, for example, Haynes and Allen (2001) and Oxenbridge and Brown (2004)), our data suggested that these predominantly early stage partnerships offered few such advantages.

When our initial survey research was first published in 2003, we suggested that these contrasting patterns were a function of the nature of union response to management strategy in the new workplace. By the latter, we meant an array of organisational and cultural changes that have taken hold in many British workplaces, including the adoption of new management techniques and new work organisation. Those unions that were better able to critically engage with these management initiatives and construct oppositional, collective action frames around patterns of worker discontent were more likely than the relatively passive partnership unions to renew and revitalise their workplace union structures (see Danford *et al.* 2003). However, these arguments were necessarily tentative in that the survey work was completed during the early stages of the promotion of 'New Unionism' in Britain. Our later case study work afforded the opportunity of a more in-depth investigation of the process and dynamics of union strategy in three salient employment sectors of the southwest economy.

The six case studies summarised in this chapter provided specific examples of the degradation of employment conditions arising from new capital accumulation strategies and intensification of market relations in private sector firms and a transition towards the market with associated use of private sector management techniques in the public sector. In the aerospace plants, the labour process became subject to new systems of financial control and matrix management involving a rationalisation of production and cost-cutting labour 'efficiencies' in the form of labour flexibility, teamworking, outsourcing and employment of agency workers. In the finance sector workplaces, similar trends could be discerned with the rationalisation of labour deployment into profit centre structures, call centre operations and customer-focused teams. The two public sector cases in local government and the NHS provided typical examples of the repercussions for labour of the privatising tendencies of 'new' Labour's 'modernisation' project. In both cases, new measures of financial control involving the specific techniques of systemic auditing, performance monitoring, benchmarking, competitive tendering and outsourcing led variously to job-cutting, work intensification and patterns of workplace stress.

To what extent were the contrasting union forms of partnership and organising able to critically engage with management strategy and influence outcomes in these highly challenging contexts of organisational change (our second research question)? In fact, the adoption by unions of co-operative approaches to relations with management seemed, at best, irrelevant and at worst, highly damaging to the interests of labour. In many respects, the outcomes for unions and their members reflected Marx's (2007: 130–131) prescient rejoinder to certain types of 'philanthropists' and 'socialists' who, in the middle of the nineteenth century, were calling for the elimination of union conflict and strikes:

[I am convinced] that the alternative rise and fall of wages, and the continual conflicts between masters and men resulting therefrom, are, in the present organization of industry, the indispensable means of holding up the spirit of the laboring classes, of combining them into one great association against the encroachments of the ruling class, and of preventing them from becoming apathetic, thoughtless, more or less well-fed instruments of production.

Whilst the different union leaderships in our workplace case studies did not see themselves as entering into a coerced form of partnership (Martínez Lucio and Stuart 2005), the expected qualitative shift in the nature of management-union relations inevitably drew on unitary action frames. In the absence of independent and oppositional union orientations, these partnerships became dominated by the employers' interests and acted as instruments of legitimisation of management policy. In the case of aerospace and finance, the partnership unions failed, eventually, to secure any sense of independent 'employee voice'. For example, their ability to maintain some influence over the regulation of employment conditions became increasingly brittle whilst their co-operative orientations to management generated very little union impact on processes of organisational restructuring and job loss. At *FinanceCo*, the one example of non-union, partnership-based employee representation, core worker concerns such as the setting of pay and conditions were left entirely to managerial discretion and excluded from partnership consultation processes. In the local government and NHS cases, we found no evidence to support the hypothesis that public sector partnership agreements contained greater potential for generating mutual gain outcomes compared to the private sector (Bacon and Samuel 2007). The tensions apparent in union co-operation with management agendas of quasi-privatisation and financial control were such that the relation of trust and accountability between member and union could not be sustained. At *CityCo*, the different workplace unions came to reject partnership following experimentation with a number of pilot projects. At *GHT*, the lack of union opposition to managerial processes that had engendered a considerable deterioration in the quality of working life on the wards caused, for many members, a process of alienation from the union to take hold. Indeed, in all of the partnership case studies, the distancing of senior union representatives from grassroots opinion became problematic.

The two examples of unions following the 'organising model' approach at *Airframes* and *JetCo* allowed direct comparisons with the contrasting partnership union groups in these plants. The dynamics of union organisation were in many respects distinctive in these cases, exemplifying Lévesque *et al.*'s (2005) argument that the process of building independent, democratic unions requires sustained attempts by activists to nurture grassroots participation and positions of worker solidarity. Union convenors regarded democratic accountability to the grassroots as paramount (a social bond that contravenes the alternative priorities of partnership). The overriding principle that governed their assessments of the contemporary role of unions at the workplace was mass membership involvement through systematic communication and debate – labour unionism was perceived primarily as an instrument of working class democracy rather than an intermediary in the regulation of the employment relationship. As a result, although these organising unions experienced their fair share of defeats and setbacks, they retained the ability to mobilise grassroots opposition to managerial actions at critical points, for example, in response to job transfers. Member participation, a degree of job control and the placing of limits on managerial prerogatives constituted the distinctive outcomes of this union form.

The contrast in dynamics between the partnership and organising union forms reinforces the argument that, as Carter (2006: 422) has put it, 'the means of renewal affect the end'. That is, and to return to our third research question, the strategic positions adopted by workplace unions are likely to have a significant long-term impact on processes of member participation and union democracy at work. It may well be the case, as Terry (2003) has argued, that unions which pursue partnership strategies may bolster their legitimacy at work and in wider society. But the problem for partnership is that legitimacy built on cooperative engagement with the employer may inevitably translate into illegitimacy in the eyes of the grassroots. We do not suggest, however, that 'grassroots' unionism constitutes the cardinal *modus operandi* for union renewal. As our aerospace case studies suggested (see also Danford *et al.* 2007), the extant traditions of 'localism' in British union relations are no longer sustainable in the face of global capital's increasing tendency to transfer jobs regionally, nationally and internationally through the use of plant relocation, outsourcing, employment agencies, and so on. This suggests that the more favourable concrete outcomes of union activity associated with an oppositional organising model may well be short-lived in the absence of a renewal of democratic processes and solidarity links beyond the confines of the single workplace. This may require a revitalisation of a broad left-led political leadership within the labour movement along with the development of new spaces of union activity and co-ordination between union members, activists, officers, union bureaucracies and trades councils. Given the current paucity of such processes in the context of neo-liberal hegemony, establishing such a dynamic of union renewal remains a daunting challenge for organised labour.

Note

1 Convenors collected recruitment data from workplace membership lists and branch records. The researchers were also able to compare these changes to head office membership data for 1998.

5
Organising, Militancy and Revitalisation: The Case of the RMT Union

Ralph Darlington

Introduction

Given that the decline of British unions over the last two decades has barely been arrested or reversed – with recent membership growth limited and overall union density still falling slightly – serious questions have been raised about the adequacy of present union organising strategies and the need for alternative approaches (Carter 2006: 415). Yet much of the academic industrial relations debate hitherto has been somewhat simplistically reduced to a dichotomy between 'partnership' and 'organising'. The partnership approach – avoiding strike action wherever possible and trying to rebuild membership and influence through collaborative relationships with employers – has been subject to critique for providing managers with the opportunity to take advantage of union moderation to restructure employment at the expense of workers' terms and conditions of employment (Fairbrother and Stewart 2005; Kelly 1996, 2001, 2004). However, the limitations of the more robust and widely-viewed more credible organising approach have also been highlighted, including the principal concern with merely short-term membership recruitment and retention, the 'top-down' approach to union building, and the failure to link organising to a more funda-mental attempt to revitalise and renew trade unionism (Carter 2000, 2006; Gall 2005; Heery *et al.* 2000a). The paradox is that many unions in recent years, supported by the TUC, have in practice pursued ele-ments of both strategies simultaneously, often involving an essentially accommodative form of unionism, albeit without much success.

By contrast, an alternative pathway to the quest for union growth and revitalisation has been provided by the National Union of Rail Maritime and Transport Workers (RMT). The RMT has combined a distinct version of the organising approach with an explicit rejection of partnership and accommodative forms of unionism in favour of the mobilisation of members through strike action, alongside a politically engaged form of left-wing trade unionism. Yet such an approach has been much neglected by academics and practitioners alike, despite appearing to be more successful in terms of basic measures such as growing membership levels, collective bargaining gains and the vibrancy of union organisation (Darlington 2001, 2007, 2008, 2009).

While there is no single organising 'model', but rather a variety of organising approaches which different unions have adopted in contrasting contexts (de Turberville 2004; Simms and Holgate 2008), the central political and strategic deficiencies of much British organising activity are threefold. First, there has been the principal concern of many unions with merely short-term individual membership recruitment and retention. Of course it is true that Unite (TGWU section), unlike some others, has long stressed that organising should not be based solely on growing membership, but on building strong workplace union organisation and shop steward representation that relates to workers' specific grievances and mobilises their collective strength. However, even this more ambitious approach is not necessarily enough to ensure that a union's presence, once obtained, is sustainable or effective in influencing managerial decision-making so as to materially improve workers' terms and conditions of employment (Simms 2007a). The nature and extent of workplace union power, and the ability and willingness of grassroots members to engage in collective resistance and struggle so as to extract concessions from management, is likely to be a crucial factor in the equation (Bagdigannavar and Kelly 2005, Taylor and Bain 2003). Moreover, the strong historical association between strike waves and periods of rapid and large union growth, notably between 1910–20, 1935–43 and 1968–75, underlines the manner in which unions have in the past been built through conflict and struggle, as opposed to partnership and compromise (Clawson 2003a; Cohen 2006; Kelly 1988, 1998). Yet the organising approaches adopted by many unions, including Unite (TGWU section), have not placed the inter-relationship between combativity and union membership growth/effectiveness at the centre of their strategic and tactical approach.

Second, there is the 'top-down' approach to union building which often characterises organising activity, with EUOs or lay full-time facility officers either substituting themselves for the engagement of members or stimulating activity in a form of 'managed activism' (Heery *et al.* 2000a). In the process, in some unions organising has become a bureaucratic and technocratic initiative that merely enhances the power of union leaderships (Carter 2000, 2006; Gall 2005). Again, the Unite (TGWU section) approach of encouraging steward leaders who can take responsibility for building union membership through collectively-driven issue-based organising has been an important countertendency in some respects. Nonetheless, arguably crucial to the success of any organising approach has to be the strengthening of membership control over decision-making at every level within the unions themselves, with the need for much deeper democratic and participative union structures than currently exists so as to facilitate such a genuinely responsive member-led movement. As Schenk (2003: 248–249) noted, there is an important link between union growth/power and union democracy: the more members have a genuine say in their union the greater their involvement in decision-making, the higher the potential for a membership interested in the issues of the day, and consequently the more vital the union is likely to be. Thus, democracy and an empowered membership can develop the capacity and confidence to build a stronger union. And unions need this increased power to fulfil their members' needs for better pay and working conditions as well as to pursue the goals of social change. In turn, advancing workers' basic needs and aspirations, further activates members and attracts non-unionised workers. Therefore, a necessary pre-requisite of a successful organising approach has to be deep-rooted membership self-activity and self-determination, something which is often sorely missing within the organising approach adopted by many unions.

Third, the interdependent links between grassroots resistance and mobilisation and membership involvement and democracy, have led some commentators to advocate the need for a fundamental revitalisation and renewal of trade unionism at workplace level and beyond. The problem with the organising approach adopted by many unions, it is argued, is that without wider ideological motivation, lay union activism has become increasingly isolated and internalised. The narrow historical focus on immediate workplace concerns has been accentuated at a time when labour unionism's withered roots suggest the need for a more external orientation on other social movements outside the workplace, and a broad political agenda, which could supplement the depleted resources of trade unions. From such a perspective 'social movement unionism' has been promoted (Fletcher and Hurd 1998; Schenk 2003) as a way of expanding the activity and appeal of trade unionism, with the potential result of the 'ideological rebirth of trade unionism as a social liberation movement' (Gall 2005: 25).

So, given these deficiencies of much current union organising activity, how and why has the RMT's alternative approach been so relatively successful, and to what extent has it overcome such limitations? Clearly, any evaluation of this needs to go beyond the single measure of growing union membership (Behrens *et al.* 2004; Kelly 2005; Stirling 2005) to embrace other dimensions such as stronger workplace organisation, increased levels of membership activism, depth of union democracy, greater combativity, success in collective bargaining, and broader political objectives and engagement. Arguably, on the basis of such a range of measures, the RMT scores fairly well, but while some, writing in an official capacity on behalf of the union, have been quite fulsome in their praise for such efforts (i.e., Berlin, 2006; Gall 2006c, 2007b), there are still important limitations and ambiguities which need acknowledging.

This chapter critically evaluates the relationship between union organising, militancy and revitalisation by specifically examining the role of the RMT within two of Britain's relatively strike-prone industries, the mainline railway and London Underground networks.[1] Methods of research included extensive tape-recorded semi-structured interviews with a range of strategically placed RMT informants at different levels of the union, analysis of documentary industrial relations and union material, and personal fieldwork observation. The chapter provides evidence of the RMT's success, and examines the key components of its union organising and strike mobilisation approach, combined with a number of other important broader contributory factors. It also explores some crucial limitations and problems with the approach, before concluding with some broader generalisations about organising, union activism, militancy, revitalisation, politics and leadership.

Union membership growth and bargaining gains

Although RMT organisation on the railways and London Underground survived Thatcherism and the 1980s without suffering any crushing strike defeats, the imposition of privatisation and Public-Private Partnership (PPP) respectively in the 1990s and early 2000s were fairly traumatic developments. They impacted negatively not only in terms of the fragmentation of bargaining, more flexible working practices and loss of jobs, but also in terms of the strength and vitality of union organisation. On the railways in 1993, in the wake of two 24-hour network-wide all-grades British Rail (BR) strikes in protest at the threat posed by impending privatisation, there was the ending of the union subscription check-off facility for the RMT (although not for Associated Society of Locomotive Engineers and Firemen (ASLEF)). This plunged the union into a financial crisis and, combined with the subsequent impact of privatisation and widespread voluntary redundancies, resulted in the union's total membership shrinking from 117,783 in 1990 to a low of 55,037 by 1999 – a loss of 62,746 or 53.3%. The ending of BR's 1956 *Machinery of Negotiations*, with its previous national, regional and local-level collective bargaining arrangements, scrapped an entire stratum of senior union officials and led, initially at least, to a widespread sense of disorientation. Likewise on London Underground, the 1992 imposition of the *Company Plan*, involving completely new contracts of employment, working arrangements, and collective bargaining structures across the network, represented a serious defeat for union organisation with the loss of some 5,000 jobs between 1993–1994 (Darlington 2001: 10). The subsequent introduction of PPP further undermined the strength of union organisation, notably with a marked decline in membership on the privatised maintenance side. Yet paradoxically, subsequent years have seen a relatively successful revitalisation of RMT membership and organisation on both the railways and London Underground. At this stage, we can note just two important features of this achievement.

First, the union has succeeded not only in stemming the relentless decline in membership it has experienced, but also, unlike many other unions, in recruiting substantial numbers of new members in recent years. Membership increased during the period 1999–2007 from 56,037 to 75,939, a rise of 37.3% (see Table 5.1). Membership levels had already started to improve slightly in the late 1990s and early 2000s, as the union began a process of reconstruction, involving a new direct-debit dues system which helped to recover lost ground amongst some lapsed members. But the election of Bob Crow as general secretary in February 2002 undoubtedly marked a significant turning point, with membership growth quickening its pace, rising from 59,277 in 2001 to 75,939 in 2007 (an increase of 28.1%). Even though the absolute numbers are not large, it means the RMT is one of the fastest growing unions in Britain. In the process, the union has successfully secured new forms of representation amongst contract cleaners on London Underground (2004) and won new union recognition agreements at Heathrow Express (2007) as well as railway infrastructure companies McGinley, Renown and Grant Rail between 2004 and 2006. Overall, there remains a relatively high level of union density on both the railways and Tube (although it inevitably varies between companies and amongst different groups of workers), an important bellwether of potential union capacity and influence.

Table 5.1   RMT membership figures, 1990–2007

Year	Membership
1990	117,783
1991	114,101
1992	105,126
1993	85,653
1994	67,981
1995	59,250
1996	60,142
1997	56,337
1998	56,470
1999	55,037
2000	57,869
2001	59,277
2002	63,084
2003	67,476
2004	71,544
2005	73,347
2006	74,539
2007	75,906

Source: Figures provided by RMT, and are at year end.
Note: The 1990 figure is a combined figure that includes the
ex-National Union of Railwaymen (NUR) and ex-National
Union of Seamen (NUS); in 1989 the NUR membership figure
was 102,639. In June 2008, RMT membership leapt to 81,000,
boosted in part as a result of the merger of the Oil Industry
Liaison Committee (OILC) as well as by continuing organising
successes across different sections of the transport industry.

Second, the RMT has provided verifiable evidence of its ability to
deliver substantial material improvements in members' pay and conditions, something which has been achieved invariably through the
threat and/or use of strike action. Thus, the union has won numerous
above-inflation pay rises, as well as the 35-hour working week on many
sectors of the railway network and London Underground (plus an annual
52 days leave entitlement on the latter). It prevented attempts by Network Rail (2004) and other rail companies (2006) to end final salary
pension schemes for new starters, and it contributed to bringing the
return of infrastructure maintenance in-house in Network Rail (2003),
stopped the privatisation by Network Rail of Merseytravel maintenance
staff (2005), prevented Metronet on the London Underground from
outsourcing maintenance staff to Bombardier (2005), and forced Transport for London to agree to take over and bring back in-house the failed
Metronet contract (2007). In addition, there have been many other forms

of collective bargaining success, including the industry-wide campaign by railways guards on train operating companies to prevent the introduction of driver-only operations that would erode guards' safety responsibilities (1999–2007). Compared with the setbacks experienced by many other unions in recent years, such gains have been impressive.

Strategic orientation

Any explanation for how and why the RMT has been able to obtain such membership growth and collective bargaining gains has to start by examining two features of the union's strategic orientation, namely, its distinct organising initiative and strike mobilisation approach.

Organising initiative

A nationally-coordinated union organising approach, backed up a small but energetic London-based 'Organising Unit' was set up shortly after Crow's election in 2002. But unlike other unions, which have employed specialist teams of paid 'organisers' trained through their own or TUC academies and sent out into the field to kick-start campaigns on the union's behalf, the RMT's 'Organising Unit' has focused more on mobilising the energies and participation of the union's reps and activists themselves to recruit new members. At the same time, organising has been conceived not merely in terms of recruiting new members, but with an emphasis on the development and creation of active, self-sufficient and sustainable reps as the foundation of the union in the workplace, able to provide effective representation.

Thus, the 'Organising Unit' has played a central role in encouraging the process of recruitment and organising, with a tremendous amount of resources made available, notably hundreds of thousands of pounds and a continuing supply of new recruitment and publicity material. Numerous different specific company/grade leaflets (for example, aimed at drivers, signallers, track workers, Network Rail, Virgin and so on) as well as general agitational literature have been produced, in each case stressing the need for an all-grades industrial union. The union has provided specially produced special RMT shoulder bags containing recruitment and organising materials such as brochures, stickers, pens, baseball caps, flags and whistles, aimed at making the union highly visible. It has produced training material aimed at helping new reps to address potential members about the virtues of membership at induction sessions for new employees. DVDs have been manufactured to help inspire existing, new and potential members by highlighting the campaigning, fighting, democratic and participative nature of the union. A union call centre has been established to phone around and re-recruit lapsed members, and a new residential training centre was opened in Doncaster (in October 2006) to provide company-specific training courses for reps (15–20 per week) on paid release from work.

Nonetheless, the main organising effort has come from the union's *own members* on the ground, and this has been manifested in a number of ways. Thus, each of the union's regions has held periodic 'organising weeks' to recruit new members and build the strength of local organisation. Planning meetings have identified recruitment targets using information gained from branch development plans and regional councils, with efforts then concentrated in specific areas with local reps and activists (some on paid leave) approaching workers in the targeted companies with a view to recruitment, usually through a 'one-to-one' approach. For example, the North West RMT regional council during one organising week in 2006 successfully recruited catering workers at a mainline station, infrastructure workers based at three depots, and cleaners at two stations. In the southwest, a local organising committee covering train operating company First Great Western studiously went through membership lists, identified weak points of organisation and successfully recruited nearly 200 members in just two months. Likewise, across the country individual branches have engaged in local recruitment and organising efforts, paying particular attention to encouraging prospective union reps to stand for election with the aim of building long-term structures that can strengthen workplace union organisation.

Of major significance has been the emphasis placed on recruiting new members beyond the traditional railway core groups (of train drivers, guards, signallers, track workers, station staff) to previously neglected groups of workers. Eurostar provides a vivid example of this broad-based recruitment and organising drive. In 1994, when the new company was formed, there were only 20 union members based at the main engineering maintenance depot. But with an increase in employment at the depot, the expansion of the Eurostar operation to other sites and the internal organising efforts of local activists, union membership increased by c.700 members to embrace the majority of the new and varied workforce, skilled and unskilled, manual and white collar, male and female. Thus, RMT membership now includes maintenance staff at the company's two engineering depots, depot-based cleaners as well as on-board cleaners (employed by private companies), Eurostar customer service staff, including many female bi-lingual staff and *bureau de change* employees, security staff (employed by Chubb Security), call centre employees, and clerical staff and IT professionals.

Meanwhile, two groups of unskilled, poorly paid and vulnerable workers specially targeted on the railways in recent years have been catering and cleaning staff. At mainline railway stations, the union has been able to win new members from amongst the growing numbers of catering staff under a sole union recognition agreement with franchisee Select Service Partners (SSP) UK Rail. The union has also put considerable effort into recruiting and building union organisation amongst train catering staff, often employed by a variety of private catering companies sub-contracted to the different train operating companies. Likewise cleaners, many of whom are immigrant workers, have been successfully targeted, including both those employed to clean railway stations and those who pick up litter on-board trains employed by private companies. On London Underground, there has also been a vigorous 'Living Wage' organising campaign aimed at cleaners employed by privatised companies, which involved network-wide strike action in 2008 and the recruitment of hundreds of new members (albeit this has involved some inter-union rivalry with Unite (TGWU section) who have also been actively recruiting cleaners).

One important feature of the RMT's organising initiative has been the attempt to invigorate new activists – to motivate not merely the union's regional officials, workplace reps and branch officers, but also a much broader layer of grassroots members, some of whom are not even integrated into formal union structures. Thus, in addition to the 2,000 registered collective bargaining and health and safety reps, the union has managed to build up a data base of another 1,200 'ambassador' activists who have independently demonstrated a willingness to help recruit and build the union in their workplace. An 'Organising Unit' officer explained:

> The big change we're making is that we're focusing much more on people who are not reps ... They're the people who don't go to the branches or regional council, but from our point of view they're a representative of the RMT in the workplace because they're the ones who often go around encouraging people to join. They've been really energised by what's been happening with the organising strategy.

A great deal of effort has gone into nurturing such union activists, supporting them with materials, advice, and training, and regularly communicating with them via text messages and email. Such a broadly-focused and activist-based organising strategy has not only paid enormous dividends in terms of recruiting new members, notably in areas from which the union had atrophied or been driven out of by privatisation, but also in building and strengthening workplace union organisation and energising a wide layer of activists.

Strike mobilisation

The second crucial ingredient to the RMT's organising approach has been the explicit rejection of social partnership and accommodative forms of labour unionism in favour of resistance and strike mobilisation as a path to the reinvigoration of union organisation. As one Bristol railway train driver explained:

> One of the reasons why people join the RMT is because in the post-Thatcher age, with the rise of managerialism, workers feel as though they need a badge of pride, sort of two fingers at the bosses. I think part of that identity is that people with no politics at all, who have never voted in their life, who don't have a parent who is in the Labour Party or on the left or anything like that, the ordinary worker wants to be a member of an organisation that they see as standing up to management. The badge of identity for an RMT member is being prepared to take strike action. They might not have always voted for strike action, but they know that being in the RMT means being prepared to take strike action. And that's different from other unions who seek to achieve by negotiation.

Not surprisingly employers, government and others have condemned such strike activity. For example, the London *Evening Standard* (29 June 2004) has commented: 'They are throwbacks to the pre-Thatcher days of militant trades unionism … with an easy formula of impossible demands followed by immediate threats of industrial action as a device to bounce managers into making concessions they cannot afford.' Nonetheless, over the last decade in many different sections of the privatised railway network and London Underground, the RMT has balloted in favour of and/or engaged in 24-hour and 48-hour strikes on numerous occasions, on issues such as pay and working conditions, pensions, and the effects of privatisation. On London Underground between January 2000 and August 2008, the RMT balloted for industrial action on 31 occasions, engaging in strikes on 17 different occasions. On the railway network during the same period, the RMT balloted for industrial action on 56 occasions, engaging in strike action on 32 different occasions. Many of these actions have been more than one-day strikes and more than single one-day strikes.[2] Per thousand members, the RMT has probably organised more ballots for industrial action and more strike action than any other union over the last 8–10 years (although this has also been encouraged by the large number of separate bargaining units created in the wake of privatisation and PPP on the railways and Underground respectively). Almost every single one of its ballots has returned overwhelming majorities in favour of action amongst those voting. As one RMT member was reported as remarking: 'The union never loses a strike ballot because we trust the union and we don't trust the management' (*Evening Standard* 27 February 2006). Even though South West Trains guards in March 2003 and Network Rail signalling staff in May 2008 both voted against strike action, the union has won majorities for industrial action in at least 82 different ballots on the railways and Underground during the period 2000–2008.

Building support for ballots for industrial action and the very process of strike mobilisation itself has provided the RMT with an important focus and opportunity to recruit new members who can be encouraged to vote and join the strike. It also obliges the union to regularly gather and update information about existing members, so that employers are less able to challenge the validity of ballot results in order to gain court injunctions (which could then force the union to call off the strike). Although strike ballots have sometimes been used as a form of sabre-rattling within the bargaining process, strike action has often been held with devastating high-profile public effect. For example, a 48-hour strike by 2,300 Metronet infrastructure workers on London Underground in September 2007, to secure guarantees over jobs, conditions and pensions, shut down the vast majority of the network, inconvenienced 3m people and caused an estimated £100m of damage to London's economy (Darlington 2008, 2009). A Metronet RMT rep explained the dramatic impact on union membership and organisation:

The strike ... helped to boost the morale and confidence of workers ... [W]e recruited literally dozens of new members across the board, mainly operational staff ... When we had our first strike ballot after PPP we had 1,500 members and in the recent dispute we balloted 2,500, so over a 2–3 year period we have gone up by 1,000 people. ... It has resulted from a lot of hard work, going round, one-to-one contact, checking membership lists, pinning down people who were in our areas and identifying non-union people ... We produced lots of our own branch literature, newsletters, branch minutes out to everyone, and anytime anyone got any information it was from us, with an RMT logo on it ... People generally believe we're the only players on the block and the only ones worth joining.

[W]e've [also] had lots of victories over recent years and there is nothing like success to bring more success. ... So if you keep winning things, even if you're not winning big things, but continually winning, it gets more and more people involved and they see it is a worthwhile endeavour. ... And we have far more reps and activists now; in fact, we have more people wanting to be reps than we have reps' positions, which has got to be a good thing because it means you have proper elections.

Other significant advances in membership and union organisation, albeit less dramatic, have occurred in a number of different parts of the railway and London Underground networks, particularly where strike action has been threatened and utilised as a means of leveraging concessions on pay and conditions from employers. For example, a one-day strike in 2004 by Eurostar customer service staff increased membership from 40 to 220. Likewise, strike mobilisation successfully forced employers to grant union recognition in some areas. In other words, the RMT's strike mobilisation strategy has been important in boosting the self-confidence of workers and their sense of collective power, which in turn has both attracted new union members and reinvigorated existing members who see that the union is prepared to fight and can demonstrably 'deliver'.

Further factors contributing to organising success

Whilst the RMT's organising and strike mobilisation approaches have been crucial ingredients to building the vitality of union organisation, a number of other objective and subjective contributory factors need to be recognised. First, a highly significant contextual industrial relations factor has been the operational vulnerability of the railway and underground networks to strike action, with the RMT's strategic position, both industrially and within society more generally, obviously providing it with enormous potential bargaining power. Even localised one-day strikes limited to individual train operating companies or one Tube line have impacted significantly, while on a more dramatic scale the prospect of an *industry-wide* railway strike has threatened to affect a complete shutdown of the network to commuters, as the RMT's planned 24-hour strikes over the defence of final salary pension systems in 2004 and 2006 vividly demonstrated. The nature of both transport industries, with their tightly integrated service networks which are not easily substitutable by other means, provides an important source of workplace bargaining power in which stoppages of work can have much greater and immediate impact than many other industrial sectors. Moreover, unlike many public and private sectors elsewhere, both rail and underground have experienced massive expansion in terms of capital investment and passenger and freight traffic. In 2007, with an estimated 3m people using the national rail network every weekday, rail travel had reached its highest level for almost 50 years, with a projected increase of 30% by 2015. Likewise on the Underground, passenger journeys have increased by over 25% over the last 15 years.[3] This buoyancy has undoubtedly contributed to boosting the RMT's bargaining leverage and confidence *vis-à-vis* employers, as well as providing union recruitment opportunities within an expanding workforce in many areas.

Second, it is of significance that the RMT is a relatively small, clearly defined and specialist 'industrial' union that organises across the transport sector (including not only the railways and Underground but also freight haulage, parcel delivery, rural bus services, licensed taxi firms, and the maritime and offshore oil industries) to include and embrace *all* grades of employees and different occupations, including skilled and unskilled. This industrial unionism and inclusive all-grades nature of the RMT has provided it with a clear core motivational identity in day-to-day organisational and political practice, encouraging a high degree of attachment and loyalty to the union, even amongst diverse groups of employees who might otherwise be members of other unions. On the railways such industrial unionism, and its related strategic and coordinated national forms of organisation, has been crucial to helping the union respond to the challenge of fragmented company-level bargaining and the spatially uneven pattern of industrial relations. As one Arriva Trains activist explained:

> When people work on the railway they develop some kind of chemistry, there is camaraderie ... people will interact from all the different companies, the platform staff will talk to the guards, and everyone talks to each other whoever they're employed by. Through that communication the trade union forms a big part – it's the union that gels everyone together in the railway industry irrespective of the company you work for.

At the same time the RMT has been able to offer members a strong occupational identity *within* the broad transport sectors in which it organises, for example with separate national committees for train crew and shunters grades, signalling grades, engineering grades, catering grades, station staff and associated grades, etc. Such intra-organisational structures have helped to increase the profile and autonomy of such occupational groups, and in turn bind them together within an all-grades industrial-wide form of identity and organisation (Wilson 2007).

Third, also of crucial significance has been the role of national leadership, primarily the general secretary, in transforming the RMT, with a change in the leadership being both cause and effect. Bob Crow has noticeably stamped his oppositionist leadership style towards the employers and the 'new' Labour government on the union and helped to shape strategic and tactical issues, with a consistent stress on so-called 'old-fashioned' virtues of collectivism, solidarity, resistance and activism. As one activist noted:

> Since his election victory, Bob Crow has taken a lead in encouraging a fighting trade union platform, supporting strike action where necessary, refuting social partnership, and breaking with the Labour Party, and so on ... Bob's election was a breath of fresh air, because the whole cautious approach that the union had had, which had done us no good whatsoever, [was overturned] ... overnight we had a figurehead who – rather than trying to block activists on the ground – wanted to take on an employer, who would actively encourage it. He would look at reasons to go into dispute rather than reasons not to, which was totally opposite to what we had seen beforehand ... I think that in itself has encouraged people to join us, because they can see that there is somebody there who does want to do something for 'me'.

Of course, managerial belligerence in the wake of privatisation and PPP has also helped to encourage such a militant union stance, with a high proportion of strike ballots and strikes essentially reactive and defensive protests against perceived managerial attempts to drive through efficiency gains, worsen conditions of work and undermine collective union organisation. In the process, there has been Crow's high-profile public face – with name recognition among the union's membership very widespread – regularly responding with press releases, radio interviews and television appearances. His open antagonism towards employers has contributed to the process of union confidence, activism, mobilisation and recruitment.

Fourth, the RMT has maintained a highly democratic form of union structure and organisation, involving a relatively high level of activism, which in turn has also contributed to the union's organising success.

In this respect, the reform of union government that occurred in the wake of Crow's election was highly significant. As a consequence, there is now election (rather than appointment) of all national and regional EUOs (who are subject to re-election after five years) and a directly elected lay-member Council of Executives (whose members must relinquish their post after a three-year term of office). In addition, central decision-making powers lie in the hands of the lay national grade conferences and the Annual General Meeting (with delegates excluded from attending for more than a three-year successive period). All of these internal democratic procedures have helped to stimulate devolved activist engagement. Meanwhile, one of the paradoxes of privatisation of the railways, with its fragmentation of organisational structure and collective bargaining, has been that it has encouraged new and wider layers of union rep and activist than existed under the old form of centralised national negotiations. As a consequence, there is a large milieu of assertive and combative lay workplace reps and activists at different levels of the union, who have played a crucial role in advocating and winning support for the mobilisation of union members in collective action against employers. Such activists have clearly been important in 'framing' issues, pitting them in antagonism to management, 'mobilising bias' (Batstone *et al.* 1977, 1978) to win strike ballot votes, and displaying leadership and organising skills.

Fifth, there is a significant layer of left-wing political activists inside the RMT who also appear to have been crucial to the task of building union organisation and industrial and political mobilisation (Darlington 2001, 2007, 2008, 2009). Such a left-wing tradition has developed in part from the ideological and practical activities of unofficial caucus groups established on both the railways and tube from the late 1980s and early 1990s. These sought to revitalise the union's internal democratic structures and to directly challenge the moderate industrial and political leadership of the incumbent general secretary, Jimmy Knapp, and the EUO grouping around him, in particular for failing to mount sufficiently robust opposition to the impending privatisation of the railways and subsequent part-privatisation of the Tube. Such networks meshed together leading union officials and activists, members of left-wing groups and a much broader layer of independent non-party industrial activists, and played a highly influential leadership role, with an industrial strategy of militant opposition to management informed by a left-wing political agenda.

One important fruit of the left's rising influence and the combative mood of the union's members in the wake of privatisation/PPP was the huge majority in support of Crow's election in 2002, following Knapp's death. Crow, who had been a supporter of the left caucus (as well as a former member of the Communist Party and Socialist Labour Party), was elected on a platform of creating a 'fighting trade union' that would campaign to roll back privatisation, and his victory was a manifestation of a new found sense of militant solidarity in the face of the perceived 'betrayals' of 'new' Labour. Despite a sustained media red scare campaign, electoral victories for the left at different levels of the union and Crow's overwhelming re-election in 2006 have further confirmed this trend. As a consequence, although it no longer has any formally organised grouping as such, the RMT has had a wide but loose network of prominent left figures (from Crow and EUOs to Council of Executive members and lay union reps and activists on the ground) with fairly explicit left-wing political values, ideology, motivation and commitment, who from the early 2000s have been increasingly influential in shaping the union's rejection of social partnership in favour of the use of strike ballots and mobilisation of members as the means to win concessions. This has made it easier for an internal union culture of militant oppositionalism directed towards employers and 'new' Labour, combined with robust collectivism and assertive style of leadership, to pervade the union (especially on the Underground).

The influence of the left inside the RMT was most decisively demonstrated in the crucial role it played – following 'new' Labour's refusal to accept the union's loyalty pledges of re-nationalisation of the railways, scrapping of part-privatisation of London Underground and repealing of anti-union legislation – in encouraging the union to progressively reduce the number of its members affiliated to Labour, cutback its affiliation fees and permit support for other political parties to the left of Labour such as the Scottish Socialist Party. This resulted in its expulsion in 2004 from the party it had helped to set up 100 years earlier. In January 2006, following an initiative from the union's left elements, the union hosted a conference open to union activists from others unions to discuss 'The Crisis in Working Class Political Representation' which made clear the gulf between the union and 'new' Labour over privatisation, employment laws, the war in Iraq and other matters. In the meantime, the union has taken the initiative to sponsor the launch of a National Shop Stewards' Network, viewed as the first step to revitalising the grassroots of unions and building a 'fighting union movement'. Finally, the RMT has taken some important steps to broaden the agenda of labour unionism by making common cause with a range of social movements, including high profile support for the Stop the War Coalition and Unite Against Fascism, and participation at the anticapitalist European and World Social Forums. All these initiatives have been well supported by left activists in the union's different regions and branches, and have marked a limited but notable attempt to reorient the union as a social actor towards a broader political agenda.

Limitations and weaknesses

Despite its undoubted successes, there remain formidable limitations and weaknesses in union organisation on both the railways and Underground. Some of the internal and external organising constraints involved are common to other unions (Heery and Simms 2008), while others are more distinctive. To begin with, the fragmentation of the industry into numerous different segments has presented formidable challenges to union organisation. As one activist commented:

> In the past under BR, you had a union branch in Carlisle which dealt with the one set of BR negotiations affecting all the different grades. But once you had privatisation and fragmentation then there were something like 20 companies operating out of Carlisle and so the union branch struggles just to get through the correspondence.

Inevitably, there is considerable unevenness in membership density between individual companies and different specific grades within companies. On the railway network, drivers, signallers and guards are some of the best organised, industrially sophisticated, and highest paid of the RMT's membership, with perhaps a stronger sense than others of their own grade cohesiveness and special interests. But the union has had varying results when it comes to organising less well paid grades of staff – such as station and booking office staff, infrastructure workers, cleaners, catering staff, and some of the fleet maintenance depot operatives. For example, whereas density among Network Rail signal staff is about 90%, amongst privatised 'permanent-way' track workers it can be as low as 20% in some companies.

Differences in levels of membership and organisation in different sections of the rail network generally can be explained by a variety of potential factors, including the nature of the job, workers' strategic position, degree of collective relations, and extent of employer opposition. For example, the highly sophisticated HRM strategy adopted by Virgin Trains on the West Coast line, with its attempt to recruit a new, young and company-loyal workforce, and to effectively undermine existing union organisation through the provision of alternative voice mechanisms, combined with the very wide dispersion of the workforce geographically, has posed a significant challenge. Likewise, South West Trains have attempted to frustrate union organising by preventing reps from attending induction courses for new employees at its large Basingstoke depot (although they continued to provide facilities for ASLEF and TSSA). But an additional contributory factor to the state of organisation is the level and quality of activism on the ground. For example, membership among the traditionally well-organised guards section at Waterloo station fell dramatically in recent years from about 70% to 40% arising from internal personal and organisational divisions, before being addressed.

The rail infrastructure sector has proved particularly difficult for the RMT. After privatisation, with the separation of the running of trains from ownership of the track, a split between operations and infrastructure, a relatively well-functioning integrated service was transformed into a highly fragmented business. Although in 2003 Network Rail took over direct ownership of infrastructure maintenance (thereby bringing 18,000 workers back 'in-house'), it still utilises the services of four private renewals companies who in turn sub-contract out work to hundreds of other companies engaged on track work, involving many thousands of workers only a minority of whom are unionised and many of whom are casually employed. Even in Network Rail, where it is a lot easier for the RMT to operate, the process of reorganisation and absorption that has taken place has resulted in a patchwork quilt of different terms and conditions of employment that has undermined the process of union collectivism.

Amongst some low-paid groups, notably catering and cleaning staff, there is also the perennial problem of turnover undermining the stability of organisation. With reference to station catering workers, one Manchester Piccadilly rep explained:

> The big problem you have – and we have recruited a lot of them from Burger King, Costa Coffee, all of them – is the turnover. You can go through a recruitment exercise and sign a load of them up, but go back another two months later and they're not there anymore.

Another obstacle has been the existence of deeply-rooted inter-union rivalries, notably with ASLEF who enjoy a higher level of membership amongst train drivers, with the consequence that the RMT have often been carved out of train operating companies' drivers' bargaining forums. Such divisions have been compounded by inter-union disputes over competitive recruitment tactics, with the RMT sometimes adopting a self-defeating hostile 'red union' approach to ASLEF. Furthermore, the RMT is now faced with the threat posed by Unite, which in 2007 announced a 'memorandum of agreement' with ASLEF and heralded the future of 'an arrangement in which [its] resources and influence nationally would work alongside ASLEF's enormous influence within the rail industry', with the sum of £15m to be spent on future organisation and recruitment. Inevitably, the RMT has been concerned that the two organisations may, indeed, be moving towards merger, further threatening its influence in the future.

But in addition to these broad constraining factors, there have also been some limitations with the RMT's approach to union organising and revitalisation. With regard to strike mobilisation, it seems that new members have only been recruited when the union appears to be winning significant gains. But when the union has proved unable to significantly influence the collective bargaining agenda through strike action it has actually lost members. This is what happened following a campaign of 14 24-hour Sunday strikes by Virgin Cross-Country guards in 2006 over payment for productivity changes. Virgin mobilised train managers from across the company (and co-franchisee South West Trains) to successfully strike-break, with the result that the dispute collapsed and a number of RMT members were lost. Although in the wake of these disputes, some of the lost members were subsequently won back, this case is illustrative of the problem faced on occasion and the high stakes that strike ballots and action can involve. Likewise, on the Underground there has on occasion been sharp criticism of RMT EUOs by local reps for settling disputes and calling off threatened strike action on terms that have been perceived as falling short of original demands (Darlington 2008).

Meanwhile, there has also been some internal resistance to the RMT's 'Organising Unit's approach by a layer of activists/reps who have raised probing questions about the perceived lack of any clearly defined or articulated organising 'strategy' as such, with the absence of a policy statement that contains strategic aims that could be subsequently assessed in the light of experience. Likewise, it has been claimed no systematic methods of data collection have been adopted to measure what progress has been made, beyond overall membership growth; for example, in terms of a detailed breakdown of membership figures in specific sectors, and evidence of increased union density or reps' representation. In addition, disquiet has been expressed at the limitations of the 'Organising Unit's all-inclusive membership recruitment approach of 'throwing the net into the sea and reeling in anything they can', with its explicit attempt to dissolve any distinctions between the so-called 'periphery' as opposed to 'core' workforce.

Nobody has opposed the attempt to recruit and organise catering, cleaning and security staff and other marginalised groups of transport workers. On the contrary, there has been a recognition that the RMT's predecessor, the National Union of Railwaymen, successfully organised early twentieth century Burger King-equivalent employees in railway hotels, stations and train buffets, as well as laundry workers, seam-stresses and any other workers who in any way had some connection with the railway industry on the basis of syndicalist-inspired industrial unionism (Bagwell 1963, 1982; Wojtczak 2005). Nonetheless, as a Council of Executives member explained:

> There is an argument ... as to whether we should be targeting the core or the periphery, and I would say within the core grades that the union has historically represented – permanent way, signallers and telecoms, guards, station staff, drivers and others – there are huge areas where we have allowed union density to plummet and union organisation to atrophy. I am told in the south-east region, the level of organisation among infrastructure workers is down to 25% in large areas, so there are big problems in some areas which we haven't addressed. But there has been a reluctance or even hostility to regarding some workers as 'core' and some as 'periphery'. Well, I think it is nonsense to say we don't make selections as to who we want to organise ... It depends on what you think a union's purpose is. If you are simply trying to recruit people in terms of trying to increase your membership then it might be a good reason, but what can you deliver? How can those workers be best organised?

As a result, a regional council took the initiative, ironically independently of the 'Organising Unit', to suggest there should be a change of emphasis towards a hitherto neglected strategic sector of the rail-way, specifically targeting the 50 nationwide train maintenance depots – employing some 20,000–25,000 workers employed by over 20 different companies. In 2008, leading local reps from the sector met and produced a *Workers' Charter* pamphlet and launched a highly successful membership recruit-ment campaign which, unlike the 'Organising Unit' approach, has been anchored around a set of specific collective bargaining demands. Similar targeted campaigns in other sectors, for example amongst engineering track workers, have now been advocated. This is posed not only on the basis that this is where the railway's core workforce is concentrated, where industrial muscle is strongest and where there is still a tremendous amount of effort needed to recruit new members and strengthen union organisation, but also in terms of the potential spill-over effect on other 'peripheral' groups of workers. Indeed, at two First Great Western train maintenance depots, not only have skilled engineering staff been recruited as a result of the new approach, but also large numbers of cleaners.

Meanwhile, the rapidly changing social composition of the industry's workforce has also posed new challenges. In addition to Virgin (see above), London Underground has undergone a similar change (with currently a 16.7% female workforce), and this has also included a significant transformation in ethnic composition, with large numbers of African, Asian, and East European workers joining a longer standing West Indian element. But such changes have not been adequately reflected within the RMT's own representative structures. For example, the union has around 8,250 female members nationally, representing less than 11% of its membership, although the proportion is higher on London Underground where there are larger numbers of female station staff. Moreover, all EUOs are male and always have been, and the national executive is all male and has only ever had two women members. Regional council and reps' organisation is highly male-dominated. Ironically, for a union that formally embraces notions of social movementism, the lack of adequate female representation may reflect not only the gendered nature of the occupational areas in which it often organises (compared to administrative grades where TSSA has a base), but also its overall 'workerist' approach, with propaganda and agitation tending to concentrate almost exclusively on traditional narrow issues, such as pay and conditions, to the neglect of a wider bargaining agenda.

Finally, there is the dilemma that having broken from 'new' Labour whom should it support politically? Although broadly sympathetic of forces to the left of Labour, the RMT has thus far been unwilling to commit itself to wholehearted support for any of the existing small parties and has not used its authority alongside other left-wing led unions (such as the FBU and PCS) to attempt to organise the nucleus of a new broader-based, union-sponsored and potentially more credible alternative left-wing political formation. Instead, it has operated a multi-faceted strategy of building political alliances with a variety of different forces, which has even included reinvigorating its parliamentary Labour group. But this approach has, for some activists at least, failed to take advantage of the potential for a new independent political party to the left of Labour that could itself form a component part of the process of revitalising the union.

Conclusion

Some conclusions and broader generalisations from the chapter can now be made in relation to current debates about union revitalisation, whereby a number of important linkages between organising, militancy and revitalisation can be identified. At a fairly simple level, the study highlights the direct link between union orientation and action (see Bacon and Blyton 2004). Thus, the ideological orientation of the RMT – involving not just its distinct application of an organising and strike mobilisation approach, but also its broader leadership and left-wing political approach – has been highly influential in shaping the specific nature of membership action and the potential fortunes of the union (see also Frege and Kelly 2004; Milkman and Voss 2004; Turner and Hurd 2001). In turn, it has been the politicisation of industrial relations arising from the process of privatisation and PPP, with all the restructuring that has been involved, which has also encouraged membership discontent and its manifestation in a 'militant' and left-wing political union orientation and leadership. In other words, the *process* by which the RMT has organised and attempted to rebuild the union – a process which stands in sharp contrast with most other unions – has been shaped by both ideological and practical factors, by both 'strategic choice' and broader environmental contextual influences.

With reference to the *outcome* and consequences of such an approach, the chapter underlines the important link between union effectiveness and membership growth. A number of studies (see, for example, Bryson 2006a, Charlwood 2003; Jowell *et al.* 1997) have suggested that one of the principal reasons why British workers generally are not joining unions in greater numbers is that they are often viewed as simply not being 'effective' enough. Kelly (1998: 48–49) noted the central problem faced by unions is the perception that they may be too weak to 'make a difference' to the solving of workplace injustices and, therefore, employees may not think they have something tangible to gain from membership. Yet if the RMT's experience of significant growth in membership in recent years is an indicator, it would seem that what has attracted workers to join has been its apparent ability to deliver in terms of obtaining manifest improvements in pay and conditions, as well as in providing some insurance against arbitrary employer actions. Of course, the relative returns to members have not been the only factor determining union membership levels, but it does appear to have been an important feature.

There also appears to have been a direct link between militancy and such union growth and revitalisation. Thus, in order to be in a position to extract concessions from employers, the RMT has adopted a combative stance, often involving collective mobilisation and the threat of, and use of, strike action. As Bob Crow has commented: 'I think when they see the unions fighting, people will join' (*Financial Times* 13 February 2004). In other words, while the union's influence in the workplace has undoubtedly been derived in part from its strategic industrial bargaining power, it has also come from the union's effective strategy and tactics, including its 'organisational effectiveness' (Bryson 2006a) as a vibrant advocate of both its members and potential members, and its ability to involve a wide activist base. Such an adversarial stance, and the benefits it has bestowed, contrasts with the more accommodative forms of trade unionism adopted by many other unions as part of their own organising approach.

Another linkage has been between revitalisation and democracy. Hyman and Fryer (1977) assessed a number of specific influences on union democracy, including the degree of membership homogeneity, extent of skill, status and educational qualifications, strength of occupational identity, and the size and distribution of membership. But in addition, it was noted that union government is affected by the prevailing conception of union purpose, whereby the broader and more ambitious the union's objectives, the more likely the members will become active participants. In the case of the RMT, the union's organising and strike mobilisation approach has been both cause and affect to such democratic tendencies. Attempts to regularly mobilise members to take strike action, the vigorous encouragement of membership activism, the union organising drive, and the broader left-wing politically-informed objectives that shape union policy have encouraged democratic processes, and in turn such democratic processes have helped to shape the union's approach, its organising success and the energising of the activists. The significance of mobilisation theory has also been underlined, notably in terms of the role of union activists in identifying, formulating and articulating grievances as well as organising collectively for redress through the mobilisation of members and through union organising and recruitment (see Kelly 1998).

Finally, the experience of the RMT appears, to some extent at least, to belie the view of commentators (see, for example, Brown 2008; Charlwood 2004; Gospel 2005; Metcalf 2005) who have assumed that unfavourable economic and political constraints severely limit the scope for unions to undergo significant revitalisation through organising, and that the unions, rather like the biblical Lazarus, will need a miracle before they can to come back to life (Coats 2005). In fact, despite continuing formidable obstacles of both an internal and external nature, a number of which are common to those unions which have adopted a more accommodative organising approach, the RMT has clearly been able to make some significant gains for both its organisation and members. The union's alternative approach to organising and revitalisation has undoubtedly been influential in this respect, albeit not without its own limitations and weaknesses. Nonetheless, the experience of the RMT also highlights some of the relatively favourable specific industrial contextual features within which it has operated, despite the overall challenges posed by privatisation and PPP, which has also been an important contributory factor to success, and which are not necessarily present elsewhere. In other words, the scale of the RMT's *subjective* accomplishments cannot necessarily be assumed to be automatically replicable by other unions (for example, PCS) that operate in less favourable *objective* contexts, although the overall organising approach may be transferable.

Acknowledgement

The research on which the chapter draws was funded by an award from the British Academy (SG: 40064).

Notes

1   The vast majority, over 60,000, of the RMT's membership, work either on the railways or London Underground.
2   Figures have been compiled from a variety of published and unpublished sources emanating from the Office for National Statistics, employers, the RMT, newspaper reports and elsewhere (see Darlington 2007, 2009).
3   Network Rail (2007) *Business Plan 2007*, Transport for London (2006) *A Rail Strategy for London's Future*, Transport for London, *Annual Report and Statement of Accounts 2006–2007*.

6
Union Organising in a Recognised Environment – A Case Study of Mobilisation

Nick McCarthy

Introduction

This chapter focuses on the presence of the 3.4m non-members in Britain who are covered by union recognition agreements (Metcalf 2003: 186). The presence of these so-called 'free riders', namely, those who benefit from improved conditions negotiated by unions through collective bargaining but choose not to be union members, is abundant evidence – were it needed – that recognition agreements with employers are alone not sufficient to make employees voluntarily decide to join the salient union there. Hypothetically, organising new members and servicing increased numbers of members covered by recognition agreements should be less resource intensive than organising non-members in workplaces without union recognition. Therefore, resources could then subsequently be released to organise in workplaces without recognition. How unions approach the challenge of organising these 3.4m non-members is examined through a case study of a medium-sized public sector union in Britain, the Public, Commercial and Services (PCS) union. It has increased its overall membership density by 3.6% between 2001 and 2007 while overall union density for the same period in Britain has fallen by 1.3% and by 0.7% in the public sector (Mercer and Notley 2008: 17, 19). The chapter explores the strategies and tactics that unions use in relation to employers and members from a radical perspective (see Inset 6.1). These strategies and tactics are broadly situated with 'organising' and 'partnership' approaches. The case study of PCS is used to explore the relationship between union behaviour and its effect on increasing membership density.

Union behaviour within recognition agreements: themes and issues

Analysing union behaviour within recognition agreements is complex, for different unions have both different approaches to growth and different relationships with employers. Therefore, it is important to attempt to define and conceptualise union approaches to membership growth within recognition agreements. The first task is, thus, to define union behaviour within recognition agreements and two broad approaches are identifiable in the literature, namely, 'organising' and 'partnership' (see Heery 2002). Each of these labels has a number of definitions and usages so that the purpose here is to define and categorise significant differences in union behaviour. Often under the influence of US developments, over the past ten years many British unions have developed organising strategies, set up organising departments and employed organisers trained by the TUC Organising Academy. 'Organising' is defined by Bronfenbrenner (in Gall 2003a: 18) in the context of US unions as:

> [a] comprehensive union building model which involves multiple elements ranging from strategic targeting, to rank and file leadership development of an active and representative organising committee to the use of adequate and numbers of trained full time organizers to escalating pressure tactics in the workplace and the broader community, [and] to the use of member volunteer organizers.

Moreover, Bronfenbrenner and Juravich (1998: 32) argued, using quantitative data from National Labor Relations Board (NLRB) certification elections, that comprehensive and strategic campaigns, which focus on 'union building' (incorporating person-to-person contact, leadership development, escalating internal and external pressure) increase the likelihood of winning elections, relative to traditional organising methods or the use of just one element of the comprehensive union building model. Others such as Gall (2003a: 16–17) and Kelly (1998, 2005) emphasised the importance of mobilisation and collective action within the organising model and union membership growth. Tilly (1978: 5–7, 54–55) developed a conceptual framework, mobilisation theory, of collective action with five major components: interests, organisation, mobilisation, opportunity and collective action. Kelly (2005: 66–67) argued that mobilisation plays a key role in union growth whereby a sense of injustice can trigger unionisation. However, this does not occur spontaneously – for union activists are required, as they help construct a sense of injustice and attribute this injustice to the employer, while encouraging group identity and cohesion. Kelly (2005: 66) also referred to 'agency' – the belief that collective action can 'make a difference', which is linked to perceptions of union instrumentality. Gall (2003a: 18) noted differences between US and British definitions of organising and the wide array of meanings which are applied to the term. It is possible to identify differences in emphasis between those who place emphasis on systematic union building strategies and tactics, which include mobilisation, and those who emphasise the centrality of mobilisation to union membership growth.

In Britain, while the main focus of organising strategies (and consequent deployment of resources) has been to win new recognition agreements with employers, organisers have also been deployed by unions within current recognition agreements to increase activity and membership density (see Colgan and Creegan 2006; Heery 2002; Wills 2004b). Wills (2004b) and Heery (2002) studied unions which tried to integrate 'organising' approaches to growth and 'partnership' approaches to bargaining. However, these studies did not focus on the potential incoherence between 'organising'-based growth strategies which focused on mobilising employees around issues of injustice, and 'partnership' approaches to bargaining which focused-on mutual gains and co-operation (rather than injustice).

There is little empirical evidence which shows a positive relationship between partnership, mutual gains and increases in membership density. At the disaggregated level, Heery, Kelly and Waddington (2003: 89) found that of some 50–80 formal partnership agreements, only five reported an increase in membership following the agreement. In this context, Kochan (1980) and Charlwood (2003) have argued that the factors which cause employees to unionise can be divided into three areas: beliefs about unions, perceptions of the work environment and perceptions of influence. Kochan (1979) tested his model and concluded that all aspects of the model were important in the decision to unionise, but beliefs that unions were instrumental in delivering improvements were the most important. Bryson and Gomez (2003: 75) analysed membership through a framework of rational choices and concluded that union membership is an 'experience good' but with benefits which are hard to observe. And, Bryson and Gomez (2003: 91) also observed that the task of the union is to convince non-members that 'the experiential benefits of membership are high quality'. Both Kochan (1980: 177) and Charlwood (2003: 70) argued that union organising strategies are unlikely to lead to a widespread resurgence of union membership levels, for dissatisfaction is not widespread and employers can resist union organising by either removing the source of dissatisfaction or through aggressive anti-union tactics, which causes workers to believe that a union will make workplace relations worse. They also concurred that organising resources are insufficient to affect aggregate union membership levels. These arguments can be taken to support the development of a positive 'partnership' relationship between unions and employers, as these will give the possibility of successful bargaining outcomes without the possible negative consequences of attempting to mobilise around issues of injustice.

Other literature on employer-union partnerships has emphasised the use of employer provided facilities to recruit members within partnership agreements. Wills (2004b) discussed the granting of union facilities, time-off and training for union reps, and access to non-members as opportunities for membership recruitment under partnership agreements, whereby she (Wills 2004b: 338) noted that membership increased at two offices in the 18 months since the Barclays-Unifi agreement was reached (albeit a study of other partnerships agreements in the finance sector in Britain concluded there was no positive relationship (Gall 2008)). Wills reported Unifi developed a sophisticated strategy including a team of organisers to work with workplace representatives and that the partnership agreement was used by the union as a 'springboard' to start rebuilding the union. Employer derived facilities provide significant additional resources for unions, given that organising is constrained by lack of resources (Heery and Simms 2008: 31). And, as Metcalf (2005: 108) pointed out, unions have to make choices in how they use their resources, which range from continuing to service current members, providing individual services and representation, organising 'free riders' within recognition agreements and organising the 14m employees outside recognition agreements. In this regard, for example, Tailby *et al.* (2007: 225), in their insurance company case study, described a union focusing on individual advocacy, where union organising was rarely mentioned. The growth strategy was limited for while the union's advocacy was highly regarded by union members, the problem for the union was convincing a large proportion of the workforce of the benefits of this support. Unions have scarce resources, so priorities must be identified, and within recognition agreements, whether resources are prioritised on individual servicing or organising is an important issue.

A pertinent issue here relates to communication. Stuart and Martinez Lucio (2005b: 108–109) in their study of MSF reps' attitudes to partnership highlighted that 66% 'strongly agreed' or 'agreed' that unions had to accept conditions of confidentiality on certain issues. Meanwhile, Oxenbridge and Brown (2005: 94–95) found in partnership arrangements that managers sought to replace union-member communications with management-employee communications. Wills (2004b) also identified the risks associated with a partnership agreement approach to growth. The agreement she studied limited Unifi's ability to communicate independently with its members and this affected the union's independence and legitimacy in the members' eyes. Indeed, 'high trust' relations of union-employer partnership usually mean that information is provided by employers on the basis of a requirement for confidentiality and joint-communication. Clearly, 'high trust' relations have implications for the bargaining process, whereby delimited communication during bargaining can constrain the mobilisation of members around issues of injustice.

Therefore, key elements of the 'organising' approach can be said to relate to foci on worker interests, employer-based injustice, mobilisation and collective action as well as using a comprehensive range of tactics which stimulate grass-roots participation in organising campaigns. However, while this approach tells us much about the strategies and tactics that unions should use to grow, it tells us little about the strategies and tactics which unions should use in collective bargaining within recognition agreements. The key elements of the 'partnership' approach relate to a focus on mutual interests and joint-working, demonstrating instrumentality and the use of employer provided facilities to recruit new members. This approach tells us much about how unions can develop productive relationships with employers but it tells us less about the strategies and tactics which unions can use to develop that relationship into increases in membership.

To summarise, a number of key differences between the two approaches emerge from the literature. First, mobilisation is central to the organising approach for membership growth. Instrumentality is central to the partnership approach and mobilisation is viewed as undesirable or counter-productive. The focus on collective mobilisation or instrumentality is the key differentiator between the two approaches, leading to other significant contradictions or choices. Second, union resources are scarce and how they are allocated is important, whereby choices must be made between union building and developing new activists to support mobilisation, or to individual representation. Third, the approach to communication with members provides a choice for unions – either campaigning on issues of injustice, or a 'high trust' approach including confidential, joint employer-union communication, emphasising mutual gains and co-operation. In this context, Bronfenbrenner and Juravich (1998) suggested compromising the essential elements of a comprehensive organising strategy may undermine the success of the strategy.

In attempting to develop a framework to examine union behaviour within a recognition agreement, it is necessary to develop the concepts which have been identified in the literature. Inset 6.1 presents an ideal-type schema which seeks to provide a comprehensive working definition of 'organising' and 'partnership' on key aspects of union behaviour (*cf.* Boxall and Haynes 1997). Its purpose is to provide polarised points on a continuum by which, heuristically, it is possible to examine union behaviour. The schema was used as the basis upon which to formulate the research tools and subsequently help to analyse the generated data from respondents.

Inset 6.1   Organising and partnership approaches

Subject/Approach	Organising	Partnership
Employer relations	Worker interests	Mutual Interests
Bargaining goals	Ambitious	Moderate
Member relations	Collective mobilisation	Individualised instrumentality
Resource priority	Developing activists	Individual representation
Growth strategy	Union building	Recruitment using employer facilities
Member communication	Open, campaigning	Confidential, elite network based
Issue framing	Injustice	Consensus

Hypotheses and research methods

PCS union has c.310,000 members and organises primarily within the civil service. Primary quantitative and qualitative data were collected through surveys in line with the schema. Internal union data on membership levels and statistical data from the British civil service archive was also deployed, and the union's annual 'Organising Strategy' was also used to provide information on strategy and data on changes to activist numbers.

From the schema, the following proposition was constructed, namely, that an 'organising', rather than a 'partnership', approach is positively associated with increased levels of membership density. Three hypotheses were then created. First, increased membership growth is positively associated with mobilisations rather than demonstrations of instrumentality. Second, decisions which focus resources on organising activities rather than servicing activities are positively associated with membership growth. Third, 'high trust' relationships with joint-communications and confidentiality during negotiations, are negatively associated with membership growth.

The chapter will test these hypotheses through comparing PCS membership of the Department of Work and Pensions group (DWP) to that of the union *excluding* the DWP group (PCSeDWP). During the period 2001 to 2007, the DWP group increased its density from 62.8% to 69.7% while PCSeDWP increased its density from 50.9% to 53.9%. Therefore, the hypotheses are designed to test whether there is evidence that behaviour approximating the 'organising' was present in the relatively higher density growth DWP group as well as to compare this behaviour with the relatively lower density growth PCSeDWP. The research methods used a series of proxies for elements of the schema namely, mobilisation, union building, and personal representation.

It is worth briefly examining the extent to which the DWP group and the PCSeDWP are valid comparators. The DWP group had c.80,000 members spread over 1,000 workplaces ranging from large workplaces in urban centres to small workplaces in small towns. The comparator PCSeDWP, is comprised of all other parts of the union, namely, its 230,000 members divided into 31 groups. The 31 groups include HM Revenue and Customs which has over 70,000 members and a density of around 80%, four groups with 10,000–20,000 members and 26 Groups with less than 10,000 members, some of which have a significantly higher density than the DWP Group and others with a lower density. Each group has a different culture, history of mobilisation and relationship with its employer. However, many factors are comparable such as the overall civil service employment environment, recognition arrangements, employer provided facility-time allocations, types of job category, gender balance and multi-site organising. Whilst the DWP/ PCSeDWP comparison has some potential flaws, it is rare to find exact comparators and the comparators have significant structural and environmental factors in common which makes the comparison valid and cautious use of the comparative data meaningful.

Hypothesis one is also tested using analysis of the effect of mobilisation and instrumentality within the PCS DWP group on the numbers of union 'joiners' which are shown in the monthly membership recruitment data between December 2005 and April 2008. The reason for using this different period of analysis is that monthly membership recruitment data is available for this period. The reason for using the DWP group is that it is possible to examine the effect of mobilisation and instrumentality within the context of a single employer-based bargaining unit. The period included both mobilisations and demonstrations of instrumentality, and the data presents an interesting and useful opportunity to isolate and identify variations in membership on a monthly basis which can be assessed against the known mobilisations and demonstrations of instrumentality affecting DWP employees.

'Joiners', the number of members who joined the union within each month, are analysed whilst 'leavers', the number of members who left PCS within each month, are not. This is, firstly, because there was a significant reduction in the numbers of employees in the DWP during the period examined and it was, therefore, not possible to determine from the data the reason for leaving. Secondly, joiners are placed on the union database within a short time of the application form being received while leavers remain on the membership system for up to three months from the member ceasing subscriptions. Consequently, it is difficult to identify associations between events and data for union leavers. Furthermore, DWP membership density increased, thereby, demonstrating in broad terms that the numbers of 'leavers' were not so significant to lead to a fall in density.

The populations surveyed were bargaining officers, employed organisers and union representatives. An on-line survey was used because all union staff and the vast majority of activists have access at work to email and the internet. At the point of the survey, PCS had 62 EUOs with bargaining responsibility, 22 EUOs with organising responsibility and 10,234 union representatives. The response rates were 82%, 77% and 12.5% respectively, giving an overall response rate of 13.2%. My own position within PCS at the time was that of a senior national officer covering a bargaining unit for which I have been responsible for organising and negotiations over the last ten years. In this regard, Thompson and Bannon (1985: 5) argued it is possible for the researcher to remain objective and critical of events in which the researcher has been personally involved, arguing that the closeness to the research subjects increased their understanding and 'in no way detracted from it'. Thus, the 'inside' researcher has some advantages; knowledge of the context of the research, awareness of the micro-politics of the environment and easy access to subjects. However there are disadvantages. Interviewing colleagues can be uncomfortable, and response may be affected by bias. Nonetheless, these were outweighed by the advantages.

Is mobilisation positively associated with membership growth?

This section examines the hypothesis that increased membership growth is positively associated with mobilisations rather than demonstrations of instrumentality, being divided into two parts. The first uses data from the membership database to analyse member recruitment patterns and mobilisations and demonstrations of instrumentality. The second uses the survey data to analyse the views of union activists towards the importance of mobilisation and instrumentality in membership growth. The two parts of the section use different methods to test the hypothesis – the first part is an analysis of the effect of mobilisations and demonstrations of instrumentality on PCS internal monthly membership recruitment data. The second part analyses survey responses and uses the DWP/PCSeDWP comparison to examine the relationship between mobilisation, instrumentality and membership growth.

Table 6.1 shows the number of PCS members and the total number of civil servants between 2001 and 2007 and the percentage change year-on-year. It also shows PCS membership as a proportion of the total number of civil servants. For the purposes of analysis, this proportion is described as 'density'. However, this does not take into account civil servants who were members of other unions which organise within the civil service (i.e., First Division Association, Prospect and Prison Officers' Association) and PCS also has a small number of members outside the civil service. The reason that these other union members have not been included in the calculation of density is that this would require detailed analysis of their memberships for not all of these members work within the civil service. Internally, PCS estimates its density to be significantly higher at 63.84% within the civil service

Table 6.1 PCS members as a proportion of civil service, 2001–2007

Year	PCS Members	Change from 2001	No. civil servants	Change from 2001	Density
2001	272,735	–	506,450	–	53.9%
2002	285,448	5%	516,200	2%	55.3%
2003	295,639	8%	542,770	7%	54.5%
2004	324,247	19%	554,110	9%	58.5%
2005	317,084	16%	562,980	11%	56.3%
2006	311,998	14%	553,560	9%	56.4%
2007	304,829	12%	530,080	5%	57.5%

Sources: PCS' annual organising strategy documents, www.civilservice.gov.uk and Office of National Statistics.

(excluding Non-Departmental Public Bodies), using a calculation based on the PCS members as a proportion of potential members. Nevertheless, the means of calculating density in this chapter allows for consistent comparisons between two sets of reliable data. The data in Table 6.1 shows that between 2001 and 2007 PCS membership increased by 12% and 'density' by 3.6%.

Strikes are the most obvious form of collective mobilisation, and collective agreements are the clearest demonstrations of instrumentality. In 2004, PCS took national strike action (5 November 2004) over threats to job security and pensions. In 2005, an agreement was subsequently reached on job cuts and pensions. The most significant increases in membership (+11%) and density (+4%) took place in 2004. During 2005, both membership (–3%) and density (–2.2%) fell. However, this sequence of events is not sufficiently detailed to reveal any relationship between changes in membership level and mobilisation or instrumentality. Additionally, in April 2005 PCS introduced a rigorous membership lapsing process, which has been applied consistently from this date. This meant that in April 2005 there was a significant one off reduction in the union's membership levels. After April 2005, membership data became more reliable as a measure of current paying members than before that date.

Monthly membership levels of the DWP group are shown in Chart 6.1 for December 2005 and April 2008 (because accurate monthly recruitment figures are available for this period). During this period the structure and boundaries of the DWP group did not change – for example, elsewhere changes in the machinery of government (such as the creation of the Ministry of Justice in May 2006) frequently result in changes of civil service departments and then internal union structures to match the employer structure. The 29-month period also coincided with the DWP group taking nine days of strike action, being the highest number of strikes of any PCS group during this period. Therefore, this 29-month period was used as month-on-month comparisons between membership recruitment and both mobilisations and demonstrations of instrumentality. Inset 6.2 summarises the key features of the nine days of strike action (seven days exclusive to the DWP and two common to PCS).

The data in Chart 6.1 shows a number of significant spikes. For nine out of 29 months where recruitment exceeded the mean monthly recruitment level (n = 582), five contained strike action, and a further three months followed directly on from a month in which strike action took place. For example, strike action took place on 26 and 27 January

Inset 6.2   Mobilisation and instrumentality events

Signifier	Year	Monthly recruitment	Event
A	2006	Jan 1612 (Feb 1005, Mar 746)	DWP strike 26 and 27 January 2006 over job cuts
B	2006	May 868	DWP strike 2 and 3 May 2006 over compulsory job cuts
C	2007	Jan 803, Feb 1102	PCS national strike 31 January 2007 over job cuts and pay
D	2007	May 633	PCS national strike 1 May 2007 over job cuts and pay
E	2007	Dec 1052	DWP strike 6 and 7 December 2007 over pay
F	2008	Mar 545	DWP strike 17 and 18 March 2008 over pay
G	2008	Mar 545, Apr 531	National agreement on job security March 2008

Source: PCS data.

2006, and both January and February were significantly above the mean level of monthly recruitment. There is one month were the recruitment level exceeded the mean (by 61 members) but there was no direct relationship to a strike and there is one month where there is a strike which does not exceed the mean (by 37 members). After 28 months in dispute over compulsory redundancies, an agreement was reached in March 2008 (but not on pay). The months of March and April of 2008 did not exceed the mean or show any significant membership change in response to the demonstration of instrumentality. In Chart 6.1, these mobilisations are marked A-G for the sake of clarity on the chart and linked to explanations in Inset 6.2. The DWP data shows an observable positive association between mobilisation and collective action and increased levels of membership recruitment, which is consistent with the analysis of Gall (2003a) and Kelly (1998, 2005). The data also shows observable diminishing returns for repeat mobilisations over the same issue. The data does not show any observable relationship between increased monthly membership recruitment levels and demonstrations of instrumentality.

This section now turns to analysing the survey data *vis-à-vis* the relationship between mobilisation, instrumentality and membership growth. The survey sought responses to a number of statements as to whether mobilisation or instrumentality would contribute to long-term membership increases. The questions asked respondents to rate the response

Chart 6.1   DWP group monthly recruitment levels, December 2005 to April 2008 (inclusive)

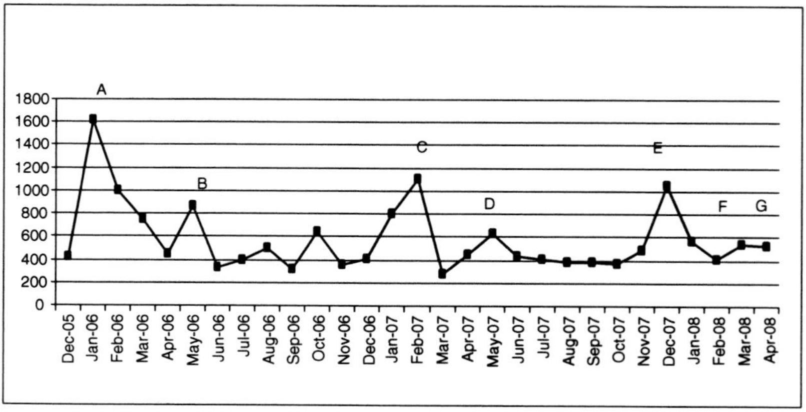

Source: PCS internal monthly membership recruitment data.

as 'very likely' (1), 'likely' (2) or 'unlikely' (3). Statement 'A' is a proxy for combining both mobilisation and instrumentality, 'B' for mobilisation without instrumentality, 'C' for instrumentality without mobilisation, and 'D' for neither instrumentality nor mobilisation. The data (Table 6.2) showed that respondents rated 'A' as most likely to contribute to long-term membership growth and 'D' the least likely. Interesting responses were found for 'B' and 'C'. The responses showed that respondents consider that it is 'likely' (1.9) that 'C' will lead to long-term increases in membership but closer to 'unlikely' (2.74) than for 'B' would do similarly. The responses demonstrated a view that in promoting long-term membership growth, instrumentality is more important than mobilisation.

A similar pattern appears in the responses for the DWP group and its PCSeDWP comparator. The DWP response pattern showed instrumentality without mobilisation has a lower average score (1.83) than PCSeDWP (1.95). Therefore, DWP respondents viewed instrumentality without mobilisation as more likely to lead to membership increases than PCSeDWP. The survey response pattern appears to confirm the analysis of Kochan (1980) and Charlwood (2003). However, the response pattern in Tables 6.1 and 6.2 contradicts the membership recruitment data analysed above (Chart 6.1) which showed a positive association between mobilisation membership increase, and no association with instrumentality and membership increases for the DWP group.

Table 6.2   Mobilisation and instrumentality

Which of the following approaches are, in your opinion, likely to contribute to long term increases in membership?	All	DWP	All – DWP
A. Running a well publicised campaign for a higher pay deal and achieving an outcome acceptable to the majority of members?	1.23	1.19	1.21
B. Running a well publicised campaign for a higher pay deal and achieving an outcome only acceptable to a minority of members?	2.74	2.73	2.74
C. Working confidentially in partnership with an employer on a pay deal and achieving an outcome which is acceptable to the majority of members?	1.9	1.83	1.95
D. Working confidentially an in a partnership with an employer on a pay deal and achieving an outcome which is only acceptable to a minority of members?	2.9	2.88	2.92

Source: Author's own data.
Note: Scores are average responses.

In testing the hypothesis that there was empirical evidence of a positive association between mobilisation and increased membership growth rather than demonstration of instrumentality, the data demonstrated an observable relationship between mobilisation and short-term 'surges' in membership recruitment, which reduced in intensity with repetition. The data showed no evidence that there are surges in membership recruitment linked to or dependent upon demonstrations of instrumentality. However, the union reps' responses placed more importance on instrumentality than mobilisation in promoting increased membership. The membership data gave significant support to the hypothesis. However, the survey data also suggested that union reps saw instrumentality as important and that they underestimated the importance of mobilisations in delivering membership increases.

Resource choices and growth

This section uses the survey data and compares responses from the DWP Group and PCSeDWP to test the hypothesis that the use of resources for organising type activities is positively associated with membership growth. Before turning to the hypothesis, the section analyses data from the entire union in order to provide an understanding of the context of resource choices within PCS. Table 6.3 outlines the responses to two questions. Question 'A' sought responses on activities respondents thought were the most important and 'B' responses on activities respondents allocated most of their union time. This allowed responses to be compared, whereby it would become evident if respondents were undertaking the activities which they had assessed as the most important. Two activities were used as proxies for individual servicing of existing members, namely, personal casework, and telephone and email advice, two were proxies for union building, namely, mapping the workplace and desk topping (face-to-face discussions in the workplace) and two were proxies for combining servicing existing members and organising new members, namely, workplace meetings and running or participating in union campaigns.

The responses to 'A' showed that personal casework (1.48) was seen as the most important activity. The least important were activities which were aimed mostly at organising current non-members, that is, mapping the workplace (2.43) and 'desk topping' (2.00). A similar pattern is evident in the responses to 'B' where personal casework was the activity on which most time is spent (1.92) and mapping the workplace (3.10) and desk topping (2.87) had the least amount of time spent on them. While all the responses to' B' were lower than 'A', showing that respondents cannot spend as much time on any of the activities that they think is needed, however, it is noticeable that the negative difference between 'A' and 'B' is greater for the organising proxies than for any other proxies. Responses to the proxies which combine servicing and organising (workplace meetings (1.70) and running or participating in union campaigns (1.83)) showed these activities were viewed as less important than personal casework, but more important than the organising proxies and more important than telephone/email advice (1.92). However, workplace meetings had the most significant negative difference (–0.96) in priority when it came to considering how respondents used their union-related time. This indicated that when resource choices have to be made, the activities which focus on existing members and particularly servicing individual members take priority over the activities which are focused solely on organising current non-members.

Table 6.4 shows a comparison between the DWP group and PCSeDWP. The difference between the comparators is insignificant. The resource choices in the DWP group are comparable with the resource choices for PCSeDWP. While responses showed that there were a slightly higher levels of importance and priority given to organising proxies and proxies

Table 6.3   Importance and priority

Which of the following activities do you believe:	A. Are the most important aspects of you union role?	B. You spend the most of your union related time	Difference
Personal casework	1.48	1.92	–0.44
Mapping the workplace	2.43	3.10	–0.67
Workplace meetings	1.70	2.66	–0.96
Desk topping	2.00	2.87	–0.87
Telephone/email advice	1.92	2.08	–0.16
Running/participating in union campaigns	1.83	2.38	–0.55

Source: Author's own data.
Note: A denotes most important activities, and B most time spent on activities. Responses on a scale of 1–4 whereby 1 denotes most important/most time spent, and 4-least important/least time spent.

which combine organising and servicing within the DWP group when compared with the PCSeDWP, there was also higher priority given to individual servicing proxies within the DWP group when compared with the PCSeDWP.

To make the scale of the comparison easier to interpret (see Table 6.4), percentage figures for the differences in responses between the DWP group and PCSeDWP were computed (response scores were divided by four and multiplied by 100). The response data from the DWP group showed higher levels of priority (Statement A) on the organising proxies (mapping the workplace – 4.25%, and desk topping – 4.5%) than PCSeDWP. The responses on time resource allocated (Statement B) on the organising proxies in Table 6.4 showed that the differences between the DWP group and PCSeDWP decrease. However, in relation to the servicing proxies, personal representation was 4.25% higher within the DWP group than PCSeDWP in relation to Statement A and 5.25% higher than PCSeDWP in relation to Statement B, which showed a higher level of importance and resource priority within the DWP group than its comparator. In relation to the other proxies, the picture is mixed and the differences between DWP and PCSeDWP are small. While the data showed that organising is considered more important within the DWP group, personal representation was also considered more important. When it comes to allocating resources, responses showed that personal representation takes precedence over organising. Finally, the differences in response

Table 6.4   Importance and priority: DWP and PCSeDWP compared

A. Which of the following activities do you believe are the most important aspects of your role?	DWP average rating	PCSeDWP	Difference between DWP-PCSeDWP	%;(Difference/4)×100
Personal casework	1.39	1.56	−0.17	−4.25
Mapping the workplace	2.37	2.48	−0.11	−2.75
Workplace meetings	1.76	1.64	0.12	3.0
Desk topping	1.9	2.08	−0.18	−4.5
Telephone/email advice	1.89	1.93	−0.04	−1.0
Running or participating in union campaigns	1.8	1.84	−0.04	−1.0
B. How do you spend the proportion of your working time that you devote to union activities?				
Personal casework	1.78	1.99	−0.21	−5.25
Mapping the workplace	3.09	3.13	−0.04	−1.0
Workplace meetings	2.67	2.66	0.01	0.25
Desk topping	2.82	2.9	−0.08	−2.0
Telephone/email advice	2.1	2.01	0.09	2.25
Running or participating in union campaigns	2.32	2.39	−0.07	−1.75

Source: Author's own data.

patterns between the DWP group and PCSeDWP are small and do not show a consistent pattern between organising and servicing proxies. The hypothesis was intended to test if the use of resources for organising type activities was positively associated with membership growth. Comparing the DWP group and PCSeDWP, the data does not support the hypothesis.

Communications

This section uses the survey data and compares the DWP group and PCSeDWP to test the hypothesis that a 'high trust' relationship, involving joint communications and confidentiality during negotiations, is

negatively associated with membership growth. But before turning to the DWP-PCSeDWP comparison, understanding the context of communication within PCS and the civil service bargaining setting is desirable. This data showed that the use of partnership-style approaches to confidentiality is widespread within the union, and the responses *vis-à-vis* confidentiality showed a pattern of high levels of confidentiality, consistent with the case study of MSF representatives in a partnership agreement (see Stuart and Martinez Lucio 2005b). Survey responses for the entire union showed that 39.5% 'strongly agreed' and 40% 'agreed' that it is often important to maintain confidentiality during negotiations. However, the data also showed some inconsistencies; over 90% of respondents 'agreed' or 'strongly agreed' that campaigning against injustice was a key function of unions, while 61% of respondents also thought that members like to see the union co-operating with the employer and this should be reflected in the communication style. The inconsistency between principle (campaigning against injustice) and practice (co-operating with the employer) indicates the degree of complexity of the power relationship within a recognised environment. This complexity was explored further and Table 6.5 outlines responses from the entire union to a question which sought to estimate the degree of influence that employers have over union communications. The responses clearly demonstrated that employers have at least a partial influence over both the timing (52.4%) and the content (48.7%) of union communications. In the experience of 25% of respondents, the employer mainly or solely influenced the timing of union responses. This employer influence is consistent with the limits on the independence of communications that was found by Wills (2004b) within the Barclays partnership agreement.

Closed survey questions were used to collect the quantitative data. However, the survey also used a small number of open questions to

Table 6.5 Influence over union communications

In you experience who has the most influence on the timing and content of union communications during important negotiations?	Solely union	Mainly union but partly employer	Mainly employer but partly union	Solely employer
Timing	21.9%	52.4%	21.9%	3.8%
Content	36.8%	48.7%	12.1%	2.4%

Source: Author's own data.

collect qualitative data. Respondents were asked: 'In what circumstances do you agree with management to maintain confidentiality over the content of negotiations?' The responses were then coded and placed in five categories (see Table 6.7 below). The qualitative responses showed a significantly more sophisticated picture than shown by the quantitative responses. Thus, while 79.4% of respondents agreed to confidentiality in some circumstances and 21.4% of respondents opposed in principle and practice to the use of confidentiality in negotiations, the make-up of the majority was more complex than at first sight. Some 16.4% of respondents only agreed to confidentiality if it involved individuals or identifiable groups of individuals while 17.9% were in principle and in practice in favour of maintaining confidentiality in all negotiations, irrespective of the circumstances. The largest category of responses (32.3%) demonstrated some degree of judgment in relation to the use of confidentiality; some in early stages of negotiations, or in critical late stages of the process. This category included responses which were in principle against confidentiality, but recognised that it was necessary in some circumstances, and those which had no problem in principle, but recognised that there are circumstances when the employer benefited and the union did not. Here a mixture of principle and pragmatism were involved. As a group these responses demonstrated the balances, strategies and tactics which union negotiators use in attempting to reach positive outcomes for members. Some 5.6% of responses stated that the only reason that they would agree to confidentiality was because the employer would not agree to negotiations on any other basis.

Turning to the hypothesis, Table 6.6 shows that the response pattern of the DWP group is significantly different to that of PCSeDWP whereby

Table 6.6   Influence over union communications: DWP and PCSeDWP

In your experience who has the most influence on the timing and content of union communications during important negotiations?	Solely union	Mainly union but partly employer	Mainly employer, but partly union	Solely employer
Timing; DWP	28.6%	51.7%	18.1%	3.8%
Timing; PCSeDWP	18.3%	52.6%	25.1%	4.0%
Content; DWP	41.9%	46.0%	10.2%	3.0%
Content; PCSeDWP	32.4%	50.8%	14.4%	2.4%

Source: Author's own data.

on both timing and content the DWP group demonstrated a greater degree of independence from the influence of the employer than PCSeDWP did.

The qualitative responses to the open question 'In what circumstances do you agree with management to maintain confidentiality over the content of negotiations?' also showed a degree of difference between DWP and PCSeDWP respondents – see Table 6.7 where the DWP showed a lower proportion of responses favouring confidentiality and a higher proportion that either opposed confidentiality or limited its application than the PCSeDWP comparator group.

In testing the hypothesis that the use of confidentiality in negotiations is negatively associated with membership growth, the response data showed that the use of confidentiality in negotiations is widespread within PCS. However, the data also showed a lower incidence of the use of confidentiality and management influence within the DWP group by comparison with PCSeDWP. The hypothesis was that a 'high trust' relationship, involving joint communications and confidentiality during negotiations, is negatively associated with membership growth. The responses to the quantitative and qualitative questions showed a higher incidence of confidentiality and employer influence over communications within the responses of PCSeDWP, by comparison with the DWP group. As PCSeDWP has a lower growth rate, the data gives some support to the negative association between a 'high trust' partnership-style approach to communications and lower membership growth rates.

Table 6.7   Comparison of qualitative responses on confidentiality: DWP and PCSeDWP

Category	DWP	PCSeDWP
Respondents would not agree to confidentiality in negotiations	25.6%	20.7%
Respondents would only agree to confidentiality in individual cases or groups of identifiable individuals	21.4%	18.3%
Respondents demonstrated a degree of tactical thinking and judgement in the use of confidentiality	22.3%	30.8%
Respondents favoured maintaining confidentiality in all circumstances during negotiations	23.5%	27.6%
Respondents only agreed to confidentiality because of employer pressure	6.7%	2.6%

Source: Author's own data.

Discussion of hypotheses

In relation to hypothesis one, there is evidence that increased membership growth is linked to mobilisations rather than demonstrations of instrumentality. Membership data shows a strong observable relationship between short-term surges in membership and mobilisations and no observable relationship between demonstrations of instrumentality and growth. Tilly's (1978) mobilisation model offers an explanation for this pattern of surges in membership growth linked to collective action, which supports the approach taken by Kelly (1998, 2005) and Gall (2003a) that mobilisation and collective action are important elements of union membership growth. It is also worth examining if this pattern of membership growth can be explained by the partnership-based models of instrumentality (Charlwood 2003; Kochan 1980) and the related concept of rational choice (Bryson and Gomez 2003). If this was the case then membership increases should be linked to demonstrations of instrumentality. There were very few demonstrations of instrumentality during the period December 2005 to April 2008, and there is no observable variation in membership that could be linked to those events. This is strong evidence which contradicts notions that union membership is an 'experience good' (Bryson and Gomez 2003: 81–83) and that demonstrations of instrumentality lead non-union members to make rational choices to join unions (see Charlwood 2003; Kochan 1980). Indeed, the membership data (Chart 6.1) reveals the sequence of membership joining decisions, whereby decisions to join are linked to mobilisation rather than instrumentality with strikes taking place before the final bargaining outcomes are known. Thus, the most plausible explanation for the DWP group membership recruitment pattern is that non-members are recruited when they are mobilised to take part in collective union organised action against employer injustice.

The survey data gave an interesting and different picture to that of the membership data. It demonstrated respondents consider that campaigns which combine both mobilisation and instrumentality are the most likely to achieve long-term membership growth. But it also appeared to show that when there is a choice between instrumentality and unsuccessful mobilisation that respondents would link instrumentality rather than mobilisation with membership growth. The experience of the DWP group, which shows repeated mobilisations and associated membership recruitment surges, over a two-year period, in the absence of demonstrations of instrumentality, appears to confound this assumption. The survey data also showed a significant gap between perceptions of the reasons why non-members join and the data on membership recruitment. This perception gap is present in equal measure both within DWP and PCSeDWP groups. The importance of the membership data is that it demonstrates that the strategies and tactics that the union uses to gain improved bargaining outcomes have a significant effect on membership recruitment. From the data, it is reasonable to conclude that when seeking increased membership levels in a recognised environment, the importance of mobilisation is underestimated and the importance of delivering the bargaining outcomes significantly over-estimated.

Can mobilisation theory also offer an explanation for the survey data? While agency and instrumentality are both linked to perceptions of union effectiveness, it is agency which is linked to perceptions of whether the collective action will be successful in delivering the aims of the collective action, and instrumentality is linked to the bargaining outcome itself. Thus, in discussing agency, Kelly (2005: 66) referred to point of the belief that collective action can make a difference. Taken together, the membership and survey data can be interpreted as demonstrating a sophisticated link between mobilisation and membership growth and a strong desire for positive bargaining outcomes. The data can be interpreted as support for this circle of union effectiveness within a recognition agreement which uses effective mobilisation to support bargaining, leading to membership growth, thus enhancing the possibility of improved bargaining outcomes. Yet, it is also important not to overstate the link between mobilisation and membership growth. During the period under study, non-members joined at times that were not directly linked to mobilisations. Further research is needed to tease out which dimensions of membership growth are linked to mobilisations as well as other factors which are not linked to mobilisations but which contribute to membership growth. Recognising that the numbers of joiners have been consistently lower between mobilisations rather than during mobilisations, the mobilisation effect also appears to reduce with repetition, thereby suggesting that there are limits to the mobilisation effect even though surges are sufficiently significant as to have a long-term effect on membership levels and contribute significantly to the increase in density. Empirically, it is difficult not to reach the conclusion that the mobilisations are a significant factor in membership growth. Although not identified by the current data, which looked at the effect of strike action, it is also possible that collective mobilisations other than strikes, such as a participative campaigning approach and action short of strike may also contribute to higher membership recruitment (but this requires further research).

The testing of hypothesis two – that resource choices which focus upon organising activities rather than servicing activities are positively associated with membership growth – through the survey data showed that organising activities were significantly constrained by individual servicing activities. Furthermore, the response patterns did not show any association between increased levels of organising and the increased membership growth within the DWP group. In fact, responses from the DWP group showed a slightly higher priority for personal casework than PCSeDWP. The data, therefore, does not find support for the contention of Bronfrenbrenner and Juravich (1998) that a comprehensive organising strategy is likely to be more successful than a single element of an organising strategy for PCS demonstrated, *inter alia*, significant membership density growth combining organising and servicing by undertaking mobilisations around collective issues and continuing to devote significant resources to individual servicing. However, it is still possible that if resources were switched from individual servicing to organising, growth rates may have been higher. It may be that the overriding influence on the increased growth pattern within the DWP group by comparison with PCSeDWP has been the mobilisation effect. Given that Kelly (2005: 66–67) argued that it is unlikely that membership increases or collective action emerge spontaneously from injustice and without an active and participative organisation in place, it is unlikely that the DWP group would be able to achieve significant and repeated mobilisations unless there was a significant level of internal organising and organisation.

If membership increases are associated with mobilisations then it would also seem logical that strategies and tactics which enhance mobilisation, support for collective action and, therefore, the chances of success of said action, would also increase membership levels. In broad terms, it would seem logical that effective organising strategies and tactics which increase activity and participation serve to enhance the mobilisation effect. However, the responses show a high level of importance attached to, and a high level of time resources devoted to, individual servicing activities and that these activities clearly constrain the level of time devoted to organising activities. Respondents viewed individual servicing as the most important activity that they undertake suggesting the main focus of the union's resources is servicing existing members, rather than organising and recruiting new members. Even within a union with a demonstrable growth record, the balance of resources between servicing and organising is complex, delicate and unresolved.

In relation to hypothesis three – that confidentiality in communications is negatively associated with membership growth – the DWP higher recruitment rates and density growth are associated with a lower level of both acceptance of confidentiality and management influence than the comparator PCSeDWP. The qualitative results also show a similar response pattern to the quantitative data and the combination of the two data sources means that the hypothesis can be confidently supported. The DWP group also has a higher level of mobilisation than PCSeDWP. Yet it is not possible to be confident about the direction of the link between mobilisation and open communications, for have the mobilisations led to open communications, or has the DWP approach to communication made mobilisation more likely? That there is an association with open communications, membership growth and mobilisation is an important element in supporting the mobilisation theorists' approach to membership growth.

Conclusion

The initial contention was that within a recognised environment a coherent 'organising' approach rather than a 'partnership' approach, as defined in the schema in Inset 6.1, would lead to increased levels of membership density. What was revealed was that surges in membership growth were linked to mobilisation, rather than a coherent 'organising' approach. Like other studies (Heery 2002; Wills 2004b), the PCS case study continues to show that unions practice a combination of organising-based growth strategies and mobilisations, and elements of partnership with employers. This chapter aimed to establish if a more coherent organising approach to employers, members and communications was positively associated with higher levels of membership growth by comparing the DWP bargaining unit with a higher level of membership growth to the union excluding the DWP group (PCSeDWP) in order to establish if the DWP group demonstrated coherent behaviour, closer to the organising ideal-type than PCSeDWP did. The chapter did not find coherent union behaviour but did find that some elements of the 'organising' model as set out in the schema are positively associated with higher recruitment levels and increased density. Rather, surges in membership growth were linked to mobilisation, rather than demonstrations of instrumentality, contradicting the proposition put forward by advocates of partnership that instrumentality has a measurable effect on membership recruitment levels. Consequently, support was found for those that attribute membership growth to mobilisation-based organising. In this respect, Gall (2007c) identified a trend within unions which highlighted that unions which have robustly defended their members' rights (like PCS, NUT, NASUWT, RMT, EIS and POA) have all increased membership levels significantly. In relation to the 'free rider' problem posed by Metcalf *et al.* (2003), the approach taken by PCS and, in particular, the DWP group has sizably increased union density (without new union recognition agreements being gained). If the PCS membership density increase had been replicated across all union recognition agreements, around 350,000 additional non-members would have been recruited and retained. This reduction in 'free-riders' would have been significant, in turn, generating significant additional resources for unions and represent a major step towards union revitalisation.

Acknowledgement

My thanks are to Gregor Gall for his considerable assistance in revising this chapter.

7
Building Stronger Unions: A Review of Organising in Britain

Paul Nowak

Introduction

The launch of the TUC Organising Academy in 1998 was meant to herald a shift in resources and culture in British union movement. Moving the motion on 'New Unionism' at the 1997 Congress, USDAW's general secretary spoke of the need for unions to go back to 'basic, grass roots organising principles', noting that:

> The drop in ... membership since 1979 has concentrated all our minds. [We] were like rabbits caught in the headlights of the on-coming Tory juggernaught. We've been content to respond by blaming the government, apathetic [or] ... part-time women workers and young people, the so-called 'Thatcher's children'. We now have to move from recrimination to determination. Organising has got to become an intrinsic and integral part of our union activity.

This chapter reviews how the union movement has progressed in its efforts to shift focus and resources towards organising, and how successful these efforts have been in reaching out to the next potential generation of members. It starts with an assessment of union membership trends over the last ten years and summarises the impact of the TUC Organising Academy and associated initiatives since 1998. It then moves to outline future prospects for union membership and the need for unions in Britain to adopt an 'organising plus' approach to membership growth (and what forms this approach may take). The chapter concludes that the organising efforts of unions over the last ten years have laid the foundations for building stronger unions in Britain.

Union membership in Britain, 1998–2008

Union density and membership peaked in 1978 and 1979 respectively. In the two decades between this peak and the launch of the Organising Academy, membership fell every single year – from a high of 12.6m to 7.1m. Density experienced a similar decline from a high of 56.1% to 27%.[1] This pattern of decline was not unique to Britain – but was mirrored in the US, Australia, New Zealand and, latterly, many European countries. Glyn (2006: 104) noted:

> ... the succession of pressures to which labour has been subjected – the turn to restrictive macroeconomic policies, the renewed emphasis on market forces and profit maximisation bringing privatisation, deregulation and the drive for shareholder value and finally the intensifying international competition in important sectors of the economy [has meant] unions were forced onto the defensive, if not into retreat

On one level, union decline in Britain has continued over the last ten years. Density amongst employees has declined by 2.5% since 1998 and individual unions have experienced serious and sustained membership losses. The GMB, for example, has experienced a 16.8% decline since 1998, the constituent unions of Unite 18.5% and the CWU by 13.6%. Job losses and industrial restructuring have had a huge impact on individual unions concentrated in 'traditional' industries such as ceramics and steel so that Unity (formerly Ceramic and Allied Trades Union (CATU)) experienced a membership decline of nearly 70%, and Community (formed from the merger of the ISTC and (National Union of) Knitwear, Footwear and Apparel Trades (KFAT)) a decline of 25%. While some of these losses may be attributed to the 'tidying up' of union membership records, it is still clear that a number of unions have struggled to retain and build membership, particularly where they predominately organise in 'declining' sectors. These trends are apparent not just in Britain but also across much of the industrialised world.

But despite these problems, it is evident that the period between 1998 and 2008 has been of a very different character to the period of membership loss between 1979 and 1998. Since 1998, total membership has remained broadly stable. In addition, the decline in density during this period has been 'shallower' than that experienced in the preceding two decades and has been predominately a function of a growing workforce than union decline. Two of the last ten years have seen very small increases in union density and a decline of 2.5% over the last decade sharply contrasts with the near 30% between 1978 and 1998. Beneath these aggregate figures, it is also apparent that some individual unions have experienced significant growth in the last ten years. Indeed, out of the 46 TUC unions that we can compare membership figures for between 1998 and 2006, 27 have grown, and all but four of these have grown by more than 10%. Even those unions who have reported aggregate decline over the last ten years have seen membership increases in recent years – for example the GMB reported membership gains between 2005 and 2008. These unions are a diverse group – representing unions large and small, public and private, blue and white-collar unions and across traditional 'left and 'right' political divide (see Table 7.1). This diversity is an important factor which will be discussed in more detail shortly.

Membership stabilisation has been underpinned by new recognition agreements with employers. Despite a recent slowdown in new recognition agreements, unions can still take heart from having been able to gain around 3,000 new recognition deals, covering 1.3m new potential members, between 1995–2005 (Gall 2007a: 83). For unions such as the NUJ, signing new recognition deals stands in stark contrast to the 'dark days' of the 1980s and 1990s when the union faced wholesale de-recognition across the sector (Gall 2006b, 2007d). Equally, the traditional 'gender gap' in union membership has been eroded to the extent that women are now more likely to be union members than men (see Mercer and Notley 2008). So, partly this is a story about the decline in union membership and density amongst men and male dominated industries, but it is also a function of unions becoming more effective at organising and representing women, particularly in the public sector.

A better external and internal environment

Many of the factors which have helped unions stabilise their membership over the last ten years are external to the union movement. Despite the ongoing tensions between unions and the post-1997 Labour governments, the last ten years have presented a more positive environment for organising than that engendered by the Conservative governments of 1979–1997. This is reflected in new union recognition legislation which, while flawed, has provided a statutory basis to gaining recognition in Britain. Other significant legislative changes with the potential to support union organising efforts include the right to accompany individuals, new information and consultation rights, and

Table 7.1   TUC affiliated membership, 1998–2007

Union	1998	2007	% change 1998–2007
ACCORD	26,217	30,145	15.0
Advance	7,612	6,763	–11.2
AFA	844	610	–27.7
ASLEF	14,426	18,033	25.0
BACM-TEAM	4,313	2,783	–35.5
BALPA	6,005	9,634	60.4
BDA	3,213	5,768	79.5
BECTU	29,243	26,210	–10.4
BFAWU	30,328	23,291	–23.2
BOS	864	1,021	18.2
CDNA	4,995	2,884	–42.3
Community	90,848	67,488	–25.7
CONNECT	16,962	19,316	13.9
CSP	30,296	35,050	15.7
CWU	273,814	236,679	–13.6
EIS	50,807	59,539	17.2
EQUITY	34,502	35,527	3.0
FBU	56,943	45,410	–20.3
FDA	10,387	17,417	67.7
GMB	709,708	590,125	–16.8
HCSA	2,268	3,108	37.0
MU	30,480	32,674	7.2
NACO	3,169	2,165	–31.7
NACODS	645	336	–47.9
NAPO	6,956	9,004	29.4
NASUWT	172,852	265,202	53.4
Nautilus	18,516	16,274	–12.1
NUJ	19,834	32,409	63.4

Table 7.1 TUC affiliated membership, 1998–2007 – *continued*

Union	1998	2007	% change 1998–2007
NUM	5,001	1,618	–67.6
NUT	191,828	282,589	47.3
PCS	265,902	304,829	14.6
PFA	1,473	2,435	65.3
POA	32,004	36,172	13.0
Prospect	104,146	102,702	–1.4
RMT	56,337	75,906	34.7
SCP	6,458	8,780	36.0
SOR	13,502	18,595	37.7
TSSA	31,132	29,102	–6.5
UCAC	3,641	3,861	6.0
UCATT	113,555	129,065	13.7
UCU	106,253	117,028	10.1
UNISON	1,300,451	1,344,000	3.3
UNITE	2,394,710	1,952,510	–18.5
Unity	20,478	6,376	–68.9
USDAW	293,470	356,046	21.3
WGGB	1,987	1,298	–34.7

Source: All figures reported to the TUC.
Notes: Where a union has merged, reported membership figures for constituent unions have been aggregated. Where figures for 2006/07 were not available, 2005/06 figures have been used. Colour used to denote those unions which have experienced membership decline.

the regulation of gangmasters. Unemployment between 1998 and 2008 averaged 5.4%, against 9% between 1979 and 1997, and the number of employee jobs grew by over 2.5m.[2] Despite recent decreases in public sector employment, overall employment in the public sector increased by nearly 600,000 between 1997–2008 – supporting public sector union growth.[3] This is perhaps well illustrated by primary and secondary education – all of the three largest TUC affiliated teachers unions have reported significant membership growth since 2001 (ATL – 6.6%, NASUWT – 44.4%, NUT – 37.1%) against a backdrop of rising teacher numbers – the number of FTE teachers rose by 35,000 between 1997–2007.[4]

But as well as these external factors, it is also the case that a significant proportion of the relative success enjoyed by British unions over the last ten years can be attributed to internal factors. These factors include an increased focus on, and investment in, organising and recruitment activity and efforts to more strategically focus on these efforts. Below are two illustrations of the depth of work undertaken by unions here. Firstly, the development of the TUC Organising Academy over the last ten years, drawing on the work of a number of academics, is summarised. Secondly, the main findings of a TUC survey of affiliated unions undertaken in 2008 to ascertain the extent to which these unions have developed their work on organising and recruitment are reported on. This survey identifies a shift in focus on, and a partial shift in resources towards, organising and recruitment. Both illustrations demonstrate the value of the work undertaken by the TUC and individual unions in this area, but both also flag up the limitations of this work to date, and suggest the need for unions to 'scale-up' their efforts around organising and recruitment, and to invest in new approaches to union growth.

The TUC Organising Academy

Since its inception, the Organising Academy and its sponsoring unions has recruited and trained some 270 new union organisers. Academy Organisers are jointly employed by the TUC and a sponsoring union on a 12-month long training programme, which involves 20 days of classroom training and practical experience derived from working on union organising campaigns. Over half (54%) of these new organisers have been women, 5% are from a BME community, and they have tended to be younger than the general union EUOs (Holgate and Simms 2008: 13). Some 70% of the Organising Academy's graduates are still employed within the union movement, which suggests retention in the programme compares well with similar programmes internationally (Rooks 2004).

A review of the work of the Organising Academy in 2003 concluded that, while the initiative faced challenges: 'the Academy has proved a success. It has produced a pool of organising talent and shown that investment in organising can lead to positive outcomes' (Heery *et al.* 2003c: 18). This report also identified that in the first year of training the first five intakes of Academy Organisers had: '[in combination]... targeted more than 1200 employers, added nearly 40,000 new members and identified nearly 2000 new activists. They have also established membership at 600 greenfield sites and helped secure or raise the question of recognition for more than 300 bargaining units' (Heery *et al.* 2003c: 9). But despite these successes the report warned that the 'achievements of the Academy are only a fraction of what is required if unions are to stabilise membership and achieve growth' (Heery *et al.* 2003c: 10).

Prompted by this research, and responding to the needs of unions, in 2004 the Organising Academy extended its provision to support existing union officers, organisers and staff as well as 'new' organisers. And, a new partnership arrangement was agreed with Newcastle College (a further education college in the north east of England) for the development and delivery of the Organising Academy programme, which provided more full-time staff resources at the TUC to support the development of the programme. The key elements of this new programme included an 'Advanced Organising Programme' consisting of modules such as 'Busting the Union Busters' and 'Strategic Campaigning', a 16-day generalist officer 'Academy' programme and, increasingly, a range of bespoke work for individual unions. Since 2004, EUOs have filled around 1,000 places on these new programmes – a significant number when one takes into account that UK unions only employ around 3,000 officers. In addition, the TUC has also developed a 'Leading Change' training and development programme for senior union officers.[5] This programme has been developed with the support of leading academics in Britain and US.

A more recent assessment of the training and support provided by the Organising Academy drew out two issues which have significance for this chapter. First of all, despite the success of the programme, many unions are still struggling to implement a more 'organising-focused' approach. This is reflected in 'the majority (69%) of [Academy Organisers] who felt there was still an absence of an integrated organising tradition within their unions which created problems in trying to instill an organising culture throughout the organisation' (Holgate and Simms 2008: 22). This, in turn, leads to other problematic issues such as the 'status' of organising and organisers within unions, problems around 'career progression' for organisers and tensions between the work of organisers and more generalist EUO. But despite these issues, progress has been made in shifting the focus of unions, due in large part to the impact of the Organising Academy upon the developing organising work of affiliated unions. Holgate and Simms (2008) noted that:

> The aim was that the Organising Academy would be a catalyst for change where a new cohort of union officials would, through their respective unions, attempt to spread a new culture of union organising.

In this respect the Organising Academy initiative has been extremely successful. Some Organising Academy graduates now occupy senior positions within the union movement and are responsible for strategic organising planning. The spread of organising programmes to generalist officers and introduction of union specific 'organising academies' – all influenced by the work started by the Organising Academy – has dramatically increased the amount of organising activity taking place.

Since 1998, 30 unions representing over 80% of the TUC's affiliated membership, have sponsored Academy Organisers – reflecting a wide range of unions, each with different organising priorities and strategies. While it would be misleading to infer that this degree of support for the work of the Organising Academy easily translates into increased focus on and investment in organising and recruitment activity, it does reflect a slow, but perhaps sure, diffusion of organising across the wider union movement in Britain over the last ten years. This point is explored in more detail below.

A shift in focus and a partial shift in resources

In the summer of 2008, the TUC undertook an interview based survey of 19 affiliated unions as part of a wider review of union organising and recruitment efforts. The unions surveyed represented the 'top 15' TUC affiliates by size plus four smaller affiliates, the smallest of which had less than 15,000 members. The surveyed unions represented some 94% of the TUC's affiliated membership. Amongst the surveyed unions, 12 reported membership growth to the TUC during the ten years to 2008, and six reported declining membership (TUC 2008). The survey found that 15 unions reported that they had a formal strategy that was either directly focused on or included distinct organising priorities. Of the four that did not, two reported that there was some form of general strategic plan or statement of strategic priorities in place that they were working to, and one reported that they were currently developing a strategy directly addressing organising priorities. Significantly, the clear majority of unions with strategies directly focusing on or including distinct organising and recruitment priorities reported that these had been introduced over the last five years. Only one affiliate reported that their organising plan had been in place since 1998.

Eleven of the unions interviewed reported that they had a nationally based/operational dedicated organising department – although as would be expected these departments varied greatly in size and scope. In two of these unions, the national team consisted of a small number of staff (single figures) responsible for the co-ordination, operation and development of national strategies. Conversely, Unite reported that they had a nationally operational team consisting of over 100 organisers. Most unions though had national organising departments consisting of headquarter-based organising officers and field organisers working on national recognition campaigns and/or supporting branches in in-fill work.

Even where the union did not have in place a nationally based/operational organising team, it was apparent that most did employ staff with specific organising and recruitment responsibilities based and managed regionally. Two of these unions reported that they had previously had a national organising team but had moved away from this model as part of their attempt to integrate organising and recruitment activity into the wider work of the union and its staff. A small number of the unions interviewed had structures that contained both a national and regional element.

One measure of how seriously or otherwise unions take their organising efforts, is to try and assess the resource they focus on this area of work. At the 2006 Congress, delegates agreed to call on unions and the TUC to: 'focus a minimum of 5% of income, and, as soon as possible, 10% of income, on measures to research and assist unions' organising' (Composite 1). However, measuring this expenditure – and in fact even agreeing what does or does not count as expenditure on organising is far from straightforward. This was borne out in the survey responses – the majority of unions interviewed reported that it was difficult to quantify the proportion of their budget spent supporting organising and recruitment activity. Most respondents either gave no response or a very general figure. Of those unions that gave more specific figures, the range was between 5% and 25% with the majority of these costs covering salaries and training. The main reason given for the lack of precision was the extent to which broader work on organising and recruitment was integrated into other areas of the unions work such as education or campaigning.

However, despite these problems, a key finding from the survey was that almost all unions giving figures estimated that the proportion spent on organising and recruitment activity had grown over recent years. All unions with national teams reported that the work of the team was linked to and supported by an element of the union's democratic structure, that is, a lay committee of their national executive. There were some differences in the role played by such committees. All unions reported that a function of such committees was the oversight of national strategies and campaigns, with a number of unions reporting that lay-committees were involved in the development and implementation as well as oversight of strategic priorities and campaigns.

The message arising from the survey responses is that the majority of UK unions have attempted to put in place some sort of national organising strategy and/or teams of staff to deliver these strategies. We have no comparable survey information for 1998, but it is safe to assume that few unions would have these strategies and structures in place prior to 1998.

What was also striking about the survey responses is that 'organising' is not the preserve of one or other type of union. Two very different unions clearly illustrate this diversity. Both USDAW and PCS have reported strong membership growth over the past decade (although PCS's membership has been hit by recent civil service job cuts). Between 1998 and 2007, USDAW reported to the TUC a net membership gain of 21.3% (65,576 members) and PCS reported a net gain of 14.6% (38,927 members). Both unions have invested heavily in organising, although they clearly operate in different sectors and also have differing industrial and political strategies.

PCS has developed a comprehensive National Organising Strategy (see McCarthy, this volume) which sets out the union's organising priorities; the roles and responsibilities of groups and committees at different levels of the union; targeted action to involve young members and other under-represented groups of members; the development of organising action plans and so on. One tangible result of this work is that PCS (2008: 6) estimated that density in the civil service stands 5% higher than overall public sector density at 63.8%. Meanwhile, at the heart of USDAW's organising strategy has been the development of its own Academy, now in its fifth year. By the end of 2007, nearly 100 USDAW reps had undertaken its six-month Academy training programme and during their time on the programme these organisers had brought in some 34,000 new members and identified 2,600 new reps and activists (USDAW 2007a). Its strategy has also leaned heavily on 'partnership' arrangements with key employers, most notably Tesco. A key feature of this agreement is a facilities agreement which provides for the paid release of almost 40 USDAW 'recruitment and development' reps for 12 weeks a year.

Common problems

Despite some of the extant diversity of organising strategies, it would appear that some of the problems facing unions trying to develop and implement such strategies are common. The TUC survey highlighted two such issues. The first focused around efforts to 'mainstream' organising and recruitment activity into the work of 'generalist' EUOs. Commonly this involved the inclusion of duties and responsibilities relating to organising and recruitment activity into the job descriptions of officers and staff. Unions also reported efforts to restructure staffing roles and responsibilities to better integrate organising work with other duties such as negotiating and handling casework. In some cases, this involved requiring EUOs to set aside a proportion of their time for 'organising' activity. Unions also reported efforts to set organising 'targets' for EUOs. While approaches to 'mainstreaming' varied, the outcomes were pretty uniform. Almost all the unions surveyed reported that their efforts to 'mainstream' organising had met with limited success and reported difficulties in delivering the practical integration of organising and recruitment activity and monitoring/measurement of outcomes. This finding is reinforced by Holgate and Simms (2008) who reported that two thirds of TUC Organising Academy graduates perceived that a lack of support from union EUOs hindered their organising work. My own experience of working with groups of EUOs over the last six years is that this lack of support is primarily not 'ideologically driven' but often rooted in practical issues, such as the addition of new responsibilities on top of an already heavy workload; targets being set arbitrarily and without any effort to assess whether they are appropriate or achievable; or a sense that the new 'organising' strategy is not related, or relevant, to their wider workload. Despite all these problems, research (Heery 2006, 2008) suggested that progress was being made, with most EUOs now reporting that the recruitment of new members and activists was now a 'central component' of their job.

The second, and arguably even more important, issue related to the engagement of lay reps and activists in the development and delivery of organising strategies. While every surveyed union reported they had on-going initiatives aimed at both increasing the numbers of reps and their involvement in organising and recruitment activities, most also reported difficulties in delivering widespread practical engagement. 'Workload' was, again, identified as a major barrier as was restrictions on the use of, or a lack of, facility time, and a lack of skills and confidence amongst lay reps. Some unions reported many of their reps simply did not see organising and recruitment activity as part of their role. This is a view borne out by other union surveys. For example, in one of Britain's largest unions less than 40% of reps thought that 'recruitment of new members' was one of their three key priorities. This lack of lay rep engagement with the organising agenda is reflected in the 2006/07 unionlearn/TUC Education putting 637 students through organising courses (including participants enrolled on the TUC Organising Academy programme) which represented barely 10% of the numbers of participants undertaking training in 'industrial relations/ collective bargaining' (6,790) and 'health and safety' (6,225) (TUC 2007a: 142). Overcoming this – and finding ways of fully involving reps and activists in union organising efforts – is perhaps the crucial issue facing unions in their attempt to step up their organising efforts.

Prospects for union membership

If the last ten years have presented a period of relative stability for membership, underpinned by increased union focus on organising and recruitment, what are the likely prospects for union membership over the next ten years? One positive reading of likely prospects in membership is based on projected trends in the occupational composition of the workforce. An assessment of these trends suggests that increases in union membership (if not density) amongst professional and associate professional will effectively offset losses amongst other occupational groups (see Wilson 2007). However, these changes in the occupational composition of the workforce need to be set against other likely trends. Sectors with high density including 'primary and utilities', 'electricity, gas and water supply', and 'public administration' are likely to see declines in employment, whilst growth is likely to be strong in areas where unions are weakest, such as 'business and other services' and retail (Institute for Employment Research/University of Warwick 2006). Manufacturing is estimated to see the loss of 400,000 jobs by 2014, and construction a loss of 100,000 (though this latter figure could be an underestimate in the face of recent shocks to the housing market). Overall public sector employment is unlikely to grow, and indeed recent years have seen significant cuts in, for example, civil service employment. No-one knows what the short-medium term impact of the current economic downturn will be upon union membership – but it would be sensible to assume it is unlikely to be positive. At the time of writing, unions have seen significant membership losses as a result of closures and/or job losses in employers as diverse as Woolworths, Waterford Wedgewood, Barclays and Nissan.

The 'demand' for union membership also presents a mixed picture. According to the *British Social Attitudes Survey*, 39% of non-union members in non-union workplaces say they would be likely to join a union if there was one in their workplace (Bryson and Freeman 2006: 2), suggesting a potential pool of some 9m union wannabes in non-union workplaces. However, a more sobering assessment of this and similar figures is made by Bryson and Freeman (2006: 2): 'If we define British workers wanting a union as those who report that they are 'very likely' to join and who believe a union would make their workplace better, just 10% of non-union employees in non-union UK workplaces would be classified as wanting unionisation'.

Taking the points made above, and considering other 'external' factors which are likely to impact upon trends in membership – including a possible change of government, changes in employer attitudes (including evidence that some employers are taking a more aggressive stance toward organising efforts, including the use of 'union busters (see Logan 2008) and the continuing fragmentation of public services – suggests that the 'climate' for organising over the next decade is unlikely to be much more favourable than it is currently. This further suggests that any substantial increases in membership are unlikely to arise as a result of external factors. Put bluntly, unions can expect no major legislative changes (certainly not in the short-term), nor substantial increases in employment in well-unionised sectors, or much change in the attitudes of potential members that will result in substantial membership gains. Instead, if unions in Britain are to grow, and grow more quickly and consistently than they have over the last decade, then the drivers for this growth will need to come from *within* the union movement rather than from *without*.

In the remainder of this chapter, three broad suggestions as to what more unions and the TUC could do to step up their organising efforts are put forward. First, putting lay reps and stewards at the heart of their organising efforts; second, increasing the resource unions commit to organising and recruitment and how this might be done; and third, the development of sectoral organising and bargaining strategies. These suggestions are by no means comprehensive or exclusive, much less a 'blueprint' for union revitalisation in Britain. Organising efforts over the last decade suggests that silver bullets are in short supply, and that efforts to find a 'one size fits all' approach to building membership and organisation are unlikely to be successful. Professional and specialist unions are likely to need to take a different approach to general unions; unions organising predominately in the public sector will face different challenges to those organising in greenfield sites in the private service sector; and unions faced with hostile employers may need to campaign in a way that makes little sense to unions with well established relations with more benevolent employers. However, while acknowledging the need for unions to develop tailored and flexible responses to their own particular organising challenges, some common themes with relevance for the wider union movement in Britain are drawn out. The chapter concludes by suggesting that significant union growth will only arise if unions are able to both step up their existing organising efforts and continue to innovate.

Union reps at the heart of union organising strategies

Good, well trained, confident, visible union reps and activists are a key element of any successful union organising strategy – and should form the basis of a broader movement-wide strategy to revitalise membership. If unions are serious about organising a significant proportion of the 20m or so non-members of the workforce, they need to better engage the 200,000 or more lay reps and stewards in this effort. Lay reps and stewards would appear ideally placed to recruit the 3m or so non-union workers working in unionised workplaces. Research for the TUC (Smeaton and Bryson 2008: 3), based on WERS data, suggested that 2m of these workers have never been asked to join the union in their current workplace. Research undertaken by the TUC (2003: 17) found that where employees had frequent contact with a union rep, 60% said that the union was 'excellent'/'good' at communicating with them (as opposed to 34% of those who had little or not contact with reps); 65% of those who had regular contact with a rep said the union was either 'excellent' or 'good' at being open and accountable (as opposed to 37% of those who reported only intermittent contact with a rep); and 60% of those who had frequent contact with a rep believed the union was taken seriously by the employer (this fell to a quarter amongst employees who did not even know of a rep in their workplace). Evidence presented to the TUC's 'Promoting Unionism Task Group' (TUC 2001) identified lack of contact from reps as the biggest issue identified by those who had left union membership due to 'dissatisfaction'.

So unions need to do more to attract members to take on rep and activist roles but they also need to ensure that support is in place for existing reps, and that reps see organising and recruitment – building the union in their workplace – as a key part of their job. But if union reps hold one of the keys to union revitalisation, it is equally clear that unions are struggling to attract and retain reps and activists, and that existing activists are under increasing pressure. The last WERS survey (Kersley *et al.* 2006: 124) reported that the proportion of union members with access to an on-site union representative had declined by 10% between 1998 and 2004 to 45%. TUC (2007b) evidence to a recent Government review of time off and facilities for union reps noted that:

> This decline [in the proportion of workplaces with a union representative] – which has occurred in both the public and private sectors –

can be explained by a number of factors, including the continued trend toward privatisation and outsourcing in the public sector, a continued tendency for workplace size to decline, and the decentralisation of collective bargaining.

In addition, many reps struggle to secure proper paid time off to train or to carry out their duties effectively. A recent TUC (2005: 5) survey found that 16% of reps say that less than a quarter of the time they spend on reps duties is paid for by the employer. A TUC/*Personnel Today* survey of union reps and HR managers found that nearly 40% of union reps reported their employer paid for less than 25% of the time spent on their duties and that 'on average just 53% of the time union reps spend on union duties is paid for by employers' (*Personnel Today* 30 January 2007). Where there are reps, they are often not 'representative'. Over half of those interviewed for the TUC organising survey cited differences between the profile of reps and their wider membership *vis-à-vis* age (reps hole tended to be older), gender (reps tended to be male) and ethnicity (reps tended not to from BME communities). Many union reps felt their employers did not value the work that they did, and a union role may impact deleteriously upon their career prospects. The TUC/*Personnel Today* survey found that 92% of union reps believed their career prospects were threatened because of their representative role. More worryingly, 36% of HR professionals admitted that this may be the case! These, and a range of other problems faced by union reps, not only impact upon the work of current reps, but also undoubtedly act as a disincentive to other members to get more involved in the day-to-day work of the union.

But despite these problems, there are many 'good practice' examples showing how unions can not only recruit and retain reps, but also get them focused on organising and building the union. The GMB (2007) put lay reps at the centre of its national organising strategy – with the union aiming to ensure that 'every workplace where we have members has a Workplace Organising Plan that is drawn up by members ... GMB workplace organisers are experts at recruiting new members, representing members and keeping members in the GMB'. USDAW (2007b) has developed 'stand down' agreements with a wide range of national employers including Tesco, Sainsbury, Morrison, Poundland and the Co-op allowing reps to take paid time off to undertake organising and recruitment activity. And, between 2005 and 2007, Unison (2007) put nearly 2,000 stewards through its 'One Step Ahead' programme which is 'designed to engage longstanding reps and to build team work in branches around organising and recruiting'.

Unions have also stepped up their efforts to recruit and activate a new layer of 'representative' union reps. The rise of the 'Union Learning Representative' (ULR) illustrates this point, whereby the TUC and individual unions have now recruited and trained nearly 20,000 ULRs over the last decade, and the proportion of these reps who have never held a union position before has 'risen massively from 9% of the overall total in 2000 to 28% in 2003 and 35.5% in 2005' (unionlearn 2006: 2). These new activists are more likely to be women and younger than union reps as a whole. Black and ethnic minority ULRs make up 7% of the total – compared to 4% of the broader representative base (unionlearn 2006: 2). Increasingly unions are beginning to think about how ULRs can contribute more broadly to building the union at a workplace level. One example of this is Unite's 'Learning for Justice Campaign' amongst migrant and vulnerable cleaning and building services workers. Working in conjunction with the union's organising department, 'Learning for Justice aims to put lifelong learning at the heart of the organising agenda by providing migrant workers with access to the learning they need and the confidence to build their union' (unionlearn 2008). This has included identifying and developing ULRs from amongst the newly unionised cleaners involved in the broader campaign – and has resulted not only in increased union activity and access to new learning opportunities but also 'pay rises for around 2,000 workers employed by five cleaning contractors in at least 11 banks' (unionlearn 2008).This latter example illustrates the latent value of union reps and stewards to union organising and recruitment strategies, and suggests there would be a positive return for increased union investment in developing new representative roles – around issues such as equalities, pensions and the environment. By providing practical demonstrations of the concrete impact unions can have in the workplace, union reps can make the difference between workers being 'union friendly' and workers joining, and staying in, the union.

Union resources

If unions are to be able to reach out effectively to the next generation of members and activists, it's essential they increase the resource available to support organising and recruitment. Making significant membership gains, particularly in private services will require investment in new organising staff, training and support for lay reps and stewards, resources to fund broader media and campaigning activity, strategic research and so on. Even in the public sector, unions will need to find additional resource to cope with the demands placed upon them by the breakdown of centralised bargaining, privatisation and an increasingly diverse workforce. Crosby's (2004: 1) analysis of the resource challenge facing Australian unions has a resonance for those in Britain:

> The cost of exercising power on behalf of working people has increased exponentially. We now suffer from the loss of union preference, increased difficulty in organising new members, decentralised bargaining, the use of expensive legal strategies by employers, far greater resistance to union demands in the light of increased competition in product markets, poor support for union training. Yet the level of income coming into unions continues relatively unchanged. We charge a similar level of dues to the fees being charged when we operated in a far more benign environment.

Between 2007 and 2008, unions in Britain had an income of around £1bn (Certification Office 2008: 60). Notwithstanding the difficulty inherent in assessing how much resource is spent on organising, the majority of TUC unions believed that they were investing more resources into this area of work than there were 10 years ago. Unite (*Press release 1* May 2007) perhaps best illustrates this trend. It indicated that it intends to set aside up to £15m pa on organising – an amount that it describes as 'unprecedented' for British union and which represents nearly 10% of the union's overall income on 2006/07 figures. But despite a likely overall increase in resources focused on organising and recruitment over the last decade, there is still much more that unions could, and should, do here.

First, there is scope to increase the proportion of current union income which is re-invested in growing and building the union movement. How best to do this? A simple directive from the TUC that unions should increase the resource they spend on organising is likely to have little practical impact. As noted before, different unions face different organising challenges, which in turn would imply they need to develop tailored strategies and allocate resources appropriately. However, there would be value in unions auditing and, where they felt appropriate, benchmarking the resources they allocate to organising. Thus, what proportion of income is dedicated to organising and recruitment; how is it spent; where do their organising strategies indicate need for additional resource; and what do unions do now, or what services do they provide, which could be done differently to free up resource for organising? The TUC could assist in this process, building on the consultancy support it already offers. This approach would allow unions to allocate resources based on organising 'need' rather than on a fixed percentage of their income or expenditure.

Second, unions need to increase the 'off-balance sheet' resource that they are able to apply to organising and recruitment. Union 'off-balance sheet' resources include the time and commitment of lay reps, support from employers in terms of paid time-off, facilities for union reps or check-off arrangements, ready access to and information about new starters etc. Willman and Bryson (2006) identified significant reductions in the 'off-balance sheet' resources available to unions between 1984 and 1998 – with a leveling off in these resources between 1998 and 2004. One result of this decline on 'off-balance sheet' resources was that unions may be 'paying for a higher percentage of total organising activity than in the past'. They go on to note that this is a serious issue, 'not just for unions, but for many charitable organisations that volunteer work is factored into viability but not accounted for' (Willman and Bryson 2006: 10).

So what can unions do here? Part of the answer concerns expanding and developing the lay rep base (see before). But this is only a partial answer. As Willman and Bryson (2006) suggest: 'off-balance sheet resources' are often factored into' viability', but they are seldom 'accounted for'. How many unions would be able to honestly estimate the value of their 'off-balance sheet' resources? A recognition agreement which contains provision for paid time-off and facilities for union reps is clearly an 'off-balance sheet resource', but it is one that most unions would be unable to quantify. Nor would most unions be able to assess whether or not this resource was being used effectively or to further their strategic objectives. But being able to recognise and quantify this is the first step in unions being able to make a concerted effort to increase it and use it effectively. And, of course, one way of unions stepping up the 'off-balance' sheet resource available to support organising activity is to extract it from employers, recovering the resource effectively lost to the union movement in the two decades or so prior to 1998.

Increasing 'off-balance sheet' support for unions – more paid time off and better facilities for union reps, positive employer support for union recruitment efforts, ready access to induction meetings and lists of new starters, rights to organise in new sites or in subsidiary companies, building access to unions into procurement policies, access to company intranet systems – should become a key bargaining priority. For many employers, these costs would be marginal (and there is evidence to suggest that whatever costs may be associated with union reps and stewards are far outweighed by the potential benefits to employers (DTI

2007)). Though these costs may be marginal to employers, they could represent a much needed, and relatively easily secured, resource for union organising.

Third, and perhaps most controversially, unions need to explore new financial models, or at the very least to look at ways of improving financial performance within current models. Crosby's point above concerning the increasing cost of exercising power on behalf of working people is as valid in Britain as it is in Australia. Willman and Bryson (2006) identified variations in union financial performance which may be explained by different resource management practices within unions. Put simply, some unions are better at managing their resources than others. They suggest that unions may benefit from information sharing opportunities and indeed benchmarking here.

Crosby's (2004) prescription is more radical, arguing that the substantial increases in union subs are required if unions are to generate the resources required to organise. Such an argument has a particular resonance in Britain where union subs are, by international standards, comparatively low. *Labour Research* (2004) estimated that union subs in Britain are roughly half of the rates found across most of Europe, a figure which is even more striking considering that in many European countries unions receive significant state funding. In common with Australian unions, British members also pay significantly less than their counterparts in the US. A typical SEIU member working in health services pays around 1.75% of their gross salary in union dues; by contrast, according to *Labour Research* (2004) in Unison 'most members will pay... 0.75% of their wages in subs'. One result of cheaper subs is that British unions are undoubtedly under-resourced – and in practical terms this hampers union organising efforts. As TGWU general secretary told the *Financial Times* (3 March 2004): 'The sinews of war are finance ... [W]e have a much better opportunity to grow if the finances are there to do it'.

Of course, no union will simply raise subs and hope that members will stomach this, but there is international evidence to suggest that when linked to building union organisation, and the capacity of the union to represent its members more effectively, members will vote for substantial increases. Crosby (2004) noted:

> Our experience is that, in unions which have done the work over recent years of getting their members to see the union as something other than a service provider, very few members resign as a result of an increase in fees. They see their union as successful, and as an

organisation that involves them in its work. They want it to grow and become more powerful. They understand that paying more money is likely to give them more power – and on that basis they are quite prepared to contribute more.

At the very least, there is value in exploring both the 'price elasticity' of membership and the 'hypothecation' of subscription increases allowing members to see a clearer link between subscriptions increases and increased union capacity.

Moving beyond organising the workplace

A barrier to unions being able to generate significant growth in Britain arises because most organising and bargaining, especially in the private sector, is configured at the enterprise or company level. Sectoral or industry-level arrangements are generally confined to the public sector, or in a very few traditionally well-organised sectors such as printing. This pattern is reflected in collective bargaining coverage in Britain – at just over a third of the workforce, and only 20% of private sector workers, compared to the EU 25 average rate of 66% (Hendy and Gall 2006: 256). Density in Germany is less than 20%, but German unions bargain on behalf of two of thirds of the workforce; in Spain density is 16% but unions bargain on behalf of 80% of the workforce; and in Italy density is 34% and unions bargain on behalf of 70% of the workforce (see Hendy and Gall 2006: 257).

The close link between bargaining coverage and density in Britain poses two key challenges for unions. First, it is hard for unions to 'break new ground' in many parts of (particularly) the private service sector as employers in these sectors are, in some cases understandably, worried about the possible impact on unionisation on their competitive ability. Employers in competitive sectors with low density and low collective bargaining coverage are effectively 'incentivised' to resist unionisation efforts. Second, organising and bargaining plant-by-plant, workplace-by-workplace or even company-by-company is resource intensive. Smaller workplaces, increased workplace fragmentation,the use of outsourcing and contracting out, agency working and sub-contracting all further drain resources. The current union recognition legislation entrenches this approach to organising. Unions have used this legislation relatively successfully in gaining new agreements (see before). But these agreements often only cover small numbers of workers – the average size of the 'bargaining unit' in statutory applications is just 119 workers – and were only secured as a result of resource intensive campaigns. Significantly boosting union membership in Britain will be almost impossible on the basis of organising 119 workers in this workplace, 119 in the next workplace and so on.

So what alternatives do unions have? One is for unions themselves to adopt strategic sectoral organising strategies, an approach yet to be fully 'tested' in Britain. Unite has adopted this approach in contract cleaning, low cost aviation and meat processing with some significant successes. Key elements of such an approach include an upfront investment in comprehensive strategic research, identifying key target employers, identifying and pressuring points of leverage within and beyond the workplace (for example, in supply chains), and focusing of resources on the campaign. Unite's director of organising, described the philosophy underlying this approach, which is at least in part modelled on the work of the SEIU and other US unions:

> Every sector campaign has the objective of winning relevant sectoral agreements within at least 75% of the companies within the targeted sector – including key companies that seek to undercut major players. The membership objective within these areas is to achieve at least 65% density within all targeted sites, as we believe that this is the minimum collective density required to ensure a sector agreement is won. This is done by organising workers on the ground and also by triggering client leverage at a suitable stage. When we pursue significant improvement for workers it is vital that we maximise the influence of customers who often control the 'ability to pay' (Graham 2007).

This approach is resource intensive and, therefore, there would be benefit in developing multi-union approaches to these sorts of long-term, resource hungry campaigns. In the early 2000s, Transport Salaried Staffs Association (TSSA)'s efforts to organise in the high street travel trade foundered partly due to the lack of resources that the union could bring to bear in a sector with low union density and no tradition of unionisation. A TUC (2006) review of the campaign for TSSA concluded: 'TSSA, as a … transport union with a membership of 35,000, did not have the strategic resources to take on large-scale organising in the travel trade'. The report suggested that: 'To unionise the travel trade requires an industry-based strategy, which may require TSSA working in partnership with other unions to extend their economic and political leverage, to deepen union support and exert pressure on employers'. Rather than one union struggling to fight on many fronts, can we develop genuine union partnerships to step up our organising efforts in the 'hard-to-reach' parts of the private service sector? There is no reason why these partnerships should be restricted to Britain – emerging international sectoral organising initiatives such as those being taken suggest that working together internationally unions can develop the capacity and resources required to tackle large multinational companies (see Bronfenbrenner 2007).

In sectors where unions are weak and low pay and low skills endemic, unions need a 'new deal' if they are to be able to play their part in representing and supporting Britain's 2m 'vulnerable workers'. Sectoral approaches to organising would be given a boost by legislative change, including the development of 'sector forums', mooted as part of the Warwick agreement in 2004 and the subsequent 2005 Labour Party manifesto (see also Hendy and Gall 2006). In addition, freeing up unions to allow groups of members to take solidarity action within and across sectors would allow unions to effectively counter the effects of outsourcing and privatisation (see Hendy and Gall 2006). Most employers are unlikely to embrace this approach, and will resist anything that they perceive to be a precursor to sectoral collective bargaining or the right for unions to take secondary industrial action – but unions should make the development of sector forums and the right to take solidarity action political priorities.

Fail to innovate, fail to grow?

Underlying the suggestions above is the belief that significant membership growth, and with this increased union effectiveness, is unlikely to come from simply stepping up investment in our existing approaches to organising and recruitment. In 2007/2008, TUC affiliates reported their largest membership increase in a decade, growing by some 65,000 members but this represented a net growth across TUC unions of just 1%. To significantly increase membership, unions will need to find new models and new approaches to membership growth to supplement increased investment in their existing efforts. This need for innovation is clearly understood by unions, both in Britain and beyond. A recent study for Federatie Nederlandse Vakbeweging (Dutch Trade Union Federation) (FNV) (Kloosterboer 2007), the Dutch national union centre, pulled together a comprehensive report with successful examples of how unions had taken on today's challenges. These innovative approaches did not start and end with organising, but included examples of unions stepping up their marketing efforts; developing new political strategies; building new coalitions with community and user groups; responding more effectively to the concerns of members by developing new approaches to representation or new services; enhancing union capacity to engage in the 'battle of ideas'; developing better ways of unions working together across international borders; and undergoing internal structural and organisational changes to make better use of resources or better implement strategic objectives.

In Britain, recent efforts by unions to organise migrant and vulnerable workers; to develop the link between union learning and organising; to develop new uses of ICT and web2.0, including the development of unionreps.org.uk and a union presence in Second Life; to positively engage with employers on issues such as the environment and climate change; and to develop new representative roles (such as equality reps), again illustrate that unions have been prepared to invest in innovation and new ways of working. But there is more that can be done. Doing more in all these areas and more effectively is necessary. Of course, simply wishing something does not make it so. All of this work will require resources and commitment, and place strains on unions already burdened by the day-to-day pressures of representing members, maintaining relationships with employers and trying to influence governments. However, the experience of the decade has shown that where unions do take conscious, strategic choices to change the way they work – and back those choices with real resources – the results can be impressive. The task now is to use the hard-earned relative stability of the last decade as the foundations for building stronger unions over the next decade.

Notes

1 Figures based on a TUC analysis of data drawn collected by the Department of Employment 1970–1991, by the Central Statistical Office from 1992–1995 and Office of National Statistics (ONS) from 1996 onwards.
2 Unemployment statistics taken from Labour Force Survey (LFS) data, seasonally adjusted, annual unweighted averages.
3 ONS figures. Total Public Sector employment in 1997 (Q2) was 5.18m, and in 2008 (Q1) was 5.67m.
4 'School Workforce in England', Department for Children, Schools and Families, 2007.
5 Between 2004–2008, the TUC 'Leading Change' programme trained 85 senior union officers.

8
Can Unions Rebound? Decline and Renewal in the US Labour Movement
Marc Dixon and Jack Fiorito

Introduction

Union decline has reached crisis proportions for the American labour movement. To be sure, union membership among private sector employees is now lower than at any point since the Great Depression (Hirsch and Macpherson 2007). The number of union elections held through the NLRB – still a key link in the primary mechanism for private sector membership recruitment – stands at about half of pre-1980s levels. Can unions rebound? If so, just what would it take? These questions are the source of much debate within and around organised labour, underlying successive shake-ups at the top of the American labour movement. The suggestions are many for a beleaguered labour movement. Some question the big picture payoff of enhanced labour organising for restoring union power and instead call for a more general rethinking of unionism and potential labour allies (Clawson 2003a; Sullivan 2007). Scholars and activists looking to build on recent innovations in labour organising still find themselves at odds over so-called 'top-down,' or more staff driven efforts, versus 'bottom up,' member driven approaches (Early 2004a; Fantasia and Voss 2004; Lerner 2003, 2007; Moody 2007; Voss and Sherman 2000). Such debates over appropriate union approach and structure are not new. As Kochan (1980) noted some time ago, unions face a critical dilemma. To wrestle concessions from large, sophisticated employers, some degree of union centralisation or top down strategy is needed. But in the absence of member involvement and effective internal political channels, centralisation is not viable for the long run and union effectiveness will diminish. With Kochan's 'caution' in mind, it is the more top down approaches of the SEIU variety which have gained the most notice of late.

Which way, then, for American unions? In this chapter, we assess recent developments within the American labour movement, the significant revitalisation attempts undertaken by national unions, and what they hold for union renewal. The first section documents how unions have fared in recent years based on traditional indicators of labour movement vitality such as membership density, militancy, and political effectiveness. Across these indicators, unions in the aggregate are down considerably from just two decades ago. If there is a silver lining for unions in any of this, it is that recent changes in membership composition also present clear opportunities, a point we return to in the conclusion. The second section considers union revitalisation attempts and their outcomes. The commitment to organising by a handful of unions has not arrested union decline or even boosted union election activity in the aggregate. Yet, labour research underscores its significant potential (Bronfenbrenner 1997, 2005; Lopez 2004a; Milkman 2006). We thus caution against calls for a complete rethinking of the 'organising project'. Perhaps more pressing, we argue, is that not all unions are equipped for the undertaking. That many unions lack the wherewithal to make necessary internal transformations suggests that revitalisation via organising is not an option available to all labour organisations, and that union innovation and gains in membership recruitment are likely to proceed in an uneven fashion.

The current state of the union

Union membership

The proportion of workers belonging to unions, which began its slow decline in the 1950s, has plummeted in recent decades. Official federal government statistics provide comparable membership and density series only since 1983, pegging that year's membership density at 20.1% in contrast to a 2007 figure of 12.1% (US Department of Labor 2008a). Unofficial estimates based on the same Current Population Survey used for the official figures put 1980 union density at 23.0% and those covered by union contracts at 25.7% (Hirsch and Macpherson 2003, 2007). Union density thus fell by roughly one-half from 1980 to 2006, and for private sector workers in 2006 stood at just 7.4%. While there is still a substantial union wage premium, unions' weakened positions have clearly diminished their effectiveness in bargaining and membership recruitment. Without some stability in public sector unionism in recent decades, the labour movement would be even worse off. In 1983, public sector workers were 32.2% of union membership, but by 2006 they were 48.0%. Disaggregated data reveal a striking uniformity in the decline across most industries and occupations. With the exception of a large private versus public sector distinction, union decline has been across the board and has not been limited to those manufacturing industries decimated by deindustrialisation. Take a growing industry like trucking, for example, which appeared to experience one of the more dramatic declines from about 37.7% density in 1983 to about 12.0% in 2006.

Several likely 'culprits' have been cited as reasons for the striking decline, including employer opposition (Fiorito and Maranto 1987), an unfavorable political climate (Western 1997), union ineffectiveness and decreased employee demand for representation (see Clawson and Clawson 1999 for a review). A recent analysis by Flanagan (2005) concurred with earlier studies in discounting the often-cited 'structural change' thesis that says shifts in employment to traditionally less unionised occupations, industries, regions and workforce participants are driving union decline. He attributes significant weight to declining employee demand for union representation due to increases in progressive human resource policies and increased government protection. Although not dismissing illegal employer opposition, Flanagan questions whether labour law reforms focused on illegal employer behavior would have a significant impact.

Whether the result of employer opposition or union ineffectiveness, there is no doubt that union organising has plummeted (Bronfenbrenner 2005). The number of NLRB union certification elections declined steeply during the early 1980s and remain at roughly half of pre-1980s levels (Fiorito and Jarley 2003; Moody 2007). While some unions have begun to pursue non-NLRB election alternatives – card check or majority sign-up where the employer agrees to recognise the union after a majority of employees have signed cards – this has not offset the decline in certification elections. Despite impassioned calls to organise, only a handful of unions appear to have made significant efforts here, and those efforts account for a small share of organising (but a potentially more important share) (Martin 2008).

There are some positive developments regarding membership composition. Unions have made some inroads among growing fields such as professional occupations and among new groups of workers. For example, gender composition of membership changed dramatically, at a time when gender composition of the workforce was relatively stable. Women's share of employed workers increased from 46% to 48% during 1983–2005, but their share of membership increased from 34%

to 43%. Some of this reflects union decline in traditional male-dominated bastions (e.g., much of heavy manufacturing). But some of this change also reflects a new organising emphasis, and the success that some unions have achieved in organising industries or occupations where women workers are common. Bronfenbrenner's (2005) work still suggests caution when interpreting these figures, noting that few unions have altered their organising practices when targeting predominantly female bargaining units.

Shifts in ethnic/racial composition were less dramatic in recent decades, although this is likely changing too. Some of the most celebrated organising gains for unions have been among mostly immigrant workers in service sector employment (Cornfield 2007). In Los Angeles, for example, immigrants have been at the forefront of union revitalisation (Milkman 2006). The SEIU, the fastest growing large union in the US, boasts significant gains amongst women and people of color. The classic US union member image in 1980 was a blue-collar, middle-aged white male employed in manufacturing, construction, or transportation, and residing in the Northeast, Great Lakes region, or on the West Coast (Lipset and Schneider 1983). By comparison, the typical union member of the early 2000s was considerably more likely to be a female, a professional, a public sector worker, and far less likely to work in manufacturing (see Fiorito 2007). If unions are to grow, they will need to make further inroads among these demographic groups. And, there appears to be a sizeable, untapped reservoir of union support from which to draw. While some attribute union density decline to decreased worker demand for representation (Flanagan 2005), there is mounting evidence of a large and possibly growing 'representation gap' between the numbers who have and want union representation (Freeman 2007; Freeman and Rogers 1999). Survey data suggests that upwards of 30% of non-supervisory workers would join a union if that option was available to them.

Labour militancy

For a long time, the strike was the critical economic weapon in labour's tactical repertoire. The public image of labour unions in the US is perhaps still defined by this tactic. But in recent years the frequency of strikes has plummeted along with the downward trend in membership. From 1981–1990, the annual number of major work stoppages (involving 1,000 or more workers) averaged 72, versus 27 for 1996–2005 (US Department of Labor 2006). Comparing the same periods, estimated lost work time from major stoppages (reflecting strike frequency, volume, and scope) dropped from about 0.04% to about 0.01%. The obvious causal suspects in strike decline include maturation and skill development among negotiators, declining union density, declining bargaining unit size – larger units being more strike-prone – and declining strike effectiveness. Some of these played a minor role, but clearly union decline and decreasing strike effectiveness were critical factors. Non-union worker strikes are not unheard of, but they are extremely rare. Thus, a 50% drop in density almost automatically implies a 50% drop in strike activity, other things equal. Yet, while union membership was roughly halved in the last two decades, strikes have dropped by about 90% (Dixon and Martin 2007). The stability of public sector density did not offset or dampen this trend since the vast majority of public sector workers do not have the right to strike.

Other things have not been equal, of course. The last three decades witnessed US central governments that were mostly hostile to unions. Through judicial and regulatory agency (e.g., NLRB) appointments and through example (e.g., the PATCO strike of 1981), the Reagan and Bush administrations created and fostered a climate that made strikes high-risk affairs for unions. Disastrous strikes at major corporations in the industrial Midwest, from Hormel in the 1980s to Caterpillar in the 1990s, the more recent disputes in the grocery industry on the West Coast and countless other cases all point to the difficulties unions now face. Globalisation and a more competitive environment are part of the story as well, providing heightened employer motivation to resist union strike threats. Balanoff (1985: 7) noted some time ago that strike had actually become an important weapon for *employers:* 'If an employer is intent upon busting a union, the strike becomes an integral part of this effort. Union-busters commonly advise employers to create strike situations as a means of creating a "union free environment"' (see also Cramton and Tracy 1998). Even more important, now, is the increased threat to both parties that a strike could result in business failure or at least permanent market share losses. In the familiar strike metaphor, the economic climate changed such that the 'pie' was greatly at risk of shrinking rapidly or even disappearing altogether if the parties failed to reach agreement. It is therefore unsurprising that while Rubin (1986) found strike frequency to positively affect the rate of compensation growth in core unionised industrial sectors pre-1980s (during the so-called 'capital-labour accord'), Rosenfeld (2006) found a complete decoupling of strike-wage relationship in more recent years, even after disaggregating to industry-region clusters.

If strikes have become a weapon of last resort for most unions (Rosenfeld 2006), there are notable exceptions. For example, just-in-time production techniques have empowered at least some sets of workers (Silver 2003). Workers in auto parts manufacturing have taken advantage of the tightly integrated supplier chains in short strikes (Rachleff 2003; *Wall Street Journal* 18 July 2008), although it is unclear whether this leverage is offset by the heightened risk of business failure or relocation in struggling manufacturing industries. There is also suggestive evidence of more aggressive unions (e.g., the SEIU, Teamsters) successfully employing intermittent striking alongside other tactics in organising and contract campaigns (Lerner 2007; Martin and Dixon 2007). In lieu of striking, unions have developed alternative strategies and tactics to pressure employers (e.g., *Labor Research Review* 1985). For example, McCammon (2001) found a sharp rise in the filing of unfair labour practices (ULPs) in response to employer intransigence during organising. Other innovations by unions include 'in plant' strategies, somewhat analogous to sit-down strikes in which tactics such as work slowdowns or 'working-to-rule' results in reduced efficiency without a formal strike and ensuing increased exposure to striker replacement. Unions' reliance on external pressure strategies, often referred to as 'corporate campaigns' or 'comprehensive campaigns,' where unions exert pressure on employers through demonstrations, advertisements, exercising stockholder rights, and in other ways generating negative publicity, have also increased (Martin 2008, and see below). At least for a handful of major national unions, it appears that an expanded tactical repertoire, which may include intermittent striking, has partially offset the declining frequency and effectiveness of the traditional strike.

Labour politics

There have been few union political victories in recent decades due to declining membership, a rightward turn in national politics, and waning union influence in the Democratic Party. The recent passage of the union-initiated *Employee Free Choice Act* in the House of Representatives – an act designed to limit management interference in organising efforts – is a notable exception, although the bill failed to pass in the Senate. It will come up again with a new Administration and Congress in 2009. Administrations under Reagan and both Bush presidencies launched various anti-union initiatives. George W. Bush's administration has made explicit efforts to revoke collective bargaining rights for thousands of federal employees in the name of 'homeland security' post-9/11, although the nexus between collective bargaining rights and threats to homeland security has never been persuasively articulated. There were brief opportunities for unions under the Clinton Administration, most notably in the *Presidential Commission on the Future of Worker Management Relations* chaired by John Dunlop. These faded with Republican gains in Congress in 1994. Clinton also attempted to use the President's executive powers to limit striker replacement, but this was struck down by the courts.

What victories unions can claim during this period came mainly in terms of the 'negative agenda,' that is in stopping legislation and other public policy or administrative initiatives intended to weaken union and worker rights. For 1996–2002, Masters and Delaney (2005: 383) derive a 35% union success rate on selected federal legislation, with a notably higher 67% success rate on legislation more directly affecting unions. There was considerable activity on labour law and public policy in states affecting both private sector and state and local public sector employees. Following the political openings for public sector unionism in prior decades, several states have repealed existing executive orders permitting collective bargaining (witness Kentucky and Indiana in the early 2000s). Oklahoma passed a Right-to-Work law in 2001 barring dues payment as a requirement of continued employment, making it the twenty-second state to do so (Jacobs and Dixon 2006), and several states saw battles over 'paycheck protection,' or as unions call it, 'paycheck deception'. These campaigns involved legislative or ballot initiatives restricting payroll deduction for union dues to bargaining activities.

There were calls in the 1980s and 1990s for unions to become more active politically and some notable efforts to do so (Delaney *et al.* 1999: 277; Fiorito 1987: 273). There were renewed efforts to form a viable labour party, but as so often in the past, these efforts foundered. Although officially non-aligned and at times endorsing Republican and minor party candidates, unions are for practical purposes 'an integral part of the Democratic Party' (Masters and Delaney 2005: 368). Unions of late have taken a more prominent role in presidential politics and have provided much of the 'muscle' for campaigning, launching sizable door-to-door get-out-the vote drives and volunteer phone banks, generally in alignment with Democratic efforts. Union members consistently favoured Democrats although less overwhelmingly than in political action committees (PACs) or mobilisation efforts. In Congressional voting over 11 biennial cycles from 1980–2000, the proportion of union-affiliated voters favouring Democrats averaged about

10% higher than for voters generally (Masters and Delaney 2005: 382). Despite the persistence of a limited union voting 'bloc,' its impact was weakened by the diminishing base of union households in the wake of declining density (Masters and Delaney 2005: 381).

Overall political activity as indicated by the level of per-member PAC contributions has been relatively constant over the last two decades in inflation-adjusted terms (Masters and Delaney 2005: 377), at less than $2 per member per biennial election cycle (federal election campaigns only). But union political spending has substantially lagged behind the growth in business-related political activity. In terms of PAC contributions to House and Senate candidates, corporate PACs outspent labour PACs by a 1.4:1 ratio in 1979–1980, and by a 2.8:1 ratio in 2003–2004 (US Census Bureau 2006). Looking at broader indices, Masters and Delaney (2005: 380) estimated that business-affiliated groups and individuals outspent their union counterparts by roughly an 8:1 margin in both 1991–1992 and 2001–2002 election cycles. There were notable changes in union political orientation, including increasing support of immigrant rights and a shift from outright opposition to trade liberalisation, after repeated defeats, to an emphasis on 'fair trade,' trying to ensure that trade agreements included meaningful labour provisions to protect US workers from foreign competition that exploited foreign workers and hastened a 'race to the bottom.' In this regard, some unions have forged alliances with other social movement organisations advocating fair trade practices (Evans *et al.* 2007; Turner 2005).

With density at 12%, unions clearly need many allies to achieve political goals, in addition to strong turnout from union households. Yet where unions are perhaps most lacking on the political front, it appears to be in their framing and the ability to champion issues that resonate with larger, non-union constituencies. For example, Masters and Delaney (2005: 383) noted that unions fared better on 'union issues' (e.g., paycheck protection/deception) than in broader issues (e.g., trade). As they concluded, unions have failed the 'critical test' of crafting a political message that inspires, championing ideas that stir passion among non-union voters as well as those from union households (Masters and Delaney 2005: 387). A 2005 Gallup Poll is telling here. Whereas 69% of American adults said unions 'mostly help' union workers, only 38% said that unions 'mostly help' non-union workers and 52% said they 'mostly hurt' non-union workers (Kiefer 2005). Union participation in living wage campaigns offers one route toward reaching larger, non-union voting blocs and alliances with sympathetic organisations and social movements (Luce 2004).

The aggregate indicators of union vitality discussed at this point highlight unions' considerably weakened position from two decades ago. Most unions remain on the defensive. Bargaining in this climate is increasingly difficult. But some unions have attempted to chart a different course marked by a commitment to organising. In the following, we examine particular strategies employed for union renewal and likely routes for labour in the near future.

Union innovation and sources of renewal

The 1995 AFL-CIO election, its first contested election ever, marked a sea change for many labour observers. Reformer John Sweeney championed a commitment to union organising from labour's highest pulpit and provided a larger stage for innovations in organising and member mobilisation developed during the decade. Remarking on the enormity of the change, Clawson and Clawson (1999: 96) underscored how rare it is that a formal organisation so publicly confronts its own demise, noting that it is even less likely for a highly bureaucratised organisation to 'attempt rejuvenation through a return to its activist roots.' What did the change entail? Sweeney encouraged affiliated unions to devote 30% of their resources to organising new members and to develop comprehensive organising programs. Innovative programs like the Organising Institute (formed under the prior administration) were allocated more resources and the new leadership reached out to a non-traditional constituency in students by forming the Union Summer program in 1996 (Van Dyke *et al.* 2007). More generally, Sweeney emphasised an activist labour orientation relative to his predecessor Lane Kirkland. Despite initial enthusiasm for Sweeney's project, labour again found itself on the retreat by the mid-2000s. Internal sparring over resource allocation, likely routes to union renewal, and the outcomes of the new leadership's reform efforts ten years on, led to another historic split in the labour movement in 2005 – this one taking more than 6m members, and the fastest growing union in the SEIU, as well as the Teamsters and handful of other unions, as part of the new 'Change to Win' coalition (CTW). The most vocal complaint of the defectors was the inability of the AFL-CIO to compel its many affiliates to organise.

The experimentation and debate within organised labour further stimulated an emerging literature on 'union revitalisation' that seeks to assess the variety of union strategies intended to revive the labour movement and their effectiveness (see Clawson 2003a; Cornfield and

McCammon 2003; Delaney *et al.* 1996; Fiorito *et al.* 1995, 2002; Lopez 2004a; Milkman 2006; Turner 2005; Voss and Sherman 2000). This work provides a window into the likely routes for US labour unions in the near future: whether a commitment to organising is worth the effort, why many unions have failed to make the necessary changes, the merits of 'top-down' versus 'bottom-up' approaches, and the ability of unions to identify and cultivate new alliances, and to expand their tactical repertoire. We examine each of these in turn.

Union organising and labour revitalisation

Most analysts agree that union revitalisation in the current climate requires some sort of transition from unions as primarily labour market institutions that 'service' existing members to an 'organising model' where unions might better resemble social movement organisations (SMOs). But is organising even worth the effort? Freeman and Rogers (2002: 9–10) noted that unions need to add 500,000 members per year just to maintain the current density level, a membership increase unions have failed to reach in years. Unions would still need to double their membership gains for the next 30 years just to reach pre-1983 density levels (Clawson 2003b). Despite the emphasis put on organising by the AFL-CIO under Sweeney as well as the new CTW coalition, there has been no spike in union election campaigns. There is evidence that organising activity has increased outside of 'official channels' (e.g., the NLRB procedures) but at best the evidence only weakly suggests this activity has risen to a point where one could say that overall union organising activity has risen (Fiorito and Jarley 2008; Martin 2008). Critics contend that these figures show the limits of current practices (Moody 2007). For example, Clawson (2003a) noted that historically labour has not grown incrementally through slow and steady organising, but rather in sudden bursts. He does not dismiss recent innovations in organising and has high praise for some SEIU campaigns. Yet he sees the fusion of labour with other social movements and community organisations as a more likely route to restoring labour power than the continual chipping away at organising under an outmoded labour relations system forged during the 'New Deal'. Similarly, and instead of strictly focusing on NLRB elections as a route to restoring density, other scholars point to examples of much smaller social movements successfully wrestling gains from employers/authorities through disruptive protest and other creative pressure tactics (Sullivan 2007; or see Piven and Cloward 1977 for an early statement).

Calls like these for a rethinking of unionism and current organising goals certainly have some merit, although they may be too quick to give up on the project. The aggregate statistics described above do not preclude effective organising, but rather reflect a labour movement where the vast majority of unions have failed to make the necessary changes. Indeed, there is mounting evidence on the *effectiveness* of recent organising. The work of Bronfenbrenner *et al.* (Bronfenbrenner 1997, 2005; Bronfenbrenner and Hickey 2004) on NLRB certification elections is compelling here for they found innovative organising tactics on the part of unions matter as much if not more than employer opposition or industry constraints. The comprehensive organising model identified by Bronfenbrenner includes tactics like strategic targeting and research, grassroots organising committees, person-to-person contact inside and outside the workplace, and creative external pressure tactics among others. To the extent that unions move away from a 'leafleting the plant gates' model to the prescribed comprehensive organising model, they significantly increased their odds of organising success.

This emphasis is supported by Fiorito *et al.*'s (1995: 631) findings on organising effectiveness, wherein a positive association between innovative tactics and effectiveness was demonstrated, again independent of employer opposition. Lopez's (2004a: 18) ethnographic research on organising among low-wage nursing home workers offered insight into how such a model may work, namely, creating a 'new vision of participatory, powerful unionism that is understood – by workers – to be different from the old-style business unionism of experience and cultural memory'. Chipping away at organising in this fashion for more than a decade, the SEIU went from near zero union density in the nursing home industry in Pennsylvania to approximately 15% (Lopez 2004b).

Research identifying 'best practices' of certain unions or organising campaigns underscores the promise of contemporary union organising. The SEIU in particular has come to resemble an ideal type for revitalisation (Nissen 2003), although not without some criticism regarding undemocratic practices. One of the most celebrated recent developments is SEIU's 'Justice for Janitors' campaign. In organising low-wage, often immigrant, janitors in large cities, the campaigns have taken on a celebratory atmosphere, often including some combination of civil disobedience and confrontational protest tactics (including intermittent striking), sophisticated media campaigns, legal challenges of employer abuses and labour-community coalition work (Greenhouse 2008; Kennett 2006).

In this light, the problem is more about unions' ability or willingness to break out of the old model than the merits of contemporary organising. This, of course, begs the question of why most unions have failed to change. This failure to commit to organising (or at least attempt to change) is surprising given that analysts and activists alike view urgent change as necessary for union survival, not to mention success (Turner 2005). Some research emphasises resources and impetus for change coming from the top, or even from outside of organised labour. Voss and Sherman's (2000) study of union locals representing service sector workers in northern California found that successful revitalisation stemmed from a) internal political crises instigating leadership change; b) the entrance of new leaders with previous social movement experience, and c) change mandated by the international union. Isaac and Christiansen (2002) and Isaac *et al.* (2006) found that overlapping personnel between civil rights and labour organisations positively affected public sector labour militancy and growth in the late 1960s and early 1970s, supporting a movement 'spillover' effect similar to that suggested by Voss and Sherman (2000).

Delaney and colleagues (1996) found union resources and rationalisation to be positively associated with union innovation. Martin's (2007) study of organisational structure and activism among union locals similarly reported that rationalisation in terms of professional staff positively influences organising expenditures and the use of non-NLRB organising strategies. The emphasis on resources, rationalisation and change from the top corresponds most closely to the SEIU experience and the breakaway unions of the CTW coalition. Leaders of this group call for the strategic organising of large industrial sectors instead of a worksite approach or a reactive strategy of opportunistically following leads from 'hot shops' – calls from desperate workers – (Lerner 2003). The 'Justice for Janitors' campaigns are often cited as a powerful example of this approach, as the targeting of commercial cleaners in an entire metropolitan area helped take wages out of competition for cleaning contractors, reducing their incentives to resist unionisation (Milkman 2006). Some unions have followed their lead; for example, the hotel and restaurant employees (UNITE-HERE) have employed similar models with hotel and industrial laundry workers with some success.

But targeting an entire metropolitan area or sector requires extensive resources and commitment from national unions. The SEIU model, in particular, involves throwing an enormous amount of staff and financial resources into a campaign. CTW unions, and especially the SEIU, have pushed for the merging of many small local unions as well as the merging of small and sometimes competing national unions in the same jurisdiction in order to marshal necessary resources for this type of undertaking. In recent years, power within the SEIU in particular has generally shifted away from local unions to the international to match this organising focus. These changes have allowed them to compel local unions via trusteeship to follow through on organising efforts and to get in line with the goals of the international (Moody 2007; Voss and Sherman 2000). Given the dire state of organised labour and the relative success of the SEIU, its approach has received much fanfare. Indeed, employers and the mainstream media have taken notice. But not everyone is on board. Critics see this 'top-down' approach as leading to a shallow form of revitalisation, one that leaves workers disempowered (Early 2004a). And, as Moody (2007) noted, in attempting to organise entire industry sectors, the SEIU has reorganised and merged local unions into large, often multi-state, 'mega locals', arguably shifting power away from grassroots employees and the worksite when the 'local union' is headquartered in some faraway city. Grassroots members are also likely to have weaker identification with, and commitment, to an amalgamated local as compared to one with more homogenous interests built on the organic solidarity that stems from shared experiences. Further, Moody contended, this disconnection diminishes active workplace representation and may actually reinforce the old model of the union as a servicing agent. Like Kochan's 'caution', Moody's concerns raise questions about whether short-term effectiveness is secured at long-term cost.

Recent reports of side agreements between SEIU, UNITE-HERE and a handful of large employers speak to this debate. The temporary agreements reached by union and company leadership reportedly extend beyond typical neutrality pacts by actually designating which sites local unions may attempt to organise and which they cannot, and by giving up the right to strike in exchange for employer neutrality (*Wall Street Journal* 10 May 2008). This increases the chances for membership gain but workers are relatively uninvolved in the process, and the development of an activist core and tradition so essential to the organising model is potentially discouraged. Not surprisingly, 'top-down' mergers and side agreements have sparked significant resistance. The SEIU faced a revolt from within by its largest health care local, United Health Care Workers West while the California Nurses Association emerged as one of its most vocal critics and competitor unions (*Wall Street Journal* 19 May 2008). Critics of the 'top-down' approach are not a unified voice, but they tend to oppose the centralisation of internal union power, being wary of staff driven campaigns, and believing workers need to be at the forefront of any union revitalisation (Moody 2007). In terms of an alternative organising model, few unions have showed much success with perhaps the exception of the Communication Workers' Association (Fiorito *et al.* 1995; Nissen and Rosen 1999). Heery (2003) addressed this in his discussion of union managerialism or managed activism *vis-à-vis* renewal strategies, contrasting various renewal perspectives, but particularly renewal as either a 'challenge from below' or a 'challenge from above.' In the former, union leaders are an obstacle to grassroots activism, while in the latter, EUOs provide the leadership that is essential for effective activism. Although the 'managerialist' terminology can be off-putting to those who tend to think of unions as inherently democratic and 'bottom-up' institutions, the need for leadership is undeniable. Further, if one stipulates that the 'management' of activism in a union context is almost inherently a bilateral process of negotiation between leaders and grassroots – leaders have little power to compel activism – objections to 'managed activism' lose much of their force.

There is no simple answer in this debate. The inability of Sweeney's leadership to increase labour's organising efforts among AFL-CIO affiliates has been used to validate both 'top-down' (Lerner 2003) and 'bottom-up' (Moody 2007) approaches. Yet, as Milkman (2006) showed, this dichotomy may be a false one. Successful union campaigns typically exhibit both extensive commitment and resources from the national union as well as significant grassroots activism (see also Fiorito *et al.* 1995). For labour to break out of its current malaise, one or the other will not be sufficient. In the absence of grassroots involvement, 'top-down' agreements lose their potency and unions become ineffective bargaining organisations. Thus, we caution that while aggressive steps by labour leaderships are dearly needed, and centralisation of the SEIU variety may be fruitful in the current climate for coaxing recalcitrant employers, by itself it is not a long-term recipe for success (Kochan 1980).

Regardless of the particular mix of staff and grassroots involvement, internal hurdles to revitalisation continue to loom large. Reformers are faced with challenging established union cultures. Member and staff resistance to internal transformation are likely as these changes often result in decreased power for certain union EUOs and fewer resources for existing members (Lopez 2004a; Nissen 2003). Furthermore, it is unclear just how often and to what extent union members are willing to mobilise as activists. The majority of evidence suggests that such member activism is exceptional, and consequently the transition or transformation from a 'servicing model' to an 'organising model' is no small task (Gallagher and Strauss 1991: 154; Nissen 1998). Finally, it is unlikely that all unions have the resources or wherewithal to change. Delaney *et al.* (1996: 609) concluded that union innovation 'is shaped more by unions' capacity to innovate rather than by their motivation to innovate.' And frequently cited successful revitalisation cases, with some exceptions, tend to share similar resource and administrative capacities (Fiorito *et al.* 1995: 632; Martin 2007; Voss and Sherman 2000, Willman and Bryson 2007). As Lopez (2004a: 220) aptly noted, despite the efforts of the SEIU and a handful of other unions: 'millions of low-wage workers who *might* support union organizing campaigns in the right context simply do not have any unions willing to make a serious attempt to organize them.'

New Alliances for Labour

If a complete rethinking of unionism and the organising project is perhaps premature, scholars agree that labour is in need of friends, and fast (Cornfield 2007). It is less clear if or how such new alliances might enhance membership recruitment. In considering union effectiveness in reaching out to other social movements and community partners, there are few systematic data sets from which to draw. Instead, we look to notable examples in recent years which suggest some potential routes. These include new ties with social movements, but also transnational union alliances, and the uneven attempts at union-employer partnerships.

Some outreach efforts would have seemed implausible just a decade earlier. For example, Clawson's (2003a) study describes how the fusion of labour and student protest organisations has given a jumpstart to unionisation campaigns by campus workers. While there are mixed views on the success of recruiting students to labour activism and organising, Van Dyke *et al.* (2007) found that outreach efforts such as 'Union Summer' helped facilitate campus-based labour activism and protest, if not membership recruitment. Organisations like Jobs with Justice (JwJ), founded in the late 1980s, explicitly seek to bridge labour and community organisations on a variety of campaigns. Local JwJ chapters have expanded in recent years, although the majority of unions still do not participate. Nissen's (2004: 78) study of labour-community coalitions in south Florida found that approximately 10% of union locals actively participated in JwJ, a tactical choice usually driven by progressive union leadership. By far the most successful and long-lived outreach effort is the living wage movement. Since 1994, more than 130 living-wage ordinances have been passed by municipalities as well as some campuses in the US (Luce 2005). Living wage ordinances typically require businesses that receive public contracts to pay a specified minimum wage, although some have been more expansive and have combined with city-wide or state minimum wage campaigns (statewide minimum wage ballot initiatives were met with some success in the 2004 and 2006 election cycles). The campaigns typically organise around faith, community and labour organisations, and combine conventional and protest politics. But unions have not been unanimous in their support of, or involvement in, living wage campaigns. The ordinances may cover few workers, or mostly non-unionised workers. But there have been notable union gains. Luce (2004, 2005) noted that some of the more expansive ordinances offer non-retaliation or neutrality clauses for union organising and have facilitated notable organising victories (with the living-wage coalition often supporting later organising efforts). The key to this appears to be keeping the coalition together to help with enforcement and to pursue other strategies to improve the conditions of low-wage workers, including organising efforts. This means considerable investment on the part of the union – organising for the long-term and unions being more than 'paper' partners with coalition members.

As unions forge ties with other SMOs, they have begun to borrow from other protest repertoires (Beckwith 2000; Martin 2008). Corporate campaigns in which unions exert pressure on employers through demonstrations, advertisements, exercising stockholder rights, and in other ways generating negative publicity have yielded some notable victories (Jarley and Maranto 1990; Juravich and Bronfenbrenner 1999). The SEIU as well as UNITE-HERE have also had some success with 'bargaining to organise' strategies, whereby unions negotiate with employers to remain neutral in organising drives among other groups of workers (Fantasia and Voss 2004). The steelworkers have found new clout by exerting their contract clauses on takeover bids, often winning board seats and taking sides with would-be private equity buyers to assure the most union-friendly transition (*Wall Street Journal* 9 May 2007).

The expansion of labour's tactical repertoire is a welcome development. Yet, many union-social movement partnerships are not geared to membership recruitment. Critics may rightly question whether such alliances are worthwhile investments. If growth is the only indicator, then the answer is clearly no. There are, of course, several reasons why unions might want to consider aligning with other SMOs. Over and above needing allies to advance legislation and to prod reluctant employers but less directly, union-community alliances can serve to bring labour and its members into the mainstream of organisational life in society. This may help to address the gap the public perceives between unions helping their members and helping non-union workers (see Kiefer 2005). And, Cornwell and Harrison (2004) highlighted profound limitations of an isolated union movement as a result of the low rate – relative to members of other voluntary organisations – of organisational embeddedness of its members *vis-à-vis* other network and organisational affiliations. This points to the diminished sources of political or popular support – exacerbating the problems associated with union decline. To the extent that union-community coalition efforts can integrate *union members* in community affairs, such efforts may provide an important, if overlooked, boost for unions.

Transnational union alliances have increased in recent years and hold potential for certain strategically placed unions (Silver 2003), with longshore workers being ahead of the curve here (see, for example, *Wall Street Journal* 26 July 2006). The recent creation of Workers Uniting by Unite in Britain and the US steelworkers may be a harbinger (*Wall Street Journal* 24 May 2008). The SEIU has also formed global union partnerships (Lerner 2007). The obvious constraint on such trends is limited 'like-consciousness' across national borders. Taira's (1980–1981) assessment of the potential for transnational union collaboration still seems pertinent. Essentially, he argued transnational unionism involving US unions was slight due to huge differentials between compensation of US workers and workers in countries that pose the greatest competitive threat to US workers (e.g., China or India) for workers with such different living standards were unlikely to find common cause and a strong sense of like-consciousness. Those 'wedge factors' are less relevant for US and western European workers, and western European workers are also not a major competitive threat to US workers. There may be a bit of a paradox here in that transnational cooperation may be most difficult where the economic incentives are greatest (under the greatest competitive 'menace' in Commons' (1909) terms).

Some scholars have theorised that globalisation provides the necessary political opportunities for transnational unionism (Kay 2005; Silver 2003). Kay (2005) found that the labour side agreement to North American Free Trade Agreement facilitated transnational alliances with Canadian, US and Mexican unions by providing a structure through which unions could engage each other and forge relationships. While the US participant in this alliance is the United Electrical Radio and Machine Workers (UE), a small national union with a long history of progressive politics, the example, nonetheless, suggests how global governance institutions may have the unintended consequence of fostering alliances across global north-south divides, potentially overcoming the paradox identified by Taira (1980–1981). There are additional factors, as Cooke (2005: 284–285) noted, including differing strategic orientations and identities, structures, governance systems, customs, 'and perhaps as a product of these differences and the political democratic nature of independent unions, unions typically have deep-rooted desires for maintaining autonomy and national identity'. Much like the commitment to comprehensive organising programs, forging lasting national and especially transnational alliances requires a significant investment from unions. Like organising, it requires certain administrative and resource capacities that are not uniform across all unions. Those unions more directly tied to global trade (e.g., longshore workers' unions) will be better positioned and/or more inclined to take advantage of these opportunities (Silver 2003).

Partnerships with employers represent another form of alliance that carries renewal connotations (see Heery 2003). While partnership as such seems to be more prominent in Britain (see Martinez Lucio and Stuart, this volume), partnership is important to several US unions and was a major topic of discussion of the AFL-CIO issued during the Kirkland years. In 1994, an AFL-CIO (1994: 11) paper noted that 'we seek partnership based on mutual recognition and respect'. Joint apprenticeship programs among many US construction craft unions, a long-standing cooperative relationship involving a UNITE-HERE predecessor and Xerox Corporation, and various UAW-auto company arrangements including most famously the GM-UAW Saturn Corporation subsidiary come to mind as some prominent examples of partnership initiatives for US unions. The partnership-renewal links in these reflect at least three distinct but sometimes overlapping main types. First, those aiming to maintain a strong union influence on labour supply and skill acquisition (e.g., apprenticeship). Second, those seeking to maintain membership levels in organised units by retaining work that is being considered for outsourcing (e.g., a contract provision allowing a union to 'bid' to retain work). And, third, those extending union recognition or membership into new units (e.g., Saturn), via various 'neutrality' or 'card check' agreements (see Eaton and Kreisky 2001), or other arrangements that facilitate union organising such as bargaining provisions that arguably subsidise competitor organising.

Though numerous and varied, partnership-renewal links generally receive only modest emphasis in the US literature. This is likely due to the high opposition to unions and extension of union recognition among US employers, even employers with substantial unionisation (Logan 2002). Indeed, the AFL-CIO (1994: 11) argued: 'Most employers have never come to terms with the legitimacy – let alone the necessity – of worker organisation or trade union representation, many employer actively seek to oust union from 'their' workplaces'. Many partnership arrangements have continued or started within specific national unions and their locals since 1994, but the 1994 AFL-CIO paper may represent the acme of partnership's prominence at peak levels. Finally, it is worth noting, some of the recent anti-democratic charges against the SEIU stem from what SEIU defenders describe as efforts to use employer alliances to enhance organising capabilities, i.e., employer neutrality type arrangements, or what could be called 'partnership as renewal' initiatives.

Conclusion

By any indicator, unions are down dramatically from the 1980s levels. Gains in membership, rare as they may be in the aggregate, tend to reflect changing labour force demographics and industrial composition. Unions have made membership gains among women and racial and ethnic minorities (Bronfenbrenner 2005), and may finally be making inroads into largely unorganised service industries where there is some untapped demand for representation (Fiorito 2007; Lopez 2004a). If labour is to move forward, unions will have to redouble their efforts in these areas. Just how unions might accomplish this has been the subject of much debate. What is needed? There are several distinct perspectives on renewal (e.g., Heery 2003), and to some extent these perspectives and their adoption reflect widely varying union circumstances (Fiorito 2004). Overall density has declined, or at best, more recently stagnated: it increased 0.1% to 12.1% in 2007 (US Department of Labor 2008a). For comparison, union density in Britain fell 0.3% to 28% in 2007 (Mercer and Notley 2008: 17). Behind such aggregate statistics, however, lies a hidden and considerable variance across national unions (Fiorito and Jarley 2008; Wilson 2007). Although Wilson's (2007: 6) conclusion that British union membership has stopped falling may be premature, it is just as important that 'the great majority' of national unions grew in the last few years. A similar disaggregation for the US shows that a large number of national unions increased both organising levels and organising success, including a majority of the largest unions.

No one strategy or tactical 'solution' readily emerges from our review. Some preliminary evidence for the US case points to employment growth and employer opposition as key environmental factors, and to organising commitment and innovation as key union factors. Importantly, most union factors cited in the literature have connections to organising, either in terms of commitment to new organising or possibly the adoption of the organising model and new organising repertoires (Martin 2008). Hence, we caution against any quick abandonment of the contemporary union organising 'project,' broadly defined. The innovations in organising described in this chapter and in recent literature have not convincingly arrested union decline. But the new models do have a clear upside. Research on the organising process documents the success of comprehensive organising programs, independent of employer opposition. These findings are compelling when considering labour's severely weakened position and a most unfavorable climate for organising. They suggest that unions have some control over their futures, a possibility of adopting reforms that can make a difference.

There has been much discussion about different approaches on the part of unions, which speaks to the merits of union centralisation. This may be a false choice for successful union organising rarely relies on just one or the other strategy. Enormous amounts of staff and financial resources on the part of national unions may, indeed, be necessary to win in the current climate. At the same time, and as labour research has long contended, union centralisation in the absence of member involvement will diminish union effectiveness and prospects for growth in the long run. The more pressing problem, we believe, is the inability of many unions to change to organise. In many ways, the call for transition to an 'organising model' is a call for unions to return to their activist roots (i.e., more aptly described as a 'mobilising model'). It is not entirely clear that today's members are willing to provide the needed activism levels and forgo staff-provided services. Further, the transition to an organising model is resource-intensive and is not an option for all unions. For this reason, we expect union innovation and membership recruitment to proceed in an uneven fashion for the foreseeable future. Among the unions best equipped for such an undertaking include those that recently left the AFL-CIO, in part because of the CTW's greater ability to compel its affiliates to organise. While it is certainly too early to assess, the development of the CTW may well reveal the full potential (and limits) of this approach. The outlook is less sanguine for other labour organisations, most notably the older industrial unions, which face an uphill battle in an economic climate that is unlikely to improve.

So what do these changes entail for the future of the labour movement? Perhaps, they are grounds for a cautious optimism. The mere fact that unions are considering, debating (in an unusually open and public fashion), and experimenting with alternatives is a sign of life and marks a sea change in the orientation of the US labour movement.

9
Union Organising and Union Revitalisation in Canada

Joseph B. Rose

Introduction

Union renewal or revitalisation has become a cottage industry. Around the world, there has been an explosion of studies examining the current state of unionism and the prospects for the future (Kumar and Schenk 2006). They have dealt with a broad range of topics, including union decline, deficiencies in union structure, organisation and leadership, and prescriptions for turning around the fortunes of organised labour. With few exceptions, the diagnosis is unions are ill, they will require extensive treatments and their recovery will be prolonged, difficult and not necessarily guaranteed. This chapter examines the plight of Canadian unions. The salient issues involve, first, considering the strength of the Canadian labour movement, both in absolute and relative terms. Over the past 30 years or so, dramatic changes in the external environment have forced unions to reassess their position and develop renewal strategies. Hence, union renewal usually involves responding to external factors (for example, making adjustments to relationships with employers, state and community) and internal ones (for example, developing new priorities and increasing member commitment and participation). It is also important to link process changes with tangible outcomes, for example increasing union membership and density (Rose and Chaison 2001). To achieve that end, unions must exploit opportunities for new organising. The chapter is organised into five sections. It begins with a brief overview of the state of Canadian labour unions. Next it examines the meaning of union renewal and the environmental forces that influence it. The third section examines the organising challenge facing Canadian unions and their response to it. In the fourth section, the chapter explores the future prospects for union organising. The final section provides an overall assessment of union organising activity and how it will impact on union renewal.

The state of Canadian unions

In relative terms, Canadian unions have fared reasonably well compared to many labour movements in the industrialised world (Visser 2006). This is especially so in relation to the US, where the Canadian union density rate is more than two times higher (Rose and Chaison 2001). Measured in absolute terms the picture is less rosy. Although union membership rose from 3.67m in 1985 to 4.48m in 2007, a 22% increase, these gains have not kept pace with employment growth. As a result, union density declined from 36.4% to 30.3% in the same period (Workplace Information Directorate 2008). While union density in the public sector has remained steady (between 70% and 73%) over the same period, the private sector density rate has fallen below 20%.

There are, to be sure, other indices of union strength. There is broad agreement that renewal must focus on internal change as well as promote social and economic change. One indicator is the degree to which unions increase membership involvement, develop and promote union democracy, encourage solidarity among members and actively support 'collective action in defence of workers' rights in the workplace and citizens' rights in the community' (Kumar and Schenk 2006: 21). Because many unions continued to grow, the Canadian labour movement did not experience a crisis similar to that of American unions. While Canadian unions faced some of the same challenges of other labour movements, there was not the same urgency to develop new strategies and initiatives. Accordingly, the *status quo* prevailed with respect to union activities such as collective bargaining and organising, the 'commitment to change on the part of leadership, staff, and even members' was often circumscribed and fragmented, and bureaucratic inertia impeded innovation and bold action (Kumar and Schenk 2006: 45).

Part of the numerical strength of Canadian labour unions can be attributed to their commitment to a broader and activist role for unions in society. In contrast to the business unionism model widely practiced by American unions, Canadian unions have traditionally embraced social unionism. As discussed below, this has enabled Canadian unions to outperform their American counterparts by achieving a greater workplace presence, better collective bargaining outcomes and the ability to exert greater political influence (Rose and Chaison 1996). In the main, Canadian unions have focused on both collective bargaining to strengthen workplace unionism and political action to promote social and economic reform. As described by Kumar and Murray (2006: 82):

[t]he former typically involved some combination of contractually-based job control and pattern bargaining ... while the latter involved the pursuit of a social and political agenda which addressed the conditions of workers in general, as both wage-earners and citizens, notably through support for a social democratic party and its policies.

In addition to pursuing goals through their affiliation with a social democratic party, Canadian unions have exerted political pressure through union-community alliances in support of workers' rights and social issues. For example, in response to restructuring, public sector unions have formed coalitions to oppose privatisation and to preserve public services such as Medicare (Stinson and Ballantyne 2006). More broadly, campaigns spearheaded by the labour movement and community groups have been engaged in epic struggles against Conservative governments. A case in point was 'Operation Solidarity' in British Columbia, which featured a threatened general strike as part of a protest against social welfare reforms and restrictions on public sector industrial relations (Thompson and Bemmels 2000). In Ontario, the labour movement was instrumental in organising one-day, citywide, rotating 'Days of Protest' to oppose the neo-liberal agenda of the Ontario government in the 1990s (Rose 2000). While these and other political protests have demonstrated the capacity of the labour movement to mobilise support for social programs and workers rights, their impact has been limited to slowing the pace of restructuring rather than altering government agendas (Camfield 2007).

Union renewal and its determinants

Interest in union renewal has been sparked by the declining role and influence of unions and the need for organised labour to develop strategies to enhance their organisational and institutional strength. Renewal can manifest itself in various ways, including:

... changes in organizational culture to promote rank-and-file activism and greater participation and involvement of members in union activities, new leadership, increased resources and new strategies for organizing, collective bargaining and political action, developing competencies to participate in workplace change, broadening the range of services, and building coalitions and networks with social and community groups for wide spread mobilization of workers to effect progressive social, economic and legislative change (Kumar and Schenk 2006: 30).

If unions are to increase their bargaining strength and political influence, renewal efforts will have to focus on achieving significant and lasting gains in membership and density (Rose and Chaison 2001). Given that a symbiotic relationship exists between union density and union effectiveness, higher densities allow unions to mobilise greater resources to achieve their organising, collective bargaining and political goals and, equally important, higher effectiveness in these spheres contributes to greater density (Rose and Chaison 1996). In relative terms, Canadian unions performed reasonably well throughout most of the 1980s and the 1990s in terms of organising and collective bargaining outcomes. In contrast to their American counterparts, organising remained a high priority and produced membership gains, and there was staunch resistance to concession bargaining. Close ties between organised labour and the social democratic party, the New Democratic Party (NDP), led to enhanced political influence and produced laws supportive of collective bargaining. That said the labour relations landscape underwent significant changes beginning in the 1990s.

In a general sense, the factors that have contributed to union decline, or stagnation in the case of Canada, also represent barriers to union renewal. There are five environmental forces shaping the union decline/ union renewal debate. First, economic forces, including capital mobility, corporate and government restructuring (amalgamation, downsizing and outsourcing), industrial and occupational shifts in employment and the rise of contingent employment have figured prominently. Second, labour legislation, which has traditionally been supportive of union organising and collective bargaining, has become more restrictive. Third, social factors, such as employer opposition to unions and worker apprehension about joining unions out of fear of job loss or employer reprisals are also relevant. Recent evidence reveals employer unfair labour practices are on the rise in Canada (Johnson 2007). Fourth, political changes such as shifts to the right of the political spectrum have reduced the influence of the NDP in many parts of Canada and contributed to the deregulation of labour standards and the adoption of more restrictive labour laws. Fifth, because Canada's industrial relations system is decentralised (the ten provinces have jurisdiction for

90% of the workforce), most labour relations activity is centered at the workplace level. Combined with deficiencies in union organisation and structure (for example, complacency, leadership and inter-union rivalry), 'the forces of globalization, new technology and related dramatic shifts in the labour market, have promoted an environment of insecurity and vulnerability leading to increasing employer hostility, state antipathy, and worker ambivalence towards unionization' (Kumar and Schenk 2006: 44).

The organising challenge

Statutory certification procedures

Before considering the organising performance of Canadian unions, it is useful to provide an overview of the means and methods of union organising in Canada and contrast it with the US system. Historically, labour policy in Canada reflected American influences (the *National Labor Relations Act 1935* – or *Wagner Act* – model) and both countries adopted statutory certification procedures. Although jurisdiction over industrial relations is diffused among the federal and provincial governments, over the course of the twentieth century, the Canadian approach diverged from the American system and provided stronger support for collective bargaining (Rose and Chaison 1995). There are two broad approaches to certification: the mandatory election procedure and the card-check procedure. Under the American election system, a union must secure majority support in a secret ballot vote to be certified. Canada traditionally relied on a card-check procedure, whereby a union could be certified without a vote provided it signed up a specified percentage of workers in a proposed bargaining unit (typically 55%). Under the card-check procedure, certification votes were rarely required. More recently, many Canadian jurisdictions have moved away from the card-check procedure in favour of certification based on expedited or quick-vote elections. While there are some similarities between the certification process in the US and the various mandatory election procedures found in Canadian jurisdictions, significant differences remain since the American law 'allows for a substantial period of time to elapse before an election' and 'institutionally, the parties appear to have more room in the US than in Canada to affect the timing of the election by agreeing or failing to agree on pre-election matters' (Campolieti *et al.* 2007: 38).

In both the US and Canada, there is substantial evidence that election delay and employer unfair labour practices are negatively related to union certification success (Bentham 2002; Cooke 1983; Riddell

2001). However, the situation is exacerbated under the US election procedure because there are no fixed time limits. Hence, not only can employers resort to legal delaying tactics, but they also have sufficient time to mount vigorous and protracted campaigns aimed at reducing the likelihood of certification success. As discussed below, election delays and employer interference have contributed to the decline of organising success by American unions and led them to pursue non-statutory organising strategies, including neutrality and card-check agreements (Eaton and Kriesky 2001). Canadian unions have not experienced the magnitude of time delays and employer opposition of their American counterparts. One reason for this is there are legislated time limits for scheduling quick votes (usually within ten days). A recent study found: 'time limit laws for elections can be an effective tool for ensuring a fair union certification process' (Campolieti *et al.* 2007: 54). As well, several Canadian jurisdictions have procedures for expediting unfair labour practice hearings. Even so, unfair labour practice complaints can lead to non-compliance with time limits and lower union certification success rates. Canadian unions also benefit because labour relations boards have greater remedial powers to regulate employer misconduct, including the authority to grant automatic certification when it is found the union would have had the requisite support for certification in the absence of employer unfair practices.

Organising performance

As noted above, the task of organising the unorganised is a cornerstone of union renewal. Although Canadian unions enjoyed considerable organising success in the period between 1970 and 2000, the more recent failure of membership gains to keep pace with employment gains and the resulting decline in density, represent clear evidence of a profound organising challenge. It is no secret that if unions are going to grow and prosper they must make significant gains in the 'harder-to-organise' sectors of the economy, for example, the private service sector, small and medium size firms and expanding segments of the labour force (such as knowledge workers in the private sector and contingent workers) (Rose and Chaison 2001). Despite some evidence of stepped up organising activity in the private service sector (Yates 2000), the adoption of innovative organising strategies (Guard *et al.* 2006), and the development of new structures to promote inter-union cooperation in organising (Weir 2006), to date that challenge has not been met.

While unions appear to be committed to organising, they have not made any significant gains in the aforementioned sectors. A compar-

ison of union density rates in 1998 and 2007 for selected characteristics of the labour force reveal there has been no appreciable increase
in union penetration and union coverage in small enterprises and
among key employee groups (see Table 9.1). The density rate for workplaces with fewer than 20 employees rose slightly from 12.4% to 13.1%
in this period (union coverage rose from 14.0% to 14.7%). Union
density for part-time employees has risen only modestly from 21.9% in
1998 to 22.9% in 2007 (union coverage went from 23.6% to 24.6%).
A broadly similar pattern is found in service producing sectors (for
example, trade; finance, insurance, real estate and leasing; professional,
scientific and technical; and accommodation and food) and for young
workers (15 to 24 year-olds). In management and sales and service
occupations, the union density and union coverage rates declined.
Taken as a whole, these figures demonstrate that union density and
union coverage are significantly below the national average and are

Table 9.1 Union density and union coverage by selected characteristics, 1998
and 2007*

| | Union Density | | Union Coverage | |
	1998	2007	1998	2007
Public Sector	71.1%	71.7%	75.3%	75.2%
Private Sector	19.1%	17.0%	21.1%	18.8%
Workplace size:				
Under 20 employees	12.4%	13.1%	14.0%	14.7%
Work Status:				
Part-time	21.9%	22.9%	23.6%	24.6%
Age: 15 to 24	11.5%	13.3%	13.3%	15.0%
Industry:				
Trade	12.5%	12.9%	14.2%	14.5%
Finance, insurance, real				
estate and leasing	7.5%	9.7%	9.5%	11.2%
Professional, scientific and				
technical	4.5%	4.3%	6.4%	5.5%
Accommodation and food	8.0%	7.4%	8.6%	8.3%
Occupation:				
Management	10.6%	8.3%	13.8%	10.9%
Wholesale	6.1%	5.4%	8.7%	6.5%
Retail	12.9%	12.3%	13.7%	13.6%
Food and beverage	9.3%	7.8%	9.7%	8.6%

*January–June average
Source: Akyeampong (1999) and Statistics Canada (2007).

largely unchanged over the past decade (Akyeampong 1999; Statistics Canada 2007).

The organising challenge has been made more difficult by changes in political climate and changes to collective bargaining laws. The rise of neo-liberal governments and their penchant for the deregulation of labour markets contributed to a political and social climate less hospitable for unions. A further development has been the declining fortunes of the NDP, especially at the federal level and in Ontario, Canada's largest province. Historically, the institutionalisation of a social democratic party within a federalised parliamentary system has produced significant labour law reforms supportive of collective bargaining (Bruce 1989). This is less so today as evidenced by the declining political influence of organised labour and the fraying of the labour-NDP alliance. In recent years, some prominent unions have pursued strategic voting strategies in federal and Ontario elections to advance labour's agenda rather than simply supporting NDP candidates. For example, in the 2007 Ontario provincial election, the Canadian Autoworkers Union, teachers unions and some building trades unions formed a coalition to oppose the Conservatives, a move seen as helping the Liberals (Urquhart 2007).

The rise of the right and the waning fortunes of the NDP highlight the importance of the political climate on union organising. As shown by Martinello (2000), political regimes can exert significant effects on the level of organising and organising success, which in turn, can impact union membership and density. This has been reflected in legal changes, most notably the shift from card-check procedure to mandatory elections. Since 1995, the percentage of the Canadian labour force covered by mandatory certification votes increased from 18% to 57% (Johnson 2004). Research indicates that union success rates are substantially lower under a mandatory vote scheme (Campolieti *et al.* 2007; Johnson 2002; Riddell 2004). In addition, mandatory votes can have an adverse impact on union density. Specifically, if all Canadian jurisdictions used mandatory votes between 1980 and 1998, a conservative estimate is union density would have been 3% to 5% lower in 1998 (Johnson 2004).

A further examination of certification activity in Ontario confirms that organising activity and success rates have declined since the introduction of mandatory votes.[1] Table 9.2 provides certification results for fiscal years 1992–1993 to 2005–2006. These figures reveal a downward trend in certification applications and the proportion of applications granted. Additionally, a study of private sector certification cases in

Ontario compared the characteristics of cases under a mandatory vote scheme and card-based certification (Slinn 2003). The findings suggest that mandatory votes may make it more difficult for unions to recruit in smaller workplaces, among part-time employees and in the service sector. Specifically, the results showed that: a) the average size of certification units attempted and certifications granted was significantly higher under mandatory vote scheme; b) units of part-time employees comprised a significantly smaller proportion of applications and a significantly lower proportion of certifications granted under compulsory votes; and c) the proportion of applications and certifications granted in the service sector was significantly lower under a mandatory vote scheme. These results may reflect a tendency by unions to only pursue units where the anticipated returns exceed the higher anticipated costs associated with votes. As well, employees in smaller and part-time units may be more reluctant to join a union or have heightened concerns about employer reprisals under a mandatory vote scheme (Slinn 2003). In any event, it is significant that organising has not kept pace with job growth in smaller enterprises, the service sector and in part-time employment.

Any assessment of organising performance would be incomplete without considering the outcomes of certification. In this regard,

Table 9.2 Ontario certification applications and results

| Fiscal year | Applications | | | Granted as proportion of cases disposed of (%) |
	Filed	Disposed of	Granted	
1992–1993	824	743	509	68.5
1993–1994	1,166	1,135	829	73.0
1994–1995	1,077	987	762	77.2
1995–1996	797	759	510	67.2
1996–1997	683	656	387	59.0
1997–1998	733	664	424	63.9
1998–1999	692	665	415	62.4
1999–2000	700	567	313	55.2
2000–2001	850	927	521	56.2
2001–2202	624	686	307	44.8
2002–2003	658	627	318	50.7
2003–2004	729	584	301	51.5
2004–2005	759	811	428	52.8
2005–2006	631	661	352	53.3

Source: Ontario Labour Relations Board, *Annual Report*, 1992–93 to 2005–06 (Toronto: Queen's Printer).

Canadian unions have been successful in two important areas. First, the availability of first contract arbitration laws has contributed to a high percentage of certifications leading to first collective agree-ments (over 90%). Second, the values of voice, dignity and security have been incorporated into first agreements as evidenced by substantive provisions on seniority, grievance procedures, union representation and union security. In doing so, these outcomes have the potential to help establish long-term collective bargaining relationships (Rose 2006; compare the situation in the US (see Jordan and Bruno (2006)).

Future prospects for organising

Whereas Canadian unions have fared reasonably well in comparative terms, union renewal represents a formidable challenge. Despite slippage in union density, gains in overall membership, albeit modest, represent a positive sign. While Canadian unions appear to have weathered the storm over the past 20 years, they must, nevertheless, confront the challenges of present and future climate change. In particular, they must respond to a more 'hostile political and economic climate created by market-oriented public policy and corporate anti-unionism that has led to a decline in union influence' (Kumar and Schenk 2006: 51). To meet this challenge, there must be a greater commitment of resources to organising and the development of new and innovative strategies and organisational structures.

What is not often discussed in the union renewal literature is this, namely, is there a numerical goal or outcome of union renewal? Union density in Canada peaked at 40% in 1983. Barring a paradigm shift created by an economic or some other crisis it is highly unlikely that figure (or a higher one) will be achieved in the foreseeable future. In the absence of centralised labour markets and a strong social democratic party that is capable of championing progressive labour laws to promote union organising, it is difficult to be optimistic about achieving a surge in union membership growth and a significantly higher union density rate (Western 1997). A more realistic prospect is that union density is unlikely to exceed about one-third of the non-agricultural labour force. While even that goal would appear ambitious, it is not outside the realm of possibility. Because of space limitations, it is not possible to provide an exhaustive treatment of the organising-renewal nexus. Accordingly, three issues are highlighted: a) the demand for unionisation among non-union workers and the failure to close the representation gap; b) alternative approaches to gaining new members and expanding union coverage; and c) the effect of legal changes on the potential to recruit unorganised workers.

Demand for unionisation among non-union workers

In a world of increasingly precarious employment and economic uncertainty, one might reasonably argue that unions would be able to extol the virtues of collective bargaining in promoting workplace justice (for example, protection against dismissal and arbitrary treatment) and job and income security (for example, protection against layoffs and enhanced severance and retirement packages). This is especially so in light of survey evidence that nearly one-third of non-union workers in Canada would vote for a union given the opportunity (Lipset and Meltz 2004; Jackson 2006). Unfortunately, converting the willingness of non-union workers to vote for a union into actual increases in union membership is not a simple matter. For one thing, many non-union workers are reluctant to join unions out of fear of employer reprisals. Additionally, it is difficult to reconcile the survey results with the practical reality that certification requires majority support in designated bargaining units.[2] Moreover, the willingness to join does not necessarily accord with a strong belief in the clear and attested benefits of unionisation in a worker's own workplace. Nevertheless, the apparent latent demand for unionisation, which is even higher for young workers, visible minorities and women (over 50%), suggests 'many workers are aware of the union advantage and could be persuaded to join unions' (Jackson 2006: 66). If union renewal is to become a reality, unions will have to penetrate these largely untapped constituencies.

Organising preferences, priorities and strategies

While most unions are engaged in new organising and recognise its importance to union renewal, especially the need to penetrate the harder-to-organise sectors of the economy, their response to the challenge suggests there are tradeoffs between organising and other union priorities and preferences. Survey evidence of union priorities indicates that protecting the current level of members' wages and benefits is far more important (95.9% rated it as extremely or very important) than organising (51.1% rated organising in the union's traditional jurisdiction as extremely or very important and 36.3% rated organising in new areas of growth as extremely or very important) (Kumar *et al.* 1998). Whereas there are numerous examples of major unions broadening their 'scope of organising' in order to increase membership, the density rates in Table 9.1 suggest these activities have not been extensive. Moreover, it appears most unions continue to organise in existing areas of strength rather than areas where density rates are substantially lower than the national rate. One survey found that 'two-thirds of the respondents (66.6%) agreed the primary organising/recruitment effort of their union is focused on traditional areas of membership strength, and only 7.3% of the respondents disagreed this was the case' (Kumar and Murray 2006: 94). Indeed, the Canadian Union of Public Employees (CUPE), Canada's largest union, prefers to increase bargaining strength by raising density in those workplaces and sectors where it already has a presence and, consequently, it does not organise outside its jurisdiction (Stinson and Ballantyne 2006). Despite their numerical strength, public sector unions have generally not made commitments to organise the private service sector. As noted more than a decade ago, 'public sector unions (or coalitions of public and private sector unions) have not responded in any significant way to this challenge' (Rose 1995: 44).

Another factor appears to be the failure to commit sufficient resources to organising or, in some cases, cutting back on organising expenditures (Yates 2006). Whereas the average percentage of revenues spent on organising is 6.8%, about one-fifth of the unions reported spending no money on organising and nearly half allocated 1% to 5% of expenditures to organising. This pattern may be because there is insufficient rank-and-file support for organising and pressure for the 'servicing' of existing memberships. A survey of union officials found: 'there is a strong possibility of membership backlash when their union puts too much effort on organising/recruitment (50.6%)' (Kumar and Murray 2006: 95).

The development and pursuit of alternative organising strategies is critical to union renewal. For example, neutrality agreements have gained prominence in the US largely out of union frustrations with government-supervised certification votes, particularly with regard to excessive time delays, employer unfair labor practices and ineffective labour relations board remedies (Doorey 2006). In Canada, the demand for neutrality agreements has been benign. However, there have been recent developments in this area. In 2008, ArcelorMittal Dofasco and the United Steelworkers reached a neutrality agreement allowing the union access to employees at its Hamilton, Ontario plant. Although the union campaign was unsuccessful, it represented a significant development since the employer had fought to keep unions out at this location for the better part of a century (Powell 2008).[3]

There has also been considerable fanfare associated with the recent agreement between the Canadian Autoworkers Union (CAW) and Magna, the country's largest automotive parts maker. To date, the union has been certified in only three of its plants and organising efforts have been strongly resisted. In October 2007, the parties reached an agreement that would allow workers at each plant to simultaneously vote on union representation and a CAW-Magna national collective agreement. The 'Framework of Fairness' agreement combines features of conventional collective agreements and aspects of Magna's 'fair enterprise corporate culture', for example, employee concerns will be handled by 'employee advocates' rather than union stewards and a 'concern resolution process' will serve as a substitute for a traditional grievance procedure. Additionally, there will be no strikes and lockouts and interest disputes will be resolved by final-offer arbitration (Van Alphen 2007).

The agreement has the potential to add 18,000 members at 45 plants and boost union revenues by millions of dollars. What is less certain is the extent to which this approach will have broader appeal or whether it merely reflects circumstances peculiar to Magna or more generally the troubled automotive sector. To some extent, there may be support for pursuing labour-management partnerships based on innovative collective agreements and labour peace. On the other hand, several CAW locals as well as other unions have criticised the agreement, particularly the abandonment of the right to strike (Van Alphen 2007). The impact of the agreement on union membership will bear watching in the future.

Legal changes

There have been two recent decisions of the Supreme Court of Canada that have the potential to alter the organising landscape. They reflect a greater recognition of international standards in interpreting the freedom of association provisions in the *Charter of Rights and Freedoms* enshrined in the Canadian constitution (Adams 2006; Barrett 2003). A 2001 decision – *Dunmore v. Ontario (Attorney General)* – dealt with the exclusion of agricultural workers from coverage under the *Ontario Labour Relations Act*. The Court held that their exclusion from a statutory labour relations scheme contravened the constitutional guarantee of freedom of association. The decision recognised that without legislative protection agricultural workers were incapable of exercising their constitutional right to freedom of association. In effect, the decision recognised the right of workers to organise without fear of reprisal and that Canadian governments have a legal obligation 'pro-actively to intervene in order to ensure that the right to organise can be freely exercised' (Adams 2003: 118). The significance of this decision is that it potentially opens the door for unions to organise employees (or assist employee associations) hitherto excluded under collective bargaining statutes.

Even more dramatic was the 2007 decision recognising that the guarantee of freedom of association contained in the *Charter* extends to the right of Canadian workers to bargain collectively (*Health Services and Support v. British Columbia*). In this case, British Columbia passed a law pertaining to the health care sector that overrode collective agreement provisions covering contracting out and seniority provisions affecting layoff and bumping rights. Reversing 20 years of jurisprudence, the Court held the law was unconstitutional. In doing so, it stressed the importance of international law and, in particular, international treaties ratified by Canada recognising collective bargaining as an essential aspect of freedom of association. The Court found that by invalidating significantly important provisions in collective agreements without engaging in good faith bargaining and consultation, the government had substantially interfered with freedom of association (Lancaster House 2007).

There would be more than a bit of irony if these decisions, and more generally if the courts, became the stimulus to organising in the fertile fields of the unorganised sectors. There are two potential implications for future union organising. The first is that previous occupation-based exclusions may be brought within the ambit of existing collective bargaining laws, thereby affording excluded groups full legal protection for exercising their right to join a union. Alternatively, other statutory models for collective representation could be adopted and might produce the similar results. It is noteworthy that Ontario recently announced it intends to introduce legislation to amend the *Colleges Collective Bargaining Act* and thereby extend collective bargaining rights to 17,000 part-time community college employees. Ontario is presently the only province that excludes part-time college staff from joining a union (Government of Ontario 2007).

A second issue is whether this might alter the way labour relations boards determine appropriate bargaining units:

> Given the constitutional importance of collective bargaining, labour relations boards may need to re-examine the way in which they define the appropriate bargaining unit to ensure that the unit is defined in a way that gives the broadest possible access to collective bargaining. More controversially, if collective bargaining is a constitutionally protected activity, does the majority-support model of industrial relations need to be re-examined? If only 20% of the employees in a bargaining unit want to be represented by a union,

should that union be certified to represent those employees who want to exercise their constitutional right to engage in collective bargaining? (Nelligan O'Brien 2007: 159).

While the full impact of these decisions will not likely be known for years to come and skeptics might argue the implications are narrower, it must be observed that not many pundits believed the Court would reverse direction and attach such significance to international standards.

Conclusion

It is difficult to be optimistic about the prospects for union renewal in Canada. Changes in the economic, political and social environment have contributed to a decline in union organising activity, bargaining power and political influence. Out of necessity, many unions have responded defensively by attaching a higher priority to servicing their current members. As was noted at the start of the twenty-first century, there are few vital signs to indicate that a surge in either union membership or density is on the horizon (Rose and Chaison 2001). It has become increasingly evident that the labour movement is adrift *and* the *status quo* will not suffice. Despite the adoption of new and innovative approaches to organising in recent years, union renewal will require higher levels of organising activity and success. To that end, the prescription remains the same, but the dosage needs to be increased. In order to be successful, this will require more resources, a stronger commitment to organising from leaders and members, new strategies, interunion organising campaigns and coalition building with community and other non-labour groups.

The organising predicament facing Canadian unions can be viewed from a comparative perspective. Despite evidence that the adoption of mandatory election procedures led to a decline in certification applications and lower union success rates, the timely processing of certification votes and unfair labour practice complaints demonstrates the Canadian approach is superior to the US system. Clearly, unions would be faced with a more daunting organising challenge if Canadian policy converged with the US certification election procedure. The American experience reveals unions have become disillusioned with the statutory certification procedure and, as a result, have pursued non-statutory alternatives. There are two important lessons to be learned from this. The first involves seeking improvements to existing certification

procedures. At present, there are variations across Canadian jurisdictions in mandatory election procedures and the investigation of unfair
labour practices. These procedures could be strengthened to increase
compliance with time limits and to expedite unfair labour practice
hearings and access to remedies. This would mitigate the 'suppression
effects of unfair labour practices and election delay' (Campolietti *et al.*
2007: 54). Canadian unions could also take a page out off the American
experience by more actively pursuing neutrality agreements. Organising pursuant to neutrality agreements also has the potential to mitigate the likelihood of unfair labour practices and election delay. While
such changes are clearly required, they represent only a piece of the
puzzle. Clearly, more profound changes will be required if union
density is to rebound in any significant way. This would include, among
other things, a resurgent NDP and the adoption of labour laws that are
more supportive of collective bargaining. Whether this results from
evolutionary change or in response to a major crisis, it is difficult to
imagine meaningful union renewal in the absence of a shift in the combined political/legal/social climate.

Notes

1 Mandatory votes were among amendments in labour legislation enacted in
   November 1995.
2 Unlike the Canadian study, an American survey, which also found one-third
   of non-union workers would vote for a union, went one step further by asking
   non-union workers whether they thought their co-workers would vote for
   a union. The study found 82% of the pro-union unorganised workers felt a
   majority of their co-workers supported a union and 10% of the non-union
   workers who opposed a union believed they were in the minority. Taken
   together, the results indicate that one-third of the non-union workers believed
   that if an election was held tomorrow, the union would win the vote. This is
   almost identical to the share of workers who themselves would vote for a
   union (Freeman and Rogers 1999).
3 The shift in corporate attitude followed the takeover of Dofasco by Arcelor-
   Mittal and reflects the global relationship it has with the union (United
   Steelworkers 2008).

10
Union Organising in New Zealand: The Near Death Experience

Robyn May and Paul Goulter

Introduction

Having endured and survived almost a decade of one of the harshest industrial relations climate amongst the Anglo-Saxon nations, primarily in the shape of the *Employment Contracts Act 1991*, New Zealand's labour unions have now had an almost similar period of time under a re-regulated regime, providing for some interesting comparisons. Since the Labour government enacted the *Employment Relations Act 2000* in October of that year, union membership has climbed slowly and steadily, reversing a decade of long decline. Whilst membership numbers are at similar levels to those of the early 1990s, density remains stubbornly at all time low levels because of strong labour market growth over the last decade. The New Zealand Council of Labour Unions (NZCTU), having learnt the hard way that reliance on the state for union fortunes was no longer a responsible strategy, has, since the late 1990s, vigorously pursued an 'organising' agenda and affiliates are currently working together with unheard of levels of cooperation. A small number of affiliates have been keen proponents of the 'organising model' since the 1980s (Oxenbridge 1998). Nonetheless, the impact of the *Employment Contracts Act 1991* has been long-lasting, however, and not just because the current government has accepted this as the *status quo* and the platform for its changes, rather than returning to what went before the 1991 Act. This raises questions about the sustainability of the current membership revitalisation and what might really be needed in order to put New Zealand's labour unions properly back on the map of important social agents. In this chapter, we look at what unions have done in order to survive, what shape they came out the other end in, and how this has informed the New Zealand movement today. We also question

191

the label 'union organising' and how helpful the 'organising model' has been as a rallying cry for unions in their quest for re-legitimacy and renewal.

In the New Zealand context, some particular questions start to emerge. Is it really possible for a movement the size of New Zealand's with a long history of dependence on the state to stand on its own feet regardless of government *per se*? Does the organising model, broadly described as a set of principles for union rebuilding and empowering workers to be active in their own workplaces and not reliant on EUOs to not only provide solutions to problems but also implement these (Bronfenbrenner *et al.* 1998; Heery 2002), require a resourcing base beyond that possible for a union movement the size of New Zealand's? Are we able to say that New Zealand labour unions are capable of fully embracing the organising model and implementing it into their own cultures and strategies, given their small size and the consequent resource constraints that flow from lack of scale? Is organising as a strategy predicated on a critical mass something more akin to that of the AFL-CIO or TUC? Or has some peculiarly New Zealand approach been crafted by unions in response to the particular circumstances they have faced and, if so, what lessons might be learnt from this by unions in other countries? We draw on our professional experience (see biographical notes on pp.xi–xii) and extant studies to examine these issues.

Background and context

The impact of the *Employment Contracts Act 1991* on New Zealand's labour unions has been well documented (Anderson 1991; Boxall 1991; Kelsey 2005). Changes to the system of compulsory arbitration, that had been the mainstay of New Zealand's industrial relations since the *Industrial Conciliation and Arbitration Act 1894*, were begun by the Labour government of 1984–1990. This government was heavily influenced by advocates for widespread market liberalisation within the public sector, and the economic conditions of the time that had lead to the rejection at the polls of the previous incumbent government (Easton 1994). The *Employment Contracts Act 1991* took decentralisation and de-collectivisation much further, prohibiting compulsory membership provisions, putting individual and collective contracts on the same footing whilst making negotiation of multi-employer contracts difficult. The *Employment Contracts Act* also gave employers veto rights over union access and allowed non-union groups or individuals to negotiate collective agreements. Within a decade, union membership and density had more than halved from a high of 55.7% in 1989 to 21.4% in 1999, and collective bargaining collapsed from being the method of pay determination for the vast majority of New Zealand workers to where it is now the method of pay determination for only an estimated one-fifth of the workforce (Harbridge and Honeybone 1996). Membership losses occurred at all levels, from workplace to industry and also from the impact of wide-scale job losses in the public sector following contracting-out and restructuring. By the end of the 1990s, union membership was highly concentrated in the public sector, manufacturing, and to a lesser extent, the transport and storage sectors, so that by 1999 these three industries accounted for 87% of all members (Crawford *et al.* 2000). New Zealand's unions effectively found themselves relegated to the status of single site bargaining agents, as the locus of bargaining shifted from multi-employer or industry-based collective agreements (known as 'awards') to the workplace. However, in maintaining the traditional bargaining function – albeit at the workplace – workloads doubled for EUOs whilst at the same time membership declines meant widespread staffing cuts at most unions.

By the time the Clarke labour coalition government was elected in 1999, New Zealand unions found themselves in an extremely difficult position. The movement was without a cohesive national structure, following a split in the peak union body in 1993, over the peak body's response to the *Employment Contracts Act 1991*, and the formation of a rival peak council. Union density was at an all time low of 21.1% of wage and salary earners, and only 302,000 New Zealander workers belonged to unions (May *et al.* 2002). Whilst Labour had pledged to replace the *Employment Contracts Act*, and the NZCTU had worked hard on restoring party/union relations, the decimation of the 1990s meant resource limitations posed huge practical constraints on union activity and capacity for renewal as well as for engagement in policy debate. The delivery of the Labour Party promise to remove the *Employment Contracts Act* marked the beginning of a turnaround in the legitimacy of the union movement, rather than a watershed in union fortunes. This was largely because the Clarke-led government, and the minority governments elected in 2002 and again in 2005, governing with the support of minority parties, have taken a measured approach to the regulation of industrial relations.

The *Employment Relations Act 2000* and the 2004 amendments to this Act, represent moderate reform within a clear *Employment Contracts Act* context. The *Employment Relations Act 2000* does not reinstate the centralised wages, conditions and disputes settling institutions lost through the late 1980s and 1990s. Instead, it carves out a 'third way' of mediation (solving employment relationship problems), embedding in the individualistic nature of grievance and dispute, and gives unions a 'hand-up' with access rights, and provision for information disclosure in relation to collective bargaining (May and Walsh 2002). Whilst unions are afforded monopoly rights to collectively bargain – with a strong emphasis on good faith – there is nothing to stop an employer from passing on union-won benefits to non-union employees, thus creating an incentive for 'free-riding' (Bryson 2006b).

Further, the exclusive right to collective bargaining awarded to registered unions, which rests essentially on a statutory declaration and just 15 members, has resulted in a potentially contradictory situation for unions (Barry and May 2002). Amendments to the *Employment Relations Act 2000* in 2004 that endeavoured to tackle this issue appear to have had little success, or at least there has been little evidence of resultant membership growth (Feinberg-Danieli and Lafferty 2007). This may be due to an ineffective education message to potential union members, or may reflect generational change in attitudes to unions and propensity to join (Haynes *et al.* 2005).

At the same time the government has strengthened the minimum employment code, increasing the minimum wage by 70% since June 2000 (from NZ$7 per hour to NZ$12 per hour from 1 April 2008 for those aged 16+ who are not new entrants or trainees (DOL 2008)), mandating four weeks annual leave effective from April 2007, introducing taxpayer funded paid parental leave of 14 weeks, improving minimum sick leave and domestic leave provisions, requiring time and a half for all work on statutory holidays and strengthening health and safety legislation.

Every year since the introduction of the *Employment Relations Act 2000* has seen an increase in membership. Overall, the seven years to December 2006 have seen membership rise by 25% or over 70,000 members. The annual increases have been variable. In 2000 membership increased by 5.4%, by 3.6% in 2001, 6.6% in 2005 and slowing to 1.4% in 2006 (Feinberg-Danieli and Lafferty 2007). In terms of union density, the raw figures, which arguably provide the clearest measure of union strength, show that strong labour force growth over recent years has meant density has effectively stalled at between 21% and 22% of all wage and salary earners. Looking further at the statistics, a distinct polarisation of membership is found, with more than half of New Zealand's labour unionists work in the public sector, where density is close to 70%, and private sector density is a low 12.4% (Fineberg-Danieli and Lafferty 2007).

New Zealand peak council union structures

In 2000, the rival peak organisations, the Trade Union Federation (TUF) and NZCTU merged amicably, ending seven years fall out over the NZCTU's response to the *Employment Contracts Act*. The TUF, with 11 affiliates, comprised some who had not joined the NZCTU on its foundation in 1987 as well as a number who left in the early 1990s arguing that the NZCTU should have been more militant in its response to the introduction of the *Employment Contracts Act 1991*. The current formation, operation and functioning of the peak body is arguably the most stable and powerful, particularly in relation to influence over affiliates, in the history of New Zealand labour unionism. The arrival of an uncontested and widely supported new leadership to the NZCTU in 1999 marked a turning point for the peak council. Currently, 39 unions, representing some 89% of labour union members, are affiliated to the NZCTU. Whilst the NZCTU has no formal power over affiliates, a high degree of mutual trust, confidence and shared vision is apparent. The lack of control over wage bargaining by the NZCTU, observed by Gardner (1995: 49), remains due to the lack of institutional structures for industry coordinated bargaining.

Despite earlier talk of a social compact or social partnership with government, the NZCTU has endeavoured to deal with government at all levels and engage on a wide range of issues in a more independent manner, often seeking to do this in an informal, rather than a formal constructed setting – as say compared with the Australian Labour Party (ALP)/Australian Council of Labours Unions (ACTU) *Accord*. Only four New Zealand unions are currently affiliated to the Labour Party with many having left over dissatisfaction with the 1984–1990 Labour government. And whilst there are a number of former union officials in government, and indeed within the Cabinet, the party and union movement do not share the same close links as between the ALP and ACTU (or certainly the link apparent during the *Accord* period). Indeed, unions may well be very cautious of adopting too much of the *Accord*-type model given the generally negative assessment of the fortunes of Australian unions under this approach (Peetz 1998). The dilemma for labour unions remains in that their capacity to genuinely participate in government policy debate at all levels is heavily constrained by their lack of resources.

Right from the outset of the new NZCTU leadership elected in late 1999, a focus on organising was promoted as the basis of union renewal. To assist with this process a NZCTU Organising Centre was developed based closely on the ACTU Organising Centre. Work at all levels within the NZCTU and with its affiliates was to be closely benchmarked to its capacity to leverage union organising and growth. The NZCTU has also promoted strongly the role of 'on the job' health and safety in building union strength and has devoted considerable resources to building up effective health and safety representatives. Finally, the NZCTU has also been particularly active in promoting a high skill/high wage agenda and attempting to get its affiliates to use this as a basis for both industry-wide engagement with employers and on the job union organising. Likewise, it has also developed workplace initiatives around the learning representatives as a basis to provide further opportunities for unions to engage with workers.

Recognising asymmetries within the movement, in particular that high growth well resourced unions are in relatively well unionised areas whilst private sector unions who have the task of reaching out to the seven in eight private sector workers who are not unionised, are resource poor and stretched beyond capacity, the NZCTU has facilitated a number of ground-breaking responses. First, via a NZCTU re-unionisation fund, resource rich public sector unions are encouraged to contribute resources, with the private sector unions allowed to draw upon the funds and resources to organise in new areas. Second, unions have been encouraged to work with other unions in their particular industries to ensure that workers are being represented in the most efficient manner, with the long-term aim that there should be fewer unions in each particular industry. This fits within the NZCTU programme of an industry-wide focus on all issues ranging from training, growth and innovation, organising and engagement with the state. One of the best examples of this initiative is the Food Sector Unions. Under the leadership of the NZCTU, this grouping has developed and implemented an inter-union relationship agreement designed to reduce or remove demarcation disputes and instead to focus on building membership growth and implement sector-wide employment standards. This grouping has also worked closely with the various government initiatives at the level of the sector. It has also established close working links with a similar food sector unions' structure in Australia.

What is organising? And, what is organising in New Zealand?

The New Zealand experience provides a number of useful insights into the ongoing debate on 'union organising'. It is helpful to consider what it is that New Zealand unions, who say they are organising unions, are doing. What are proving to be the barriers to organising for New Zealand unions? Heery and Simms (2008) noted a range of internal barriers, including lack of resources, ineffective methods, internal opposition and competing priorities, and finally, internal management issues. Given the low levels of density in the private sector, currently around 13%, does that therefore mean that organising is likely to be a failure or does it indicate that union membership and activity is essentially a public sector phenomenon?

There are three key factors that have shaped the New Zealand response to organising and which are separate from that which has occurred in other Anglo-Saxon nations, New Zealand's closest comparators. First is the 'question' of scale. The New Zealand movement is small and frag- mented. With a total membership of just under 400,000, New Zealand has 169 registered unions, half of whom have less than 100 members (DOL 2008). This is a direct result of the legislative requirements that only registered unions can collectively bargain on behalf of workers, and to be a registered union there simply needs to comprise more than 15 members, as well as a union needs to be an incorporated society and to fill out an annual membership return with the Department of Labour (DOL 2008). Thus, the bar to creating a union is very low and does not require an extensive organisational base. Rather the formation of a union can be simply to provide a vehicle for 'negotiating' a collec- tive agreement, or, in reality, accepting the terms of an employer pro- posed agreement, and thus not much else.

Second is the *Employment Contracts Act 1991* legacy, what we describe as 'bargaining agent unionism'. The difficulty of shrugging off the mantle of bargaining agent unionism is one of the main reasons why the New Zealand movement in the private sector has not prospered. Bargaining agent unionism developed in the *Employment Contracts Act* years as unions struggled to maintain their presence and relevance through collective bargaining at an enterprise level against a backdrop of a complete breakdown of industry or sector-wide industrial instru- ments. A bargaining agent union can be defined as a union that just turns up to bargain the (enterprise) agreement and then moves onto the next agreement without any sense of an underpinning or inter- linked strategy for the sector or industry. The union acts essentially as a third party bargaining agent on behalf of its members. Faced with the endless grind of enterprise bargaining, the union essentially does the deal and moves on, hoping that the process might deliver new members but acutely aware that the employer was likely to pass on the benefits of bargaining outcomes to all employees despite their varying union

membership status. While this approach was completely understand-
able during the *Employment Contracts Act* years, unions have become
locked into it and seem unable to effectively break the cycle. Thus, 'servicing' writ large appeared to dominate. Even in industries such as
manufacturing, the Engineering, Printing and Manufacturing Union
(EPMU) struggled to maintain and build on the multi-employer
'metals' agreement. The manufacturing industry in New Zealand was a
relatively cohesive industry with a long tradition of single agreement
coverage negotiated by the EPMU. While this broke down in the *Employment Contracts Act* years, there was still a residual multi-employer agreement. However, it proved very difficult to get additional employer
parties added to the agreement due to strong employer opposition and
a desire by some employees to continue with their 'own' enterprise
agreements. Before explaining the third reason, it is useful to elaborate
upon a number of the issues contained within, and associated with,
the move to enterprise-based bargaining.

The enterprise approach deployed typically mirrored the approach of
'hot shop' organising whereby an organising approach is applied to
particular workplaces on the basis of an issue that has arisen there. It
has been this approach that New Zealand unions have largely relied upon
as their organising approach, but we argue that this reactive approach
lacks any context of an industry or sector-wide strategy. Fundamentally,
it will not work to rebuild union power in New Zealand industries and
sectors. Thus, it is difficult for a union to be powerful in an industry
or sector if it has no capacity to influence and control key industry or
sector-wide transactions – including but not limited to the traditional
wages and conditions. The dynamics of industries or sectors mean that
wages (and other labour costs) cannot be taken out of competition
if the basis for organising and bargaining is enterprise-by-enterprise.
Labour costs get caught up in the relentless pressures of competition
between enterprises. Our preferred approach, nee strategy, is an industry or sectoral one where membership and allied mobilisation exist
around a pro-active agenda for that industry or sector.

Much of the attention of New Zealand unions has been on trying to
build density around bargaining, with most unions experiencing an
increase in membership during bargaining. This means a focus on sites
or enterprises where there is already some level of union membership.
It also accords with the enterprise approach developed in the *Employment Contracts Act* years. The resource demands of organising in the
context of this regime of bargaining leave little room to develop and
implement successful industry or sector-wide campaigns. In these cir-

cumstances, servicing existing members' issues and bargaining pre-dominate over organising initiatives outside in greenfield or brownfield enterprises and sites. Moreover, in the private sector, there has been intense employer opposition to multi-employer collective bargaining. This, combined with the technical difficulties of multi-employer bar-gaining under the *Employment Relations Act 2000*, has dissuaded most unions away from such an industry or sector approach and to continue with enterprise bargaining. By contrast, multi-employer bargaining in the public sector has been more successful. Some of the notable exam-ples are in the health sector and education sector. The campaigns to achieve these collective agreements are usually based on already high levels of union membership with the campaign organising focusing on mobilising those members and activists.

More generally, many New Zealand unions – in both the private and public sector – report continued strong opposition from employers to any role for the union or collective bargaining. It is often stated that employers are still acting as if the *Employment Contracts Act* was still law. This has made it very difficult for unions to extend into greenfield areas as protection of the union's presence in existing areas is foremost. The resource demands of greenfield organising on a consistent basis are beyond most unions while they face constant pressure on their exist-ing sites of organisation. This is despite the various organising rights such as right of entry that are provided under the *Employment Relations Act*. The 2006 strike and subsequent lockout at the distribution centres of the giant Australian owned retail chain, Progressive Enterprises, involving the National Distribution Union (NDU) and EPMU is a good example of just how difficult it has been for unions in New Zealand when confronted by hostile employers intent upon not dealing with unions or collective bargaining.

Another salient aspect of organising is that it is carried out primarily around bargaining campaigns at sites or enterprises where there is already some measure of union density and it has usually involved existing delegates or representatives. It is not common for recruitment to be driven by a systematic contact strategy utilising extensive mapping. Various organising capacity initiatives have been taken up by unions in both the private and public sectors. Membership service centres (call centres) have been picked up by a few large unions and are based pri-marily on the Australian models. In some instances, Australian union call centres have been used for union campaigns. Member organisers have also been utilised by some unions with some success. How-ever, most organising is carried out by EUOs. Delegates or workplace representatives are usually engaged at the time of bargaining to assist with the organising, albeit this does vary considerably between unions. Delegate education is extensively promoted by the NZCTU and paid union education leave is available under the *Employment Relations Act*. The NZCTU also provides an organiser traineeship scheme again closely linked to the Australian *Organising Works* program. This is intended to provide a steady stream into unions of organisers trained extensively in organising skills. Lead organisers are also not common with only a few unions in the private sector using a lead organiser model to lead organising campaigns.

An interesting organising initiative has been the extensive mobilising of young workers by the Unite union. This union has run a number of successful campaigns in the hospitality industry based on activating large numbers of young workers and supporters. While actual numbers of paying union members are low, the campaigns attract and mobilise large numbers of supporters. How to combine the successes of this approach with the practicalities of ongoing servicing of those workers is a matter that is still under consideration. A combination of linking this approach to the resources of a larger union either through direct amalgamation or some other arrangement may be the way forward.

Turning to the third point, and flowing directly from the first two points, is the issue of capacity building and how unions can get beyond capacity building when the ramifications of size, scale, culture and history are difficult to overcome. Most New Zealand unions of any consequence, especially in the private sector, would describe themselves as 'organising' unions largely because of an actual or desired focus on membership. For most unions, there is a wide range of different activities that fall under the rubric of 'organising union'. Generally, however, it draws on a view of increased membership involvement, often through delegates in matters that directly affect them, the so-called 'hot shop' or 'hot issue' approach focusing on existing members, but using the issue to encourage new membership by advertising the union's relevance. This 'hot issue' approach, combined with the focus on enterprise bargaining where coverage already exists, leaves little room to organise in new areas, or so-called greenfield sites.

Most New Zealand private sector unions can point to some success with this approach with increased participation during bargaining rounds and often a lift in membership. However, this does not translate into a union exercising significant power and influence in the relevant industries or sectors. Unions would certainly claim that without this rallying cry they may not have survived the last few decades as they did, but many unions typically struggle to get beyond this point. The extension of organising into changing the union's internal systems and redirecting resources into organising has been difficult because of the ongoing demands of servicing and bargaining.

There has been a very low take up of organising teams directed only to membership growth. The ongoing servicing and bargaining demands leave little room to transfer resources into new growth areas. In trying to deal with this resource dilemma, some unions like the finance union, Finsec, and the Service and Food Workers Union (SFWU) have gone to their members and successfully sought an additional increase in union fees devoted solely to organising for growth. This has had some success in increasing resources for growth. But again, this has been devoted to increasing membership within existing areas of coverage either through infill organising or organising in non-union enterprises in an industry or sector where there is already some level of union membership in other enterprises.

Specialist servicing through deploying call centres or specialised industrial officers is rare. Scale is a problem due to the high establishment costs of membership service centres. Also many unions struggle with the internal systemic changes necessary to move to this more specialist approach. EUO resistance to these changes in some cases is also high. These negative factors represent yet another version of the strong focus on existing sites and the associated servicing and bargaining demands of these sites. As a consequence, EUOs struggle to break through the excessive workloads around enterprise bargaining and, therefore, 'organising' becomes a luxury to which few can devote time.

Furthermore, ongoing restructuring of the private sector, through such factors as globalisation and offshoring often means private sector unions are continually on the backfoot dealing with these impacts. Unfortunately, for many unions the restructuring usually focuses on existing unionised worksites, leaving unions with the dual problem of losing membership and the necessity to organise greenfield sites to replace the membership.

The unions are continually stretched by these changes leaving little time and resources to focus on and develop a more sophisticated industry wide approach. For the New Zealand industry unions such as Finsec and the Dairy Workers' Union (DWU), which only operate in one industry or sector, the development of an industry wide strategy is more advanced than in some of the general unions. The Finsec campaign entitled *Better Banks* focused on all of the major banks and sought to use community and political leverage to improve terms and conditions of employment across the sector through changing the ways that banks operate, for example, performance-based payment systems based on selling an increasing number of bank products and services. The DWU, through its close links with the giant dairy multi-national company, Fonterra, has engaged in significant initiatives around work restructuring. However, in the major general unions – the EPMU, NDU and SFWU – there have been interesting internal changes to allow for a greater focus on an industry-wide approach to their organising and campaigning. The EPMU has internally restructured into a series of industry sections to allow for an organising and campaigning focus in those industries. The NDU has put resources into growth in particular sectors as well as focusing on an industry approach where possible (for example, in retail). The SFWU has devoted considerable resources to building growth and is part of a number of Australasian campaigns with their counterpart union in Australia. These campaigns in the contract cleaning and hospitality industries reflect the trans-Tasman nature of the employers and the need to organise accordingly.

Seen in this light organising has not failed or succeeded in New Zealand because it has not really started. It is still largely at the stage of building capacity for organising – that is, development of lead organisers, membership service centres, a focus on delegates and member activism and so on. Only in isolated instances have private sector unions confronted the realities of industry-wide campaigning to build sustainable power. Indeed, it is most likely that there has been little discussion on what such power would look like. An industry-based approach to building power makes redundant the arguments over whether unions should be 'organising' or 'servicing' unions or whether a move to 'social movement' unionism or 'community' unionism or geographical organising is going to save unionism. Rather, it is a clinical look at what power is, where it can be built, where it can be leveraged and what is necessary to achieve it. It may involve any or all of these different models, just as it may involve political strategies, regulatory strategies as well as capital strategies. But the reality is effective industry-wide comprehensive campaigns utilising a wide range of points of leverage are far beyond the resources of most New Zealand unions. So unions there need to look beyond their own nation-state borders for allies, and with Australia and New Zealand operating as a single labour market, the union movement is beginning to think on the same terms. A good example is the *Clean Start* campaign mounted by the SFWU in New Zealand to organise contract cleaners in central business districts, which was an offshoot of a wider campaign mounted by the Liquor, Hospitality and Miscellaneous Workers Union (LHMU) in Australia with assistance from the American union, the SEIU. This campaign, based on the US *Justice for Janitors* campaign, has demonstrated the success of a sector-wide comprehensive campaigning. Because the resources demanded of these comprehensive campaigns are far beyond those of most New Zealand private sector unions, in the *Clean Start* campaign, the SFWU was able to take part in and access the considerable resources of the other unions. Indeed, the research demands alone that precede these comprehensive campaigns are huge and beyond the capacity of New Zealand unions, making co-operation at the first stage essential.

In contrast to the private sector, there has been considerable growth in union density in the public sector in New Zealand. This reflects the influence of a Labour-led government – both as the employer and in its overall relationships with the unions as well as a number of successful campaigns by unions in the state sector. Despite the ongoing attacks on public sector unions in the 1990s by a hostile government, these unions were able to emerge from that time in better heart and health than the private sector unions. It is possible that these unions were more embedded into their sectors than private sector unions and, hence, more difficult to break or remove. The capacity of public sector unions to act in both the professional and industrial streams in their sectors is also a definite strength which also mirrors experience elsewhere.

It is difficult to generalise about the public sector and the approach there to organising as each union has taken different routes. The Public Sector Association has developed and implemented a number of partner-ship arrangements with the government. In the health sector, vigorous campaigning from the unions has led to a number of multi-employer agreements for specific sub-sectors. In the compulsory part of the education sector, large national agreements have allowed for effective national campaigns. The degree to which the success of these unions is related to that influence, and how the professional and industrial sides meet in campaigns, and on the ground organising, needs to be further explored. A principle issue for these unions is how to prevent the 'siloing' of work in each of these streams. Unions need to leverage their respective strengths in each of these streams and this is best done by using one to leverage the other – for example, using professional issues to create a basis for members and non-members engaging with the union and using that engagement to build membership and activism.

The New Zealand experience to date reveals that the focus on organis-ing as a capacity building exercise within a reactive 'hot shop' context is flawed. There is little or no evidence of a union building sustainable power inside and industry or sector based on this approach. The low state of union density in the private sector even after nine years of a relatively more supportive government indicates the problem(s). The primary focus must rather be on building power in the context of an industry or sector. The problems that most of the New Zealand private sector unions experience derive principally from the fact that they are not powerful players in their industries and sectors – as evidenced by low densities within their sectors and, thus, low influence. Unions in the retail sector are a case in point, despite an impressive 24% increase in membership during 2006, density is incredibly low at around 5%, fuelled in part by strong labour market growth. In contrast, many of the public sector unions have high density and are seen as powerful in their sectors. Important variables here are employer attitudes, employment structure, employee composition and receptiveness to political campaigning.

Conclusion

The New Zealand union movement came through the *Employment Contracts Act* years leaner but more focused. Part of the change in focus was a shift to some hybrid version of 'organising'. The NZCTU promoted and resourced this approach. The approach has tended to languish, however, as it has not got past the capacity building elements of organising, and struggles against the demands of continuous enterprise bargaining. It seems that in the absence of extensive legislation prescribing a broader set of union rights than exist at present, the only effective approach in the New Zealand context is to develop the scale of operation and presence to allow for the development and implementation of effective industry or sector-wide campaigning and organising that can transcend the lack of institutional support. But as industries change, even the benefits allowed to single-industry unions of a single-industry focus are being lost though. This is shown up most clearly in logistics where the move from a transport focus to a total logistics focus challenges the capacity of the existing unions who are each narrowly focused in one particular part of the logistics chain.

The union movement now needs to take up the challenges of organising and campaigning in the context of an industry or sector strategy to build power. This requires both resources and leadership. Demarcation matters must be addressed to allow an effective singular focus on a particular industry or sector. The necessary scale is lacking and the movement must confront the urgent need to build that scale through further amalgamations. These amalgamations can be domestic or international. Some progress is being made in a possible amalgamation of two of the larger general unions – NDU and SFWU. Australia is an obvious place to look for international amalgamations. Most New Zealand unions have close relationships to their Australian counterparts and already there is in many sectors ongoing sharing of information and sometimes resources. While this is evolutionary in approach, maybe fresh initiatives could be looked at. One of the interesting developments is the Australian Media, Entertainment and Arts Alliance (MEAA) setting up a branch in New Zealand to organise New Zealand actors. This is in response to the reality that this sector does operate as a genuinely trans-Tasman labour market. A further longstanding example is the close relationships between the transport unions on both sides of the Tasman. Driven primarily by the maritime sector unions on both sides, many unions now belong to the trans-Tasman Transport Unions Federation. Again in the transport/logistics sector, the market is seen as a single market and the unions needed to respond accordingly. But whether that results in trans-Tasman amalgamations is a secondary issue to effective collaboration and resource sharing.

Despite government initiatives in renationalising significant parts of the economy – New Zealand rail, Air New Zealand, the accident compensation system and creating new government owned institutions such as Kiwibank – the economy is still very closely linked to the Australian economy and further liberalisation of labour and services between the two countries will only further that link. It is now widely accepted that there is a single trans-Tasman labour market and union organising needs to reflect that reality. Ultimately though, the answer must be found in the first instance within the New Zealand movement itself. If it is to break out of is current depressed state (especially in the private sector) then New Zealand unions, through the NZCTU, must confront the hard domestic issues around lack of scale of resource.

References

Adams, R. (2003) 'The revolutionary potential of *Dunmore*', *Canadian Labour and Employment Law Journal*, 10/1: 117–134.

Adams, R. (2006) *Labour Left Out*, Canadian Centre for Policy Alternatives, Ottawa.

AFL-CIO (1994) *The New American Workplace: a labor perspective*, Committee on the Evolution of Work, AFL-CIO, Washington, DC.

Akyeampong, E. (1999) 'Unionization – an update', *Perspectives on Labour and Income*, Autumn (Statistics Canada, Catalogue no. 75-001-XPE), pp.45–65.

Anderson, G. (1991) '*The Employment Contracts Act 1991*: an employers' charter?', *New Zealand Journal of Industrial Relations*, 16/2: 127–142

Australian Bureau of Statistics (1996) 'Trade union statistics', Catalogue 6323.0 <www.abs.gov.au/AUSSTATS/abs@.nsf/DetailsPage/6323.0June%201996?Open Document>.

Australian Bureau of Statistics (2000) 'Australian social trends', Catalogue 4102.0 <www.abs.gov.au/ausstats/abs@.nsf/2f762f95845417aeca25706c00834efa/243 31db49dae9bb4ca2570ec000e4155!OpenDocument>.

Australian Bureau of Statistics (2006) 'Employee earnings, benefits and union membership', Catalogue 6310.0 <www.abs.gov.au/AUSSTATS/abs@.nsf/Previous-products/6310.0Main%20Features2Aug%202006?opendocument&tabname= Summary&prodno=6310.0&issue=Aug%202006&num=&view=>.

Bacon, N. and Blyton, P. (2004) 'Trade union responses to workplace restructuring: exploring union orientations and actions', *Work, Employment and Society*, 18/4: 749–773.

Bacon, N. and Blyton, P. (2006) 'The effects of co-operating or conflicting over work restructuring: evidence from employees', *Sociological Review*, 51/1: 1–19.

Bacon, N. and Blyton, P. (2007) 'Conflict for mutual gains', *Journal of Management Studies*, 44/5: 814–834.

Bacon, N. and Samuel, P. (2007) 'Partnership agreements: adoption, form and survival in Britain', paper presented to the International Industrial Relations Association, 8th European Congress, University of Manchester.

Bagdigannavar, V. and Kelly, J. (2005) 'Why are some union organising campaigns more successful than others?', *British Journal of Industrial Relations*, 43/3: 515–536.

Bagwell, P. (1963) *The Railwaymen: the history of the national union of railwaymen*, Allen and Unwin, London.

Bagwell, P. (1982) *The Railwaymen: the history of the national union of railwaymen – Volume 2 –The Beeching Era and After*, Allen and Unwin, London.

Balanoff, T. (1985) 'The cement workers' experience', *Labor Research Review*, 7: 5–32.

Balibar, E. (1996) *The Philosophy of Marx*, Verso, London.

Banks, A. and Metzgar, J. (2005) 'Response to "Unions as Social Capital"', *Labor Studies Journal*, 29/4: 27–35.

Barrett, S. (2003) '*Dunmore v. Ontario (Attorney General)*: Freedom of Association at the Crossroads', *Canadian Labour and Employment Law Journal*, 10/1: 83–116.

Barry, M. and May, R. (2002) 'New employee representation: legal developments and New Zealand unions', *Employee Relations* 26/2: 203–223.

Batstone, E., Boraston, I. and Frenkel, S. (1977) *Shop Stewards in Action: the organisation of workplace conflict and accommodation*, Blackwell, Oxford.

Batstone, E., Boraston, I. and Frenkel, S. (1978) *The Social Organisation of Strikes*, Blackwell, Oxford.

Beckwith, K. (2000) 'Hinges in collective action: strategic innovation in the Pittstown coal strike', *Mobilization*, 5/2: 179–200.

Behrens, M., Hamman, K. and Hurd, R. (2004) 'Conceptualizing labour union revitalization' in Frege, C. and Kelly, J. (eds) *Varieties of Unionism: strategies for union revitalisation in a globalising economy*, Oxford University Press, Oxford, pp.11–29.

Bentham, K. (2002) 'Employer resistance to union certification', *Relations Industrielles*, 57/1: 159–187.

Berlin, M. (2006) *Never on Our Knees: a history of the RMT 1979–2006*, Pluto Press, London.

Beynon, H. (1984) *Working for Ford*, second edition, Penguin, London.

Boxall, P. (1991) 'New Zealand's Employment Contracts Act 1991: an analysis of background, provisions and implications', *Australian Bulletin of Labour*, 17/4: 284–309.

Boxall, P. and Haynes, P. (1997) 'Strategy and trade union effectiveness in a neo-liberal environment', *British Journal of Industrial Relations*, 35/4: 567–591.

Bronfenbrenner, K. (1997) 'The role of union strategies in NLRB certification elections', *Industrial and Labor Relations Review*, 50/2: 195–212.

Bronfenbrenner, K. (2005) 'Organizing women: the nature and process of union-organizing efforts among US women workers since the mid-1990s', *Work and Occupations*, 32/4: 441–463.

Bronfenbrenner, K. (2007) (ed.) *Global Union: challenging transnational capital through cross-border campaigns*, ILR Press, New York.

Bronfenbrenner, K. and Hickey, R. (2004) 'Changing to organize: a national assessment of union organizing strategies' in Milkman, R. and Voss, K. (eds) *Organize or Die: labor's prospects in neoliberal America*, Cornell University Press, Ithaca, pp.17–61.

Bronfenbrenner, K. and Juravich, T. (1998) 'It takes more than house calls: organising to win with a comprehensive union-building strategy' in Bronfenbrenner, K., Friedman, S., Hurd, R., Oswald, R. and Seeber, R. (eds) *Organising to Win – new research on union strategies*, ILR Press, Ithaca, pp.19–36.

Bronfenbrenner, K., Friedman, S., Hurd, R., Oswald, R. and Seeber, R. (1998) *Organising to Win – new research on union strategies*, ILR Press, Ithaca.

Brown, W. (2008) 'The influence of product markets on industrial relations' in Bacon, N., Blyton, P., Fiorito, J. and Heery, E. (eds) *The Sage Handbook of Industrial Relations*, Sage, London, pp.113–128.

Bruce, P. (1989) 'Political parties and labor legislation in Canada and the US' *Industrial Relations*, 28/2: 115–41.

Bryson, A. (2006a) 'Working with dinosaurs? Union effectiveness in Britain' in Gall, G. (ed.) *Union Recognition – organising and bargaining outcomes*, Routledge, London, pp.25–43.

Bryson, A. (2006b) 'Union free-riding in Britain and New Zealand' Discussion Paper 713, Centre for Economic Performance, LSE, London.

Bryson, A. and Freeman, F. (2006) *Worker Needs and Voice in the US and the UK*, NBER Working Paper No. 12310, Cambridge, Mass.

Bryson, A. and Gomez, R. (2003) 'Buying into union membership' in Gospel, H. and Wood, S. (eds) *Representing Workers: trade union recognition and membership in Britain*, Routledge, London, pp.72–91.

Camfield, D. (2007) 'Renewal in Canadian public sector unions: neo-liberalism and union praxis', *Relations Industrielles*, 62/2: 282–304.

Campolieti, M., Riddell, C. and Slinn, S. (2007) 'Labor law reform and the role of delay in union organising: empirical evidence from Canada', *Industrial and Labor Relations Review*, 61/1: 32–58.

Carter, B. (1995) 'A growing divide: Marxist class analysis and the labour process', *Capital and Class*, 55: 33–72.

Carter, B. (2000) 'Adoption of the organising model in British trade unions: some evidence from Manufacturing, Science and Finance (MSF)', *Work, Employment and Society*, 14/1: 117–36.

Carter, B. (2006) 'Trade union organizing and renewal: a response to de Turber-ville', *Work, Employment and Society*, 20/2: 415–425.

Carter, B. and Cooper, R. (2002) 'The organizing model and the management of change: a comparative study of unions in Australia and Britain', *Relations Industrielles*, 57/4: 712–742.

Carter, B. and Poynter, G. (1999) 'Unions in a changing climate: MSF and UNISON experiences in the new public sector', *Industrial Relations Journal*, 30/5: 499–513.

Certification Office (2008) *Annual Report of the Certification Officer 2007–2008*, Certification Officer, London.

Charlwood, A. (2003) 'Willingness to unionise amongst non-union workers' in Gospel, H. and Wood, S. (eds) *Representing Workers: trade union recognition and membership in Britain*, Routledge, London, pp.51–71.

Charlwood, A. (2004) 'The new generation of trade union leaders and prospects for union revitalisation' *British Journal of Industrial Relations*, 42/2: 379–398.

Clawson, D. (2003a) *The Next Upsurge: labor and the new social movements*, ILR Press, Ithaca.

Clawson, D. (2003b) 'We shall overcome', *New Labor Forum*, 12/3: 38–48.

Clawson, D. and Clawson, M. (1999) 'What happened to the US labor movement? Union decline and renewal', *Annual Review of Sociology*, 25: 95–119.

Coats, D. (2005) *Raising Lazarus: the future of organized labour*, Fabian Society, London.

Cohen, S. (2006) *Ramparts of Resistance: why workers lost their power and to get it back*, Pluto Press, London.

Colgan, F. and Creegan, C. (2006) 'Organising in banking and insurance' in Gall, G. (ed.) *Union Recognition: organising and bargaining outcomes*, Routledge, London, pp.64–82.

Commons, J. (1909) 'American shoemakers, 1648–1895: a sketch of industrial evolution', *American Economic Review*, 24/1: 39–84.

Cooke, W. (1983) 'Determinants of the outcomes of union certification elections', *Industrial and Labor Relations Review*, 36/3: 402–414.

Cooke, W. (2005) 'Exercising power in a prisoner's dilemma: transnational collective bargaining in an era of corporate globalisation', *Industrial Relations Journal*, 36/4: 283–302.

Cooper, R. (2002) 'To organise wherever the necessity exists: the activities of the organising committee of the Labor Council of NSW, 1900–10', *Labour History*, 83: 43–65.

Cornfield, D. (2007) 'Seeking solidarity ... why, and with whom?' in Evans, P., Turner, L. and Cornfield, D. (eds) *Labor in the New Urban Battlegrounds: local solidarity in a global economy*, Cornell University Press, Ithaca, pp.235–253.

Cornfield, D. and McCammon, H. (2003) (eds) 'Revitalising Labor: global perspective and a research agenda', *Research in the Sociology of Work*, 11/1.

Cornwell, B. and Harrison, J. (2004) 'Union membership and voluntary associations: membership overlap as a case of organizational embeddedness', *American Sociological Review*, 69/6: 862–881.

Cramton, P. and Tracy, J. (1998) 'The use of replacement workers in union contract negotiations: the US experience, 1980–1989', *Journal of Labor Economics*, 16/4: 667–701.

Crawford, A., Harbridge, R. and Walsh, P. (2000) 'Unions and union membership in New Zealand: annual review for 1999' IRC Working Paper 1/99, Victoria University Wellington, New Zealand.

Crosby, M. (2004) 'Running on empty: union fees and what to do about them in Australia and New Zealand' ACTU Organising Centre, ACTU, Melbourne.

Cully, M., Woodland, S., O'Reilly, A. and Dix, G. (1999) *Britain at Work – as depicted by the 1998 Workplace Employee Relations Survey*, Routledge, London.

Danford, A., Richardson, M., Stewart, P., Tailby, S. and Upchurch, M. (2007) 'Capital mobility, job loss and union strategy: the case of the UK aerospace industry', *Labor Studies Journal*, 32/3: 298–318.

Danford, A., Richardson, M., Stewart, P. Tailby, S. and Upchurch, M. (2005) *Partnership and the High Performance Workplace – work and employment relations in the aerospace industry*, Palgrave Macmillan, Basingstoke.

Danford, A., Richardson, M. and Upchurch, M. (2003). *New Unions, New Workplaces – a study of union resilience in the restructured workplace*, Routledge, London.

Darlington, R. (2001) 'Union militancy and left-wing leadership on London Underground', *Industrial Relations Journal*, 32/1: 2–21.

Darlington, R. (2002) 'Shop stewards, leadership, left-wing activism and collective workplace union organisation', *Capital and Class*, 76: 95–126.

Darlington, R. (2007) 'Leadership and union militancy: the case of the RMT', paper presented to the 8th European Congress of the International Industrial Relations, University of Manchester.

Darlington, R. (2008) 'Striking against PPP: RMT organisation in Metronet on London Underground 2003–8', paper presented to British Universities' Industrial Relations Association Conference, University of the West of England, Bristol.

Darlington, R. (2009, forthcoming) 'RMT leadership and union militancy' *Capital and Class*, 98.

Delaney, J., Fiorito, J. and Jarley, P. (1999) 'Evolutionary politics? Union differences and political activities in the 1990s', *Journal of Labor Research*, 20/3: 277–295.

Delaney, J., Jarley, P. and Fiorito, J. (1996) 'Planning for change: determinants of innovation in US national unions', *Industrial and Labor Relations Review*, 49/4: 597–614.

Deleuze, G. (2006) *Nietzsche and Philosophy*, Continuum, London.

Deleuze, G. and Guattari, F. (2003a) *Anti-oedipus – capitalism and schizophrenia*, Continuum, London.

Deleuze, G. and Guattari, F. (2003b) *A Thousand Plateaus – capitalism and schizophrenia*, Continuum, London.

de Turberville, S. (2004) 'Does the 'organizing model' represent a credible union renewal strategy?', *Work, Employment and Society*, 18/4: 775–794.

de Turberville, S. (2007a) 'Union organizing: a response to Carter', *Work, Employment and Society*, 21/3: 565–576.

de Turberville, S. (2007b) 'Reorganising Unison within the NHS', *Employee Relations*, 29/3: 247–262.

de Turberville, S. (2007c) 'Union decline and renewal in Australia and Britain', *Economic and Industrial Democracy*, 28/3: 373–399.

Dixon, M. and Martin, A. (2007) 'Can the labor movement succeed without the strike?', *Contexts*, 6/2: 36–39.

DOL (2008) 'Union Membership return 2007' <www.ers.dol.govt.nz/union/registration.html>.

Doorey, D. (2006) 'Neutrality agreements: bargaining for representation rights in the shadow of the state', *Canadian Labour and Employment Law Journal*, 13/1: 41–105.

DTI (2007) 'Workplace Representatives: a review of their facilities and facility time', Department of Trade and Industry, London.

Dunlop, J. (1948) 'The development of labor organization: a theoretical framework' in Lester, R. and Shister, J. (eds) *Insight into Labor Issues*, Macmillan, New York, pp.163–193.

Dunmore v. Ontario (Attorney General) (2001), 207 D.L.R. (4ᵗʰ) 193 (S.C.C.).

Early, S. (2004a) 'Reutherism redux: what happens when poor workers' unions wear the color purple?', *Against the Current*, 19/4: 31–39.

Early, S. (2004b) 'What happens when poor workers' unions wear the color purple?', *Labornotes*, <www.labornotes.org/archives/2004/09/articles/j.html>.

Easton, B (1994) 'Economic and other ideas behind the New Zealand Reforms', *Oxford Review of Economic Policy*, 10/3: 78–94.

Eaton, A. and Kriesky, J. (2001) 'Union organizing under neutrality and card check agreements', *Industrial and Labor Relations Review*, 55/1: 42–59.

Evans, P., Turner, L. and Cornfield, D. (2007) (eds) *Labor in the New Urban Battlegrounds: local solidarity in a global economy*, Cornell University Press, Ithaca.

Fairbrother, P. (1996) 'Workplace trade unionism in the state sector' in Ackers, P., Smith, C. and Smith, P. (eds) *The New Workplace and Trade Unionism: critical perspectives on work and organisation*, Routledge, London, pp.110–148.

Fairbrother, P. (2000) 'British trade unions facing the future', *Capital and Class*, 71: 47–78.

Fairbrother, P. and Stewart, P. (2005) 'The dilemmas of social partnership and union organisation: questions for British trade unions' in Fairbrother, P. and Yates, C. (eds) *Trade Union Renewal*, Routledge, London, pp.158–179.

Fantasia, R. and Voss, K. (2004) *Hard Work: remaking the American labor movement*, University of California Press, Berkeley.

Feinberg-Danieli, G. and Lafferty, G. (2007) 'Unions and union membership in New Zealand: annual review for 2006', IRC Working Paper, 1/07, Victoria University Wellington, New Zealand.

Findlay, P. and McKinlay, A. (2003) 'Organising in electronics: recruitment, recognition and representation – shadow shop stewards in Scotland's "Silicon Glen"' in Gall, G. (ed.) *Union Organising: campaigning for trade union recognition,* Routledge, London, pp.114–132.

Fine, J. (2006) *Worker Centres: organizing communities at the edge of the dream,* Cornell University Press, Ithaca.

Fiorito, J. (1987) 'Political instrumentality perceptions and desires for union representation', *Journal of Labor Research,* 8/3: 271–289.

Fiorito, J. (2003) 'Union organizing in the United States' in Gall, G. (ed.) *Union Organizing: campaigning for trade union recognition,* Routledge, London, pp.191–210.

Fiorito, J. (2004) 'Union renewal and the organizing model in the United Kingdom', *Labor Studies Journal,* 29/2: 21–53.

Fiorito, J. (2007) 'The state of unions in the United States', *Journal of Labor Research,* 28/1: 43–68.

Fiorito, J., Gramm, C. and Hendricks, W. (1991) 'Union Structural Choices' in Strauss, G., Gallagher, D. and Fiorito, J. (eds) *The State of the Unions,* IRRA, Madison, WI, pp.103–137.

Fiorito, J. and Jarley, P. (2003) 'Union organizing commitment: rhetoric and reality', *Proceedings of the Fifty-fifth Annual Meeting of the Industrial Relations Research Association,* IRRA, Champaign, IL, pp.283–293.

Fiorito, J. and Jarley, P. (2008) 'Union organizing and revitalisation in the US', *Proceedings of the Sixtieth Annual Meeting of the Labor and Employment Relations Association,* LERA, Champaign, IL., in press.

Fiorito, J., Jarley, P. and Delaney, J. (1995) 'National union effectiveness in organizing: measures and influences', *Industrial and Labor Relations Review,* 48/4: 613–635.

Fiorito, J. and Maranto, C. (1987) 'The contemporary decline of union strength', *Contemporary Policy Issues,* 5/3: 12–27.

Flanagan, R. (2005) 'Has management strangled US unions?', *Journal of Labor Research,* 26/1: 33–63.

Fletcher, B. and Hurd, R. (1998) 'Beyond the organizing model: the transformation process in local unions' in Bronfenbrenner, K., Freidman, S., Hurd, R., Oswald, R. and Seeber, R. (eds) *Organizing to Win: new research on union strategies,* Cornell University, Ithaca, NY, pp.37–54.

Foucault, M. (1991) *Discipline and Punish – the birth of the prison,* Penguin Books, London.

Freeman, R. (2007) 'Do workers still want unions? More than ever', EPI Briefing Paper 182, Economic Policy Institute, Washington DC, available at <www.sharedprosperity.org/bp182.html>.

Freeman, R. and Rogers, J. (2002) 'Open source unionism', *WorkingUSA,* 5/4: 8–40.

Freeman, R. and Rogers, J. (1999) *What Workers Want,* Cornell/ILR Press, Ithaca.

Frege, C. and J. Kelly (2004) (eds) *Varieties of Unionism: strategies for union revitalisation in a globalising economy,* Oxford University Press, Oxford.

Gall, G. (2003a) 'Introduction' in Gall, G. (ed.) *Union Organising: campaigning for trade union recognition,* Routledge, London, pp.1–19.

Gall, G. (2003b) 'Organising in the offshore oil and gas industry in Britain, c.1972–1990: a long burning flame or spark that has gone out?' in Gall, G.

(ed.) *Union Organising: campaigning for trade union recognition*, Routledge, London, pp.39–55.

Gall, G. (2003c) 'Conclusion: drawing up a balance sheet' in Gall, G. (ed.) *Union Organising: campaigning for trade union recognition*, Routledge, London, pp.191–210.

Gall, G. (2003d) (ed.) *Union Organising: campaigning for trade union recognition*, Routledge, London.

Gall, G. (2004) 'Trade union recognition in Britain, 1995–2002: turning a corner?', *Industrial Relations Journal*, 35/3: 249–270.

Gall, G. (2005) 'Organised enough', *RMT News*, December, pp.24–25.

Gall, G. (2006a) 'Conclusion: issues and prospects' in Gall, G. (ed.) *Union Recognition: organising and bargaining outcomes*, Routledge, London, pp.232–237.

Gall, G. (2006b) 'The National Union of Journalists and the provincial newspaper industry – from derecognition to recognition to fraught bargaining' in Gall, G. (ed.) *Union Recognition: organising and bargaining outcomes*, Routledge, London, pp.115–133.

Gall, G. (2006c) 'Organising for the future. Today', *RMT News*, September, pp.10–11.

Gall, G. (2007a) 'Trade union recognition in Britain: a crisis of union capacity?', *Economic and Industrial Democracy*, 28/1: 78–109.

Gall, G. (2007b) 'Putting the cool back into trade unionism', *Morning Star*, 26 June, p.7.

Gall, G. (2007c) 'Union membership in Britain: the larger unions – who's up and who's down and why', Research Report No. 11, *Employment Research Service*, Centre for Research in Employment Studies, University of Hertfordshire, Hatfield.

Gall, G. (2007d) 'Turning full circle? Changing industrial relations in the magazine industry in Britain', *Personnel Review*, 36/1: 91–108.

Gall, G. (2008) *Labour unionism in the financial services sector – struggling for rights and recognition*, Ashgate, Aldershot.

Gallagher, D. and Strauss, G. (1991) 'Union membership attitudes and participation' in Strauss, G., Gallagher, D. and Fiorito, J. (eds) *The State of the Unions*, IRRA, Madison, WI, pp.139–174.

Gardner, M. (1995) 'Labour movements and industrial restructuring: Australia, New Zealand and the US' in Wever, K. and Turner, L. (eds) *The Comparative Political Economy of Industrial Relations*, Cornell University Press, Ithaca, NY, pp.33–70.

Glyn, A. (2006) *Capitalism Unleashed: finance, globalisation and welfare*, Oxford University Press, Oxford.

GMB (2007) *GMB Workplace Organisers Tool-kit*, GMB, London.

Gospel H. (2005) 'Markets, firms and unions: a historical-institutionalist perspective on the future of unions in Britain' in Fernie, S. and Metcalf, D. (eds) *Trade Unions: resurgence or demise?*, Routledge, London, pp.19–44.

Government of Ontario (2007) 'McGuinty government announces intention to recognize bargaining rights for part-time college workers' <www.ogov.newswire.ca/ontario/BPOE/2007/08/30/c3948.html>.

Graham, I. (2002) 'It pays to be union, US figures show' <www.ilo.org/public/english/dialogue/actrav/publ/128/>.

Graham, S. (2007) 'Organising out of decline – the rebuilding of Britain and Ireland shop stewards movement', *Union Ideas Network*, available at <www.uin.org.uk>.

Grainger, H. and Crowther, M. (2007) *Trade Union Membership 2006*, Employment Market Analysis and Research, Department of Trade and Industry, London.

Greenhouse, S. (2008) *The Big Squeeze: tough times for the American worker*, Alfred A. Knopf, New York.

Greer, I., Stuart, M. and Greenwood, I. (2008) 'Community unionism as a revitalisation strategy? A British case of Innovation', paper presented 103rd *American Sociological Association Annual Meeting: World of Work*, Boston.

Guard, J., Garcia-Orgales, J., Steedman, M. and Martin, D. (2006) 'Organising call centres: the steelworkers' experience' in Kumar, P. and Schenk, C. (eds) *Paths to Union Renewal: Canadian experiences*, Broadview Press, Toronto, pp.277–292.

Halsey, A. (1988) *British Social Trends since 1900*, Macmillan, London.

Harbridge, R. and Honeybone, R. (1996) 'External legitimacy of unions: trends in New Zealand', *Journal of Labour Research*, 17/3: 425–444.

Haynes, P. and Allen, M. (2001) 'Partnership as union strategy: a preliminary evaluation', *Employee Relations*, 23/2: 164–187.

Haynes, P., Vowles, J. and Boxall, P. (2005) 'Explaining the younger-older worker union density gap: evidence from New Zealand', *British Journal of Industrial Relations*, 43/1: 93–116.

Heery, E. (2002) 'Partnership versus organizing: alternative futures for British trade unionism', *Industrial Relations Journal*, 33/1: 20–35.

Heery, E. (2003) 'Trade unions and industrial relations' in Ackers, P. and Wilkinson, A. (eds), *Understanding Work and Employment*, Oxford University Press, Oxford, pp.278–304.

Heery, E. (2005) 'Sources of change in trade unions', *Work, Employment and Society*, 19/1: 91–106.

Heery, E. (2006) 'Union workers, union work: a profile of paid union officers in the United Kingdom', *British Journal of Industrial Relations*, 44/3: 445–471.

Heery, E. (2008) 'A profile of union officers', *Forefront*, 7: 5, Unions 21, London.

Heery, E. and Kelly, J. (1994) 'Professional, participative and managerial unionism: an interpretation of change in trade unions', *Work, Employment and Society* 8/1: 1–22.

Heery, E. and Simms, M. (2008) 'Constraints on union organizing in the United Kingdom', *Industrial Relations Journal*, 39/1: 24–42.

Heery, E., Simms, M., Delbridge, R., Salmon, J. and Simpson, D. (2000a) 'Union organizing in Britain: a survey of policy and practice', *International Journal of Human Resource Management*, 11/5: 986–1007.

Heery, E., Simms, M., Delbridge, R., Salmon, J. and Simpson, D. (2000b) 'The TUC's *Organizing Academy*: an assessment', *Industrial Relations Journal*, 31/5: 400–415.

Heery, E., Simms, M., Simpson, D., Delbridge, R. and Salmon, J. (2000c). 'Organizing unionism comes to the UK', *Employee Relations*, 22/1: 38–57.

Heery, E., Simms, M., Delbridge, R., Salmon, J. and Simpson, D. (2003a) 'Trade union recruitment policy in Britain: form and effects', in G. Gall (ed.) *Union Organising: campaigning for trade union recognition*, Routledge, London, pp.56–78.

Heery, E., Delbridge, R., Simms, M., Salmon, J. and Simpson, D. (2003b) 'Organising for renewal: a case study of the UK's Organising Academy' in D. Cornfield and H. McCammon (eds) *Labor Revitalization: global perspectives and new initiatives*, Elsevier, Oxford, pp.79–110.

Heery, E., Delbridge, R. and Simms, M. (2003c) *The Organizing Academy – five years on*, Trade Union Congress, London.

Heery, E., Kelly, J. and Waddington, J. (2002) 'Union revitalization in the United Kingdom', *International Institute for Labour Studies Discussion Paper*, Geneva.

Heery, E., Kelly, J. and Waddington, J. (2003) 'Union revitalization in Britain', *European Journal of Industrial Relations*, 9/1: 79–97.

Hendy, J. and Gall, G. (2006) 'Workers' rights today and the Trade Union Freedom Bill' in Hendy, J. (ed.) *The Right to Strike: from the Trades Disputes Act 1906 to a Trade Union Freedom Bill 2006*, Institute of Employment Rights, London, pp.247–278.

Hinton, J. (1973) *The First Shop Stewards' Movement*, George Allen & Unwin, London.

Hirsch, B. and Macpherson, D. (2003) 'Union membership and coverage database from the current population survey: note', *Industrial and Labor Relations Review*, 56/1: 349–54.

Hirsch, B. and Macpherson, D. (2007) 'Union coverage and membership database', <www.trinity.edu/bhirsch/unionstats/>.

Hirsch, B. and Macpherson, D. (2008) 'Union membership and coverage database from CPS', <unionstats.gsu.edu/contents.htm>.

Hobsbawm, E. (1981) 'The forward march of labour halted?' in Jacques, M. and Mulhearn, F. (eds) *The Forward March of Labour Halted?*, Verso, London, pp.1–19.

Holgate, J. (2009, forthcoming) 'Contested terrain: London's living wage campaign and the tensions between community and union organising' in Macbride, J. and Greenwood, I. (eds), *Community Unionism: a comparative analysis of concepts and contexts*, Palgrave, Basingstoke.

Holgate, J. and Simms, M. (2008) *The Impact of the Organising Academy on the Union Movement*, TUC, London.

Howells, K. (2006) *Trade Unions and the State: the construction of industrial relations institutions in Britain 1890–2000*, Princeton University Press, Princeton.

Hurd, R. (1998) 'Contesting the dinosaur image: the labor movements search for a future', *Labor Studies Journal*, 22/4: 5–30.

Hyman, R. (1989) *The Political Economy of Industrial Relations: theory and practice in a cold climate*, Macmillan, London.

Hyman, R. (2007) 'How can trade unions act strategically?', *Transfer*, 13/2: 193–210.

Hyman, R. and Fryer, R. (1977) 'Trade unions: sociology and political economy' in Clark, T. and Clements, L. (eds) *Trade Unions under Capitalism*, Fontana, Glasgow, pp.162–165.

Institute for Employment Research/University of Warwick (2006) *Working Futures: 2004–2014*, London/Coventry.

Isaac, L. and Christiansen, L. (2002) 'How the civil rights movement revitalized labor militancy', *American Sociological Review*, 67/5: 722–746.

Isaac, L., McDonald, S. and Lukasik, G. (2006) 'Takin' it from the streets: how the sixties mass movement revitalized unionization', *American Journal of Sociology*, 112/1: 46–96.

Jackson, A. (2006) 'Rowing against the tide: the struggle to raise union density in a hostile environment' in Kumar, P. and Schenk, C. (eds) *Paths to Union Renewal: Canadian experiences*, Broadview Press, Toronto, pp.61–78.

Jackson, H. (2004) *SEIU: Big Brother? Big Business? Big Rip Off?* AuthorHouse, New York.

Jacobs, D. and Dixon, M. (2006) 'The politics of labor-management relations: detecting the conditions that affect changes in right-to-work laws', *Social Problems*, 53/1: 118–137.

Jarley, P. and Maranto, C. (1990) 'Union corporate campaigns: an assessment', *Industrial and Labor Relations Review*, 43/5: 505–524.

Jenkins, J. (2006) '"Robust" partnership: processes and outcomes', paper presented to the British Universities Industrial Relations Association Conference, National University of Ireland, Galway.

Jenkins, J. (2007) 'Gambling partners? The risky outcomes of workplace partnerships', *Work, Employment and Society*, 21/4: 635–652.

Johnson, S. (2002) 'Card check or mandatory vote? How the type of recognition procedure affects union certification success', *The Economic Journal*, 112/479: 344–361.

Johnson, S. (2004) 'The impact of mandatory votes on the Canada-US union density gap: a note', *Industrial Relations*, 43/2: 356–63.

Johnson, S. (2007) 'Unfair labour practices in Canada 1975–2005: empirical evidence', paper presented at the 44th Annual Meeting of the Canadian Industrial Relations Association, Calgary.

Jordan, L. and Bruno, B. (2006) 'Does the organising means determine the bargaining ends?' in Gall, G. (ed.) *Union Recognition: organising and bargaining outcomes*, Routledge, London, pp.181–197.

Jowell, R., Curtice, J., Park, A., Brook, L., Thompson, K. and Bryson, A. (1997) (eds) *British Social Attitudes*, Gower/Dartmouth, Aldershot.

Juravich, T. and Bronfenbrenner, K. (1999) *The Steel Workers Victory and the Revival of American Labor*, Cornell University Press, Ithaca, NY.

Kay, T. (2005) 'Labor transnationalism and global governance: the impact of NAFTA on transnational labor relationships in north America', *American Journal of Sociology*, 111/3: 715–756.

Kelly, J. (1988) *Trade Unions and Socialist Politics*, Verso, London.

Kelly, J. (1996) 'Union militancy and social partnership' in Ackers, P., Smith, C. and Smith, P. (eds) *The New Workplace and Trade Unionism: critical perspectives on work and organisation*, Routledge, London, pp.77–109.

Kelly, J. (1998) *Rethinking Industrial Relations: mobilization, collectivism and long waves*, Routledge, London.

Kelly, J. (2001) 'Social partnership agreements in Britain: union revitalisation or employer counter-mobilisation?' in Martinez Lucio, M. and Stuart, M. (eds) *Assessing Partnership: the prospects for and challenges of 'modernisation'* LUBS, Leeds University, Leeds.

Kelly, J. (2004) 'Social partnership agreements in Britain: labour co-operation and compliance', *Industrial Relations*, 43/1: 267–92.

Kelly, J. (2005) 'Social movement theory and revitalization in Britain' in Fernie, S. and Metcalf, D. (eds) *Trade Unions: resurgence or demise?* Routledge, London, pp.62–82.

Kelly, J. and Heery, E. (1989) 'Full-time officers and trade union recruitment', *British Journal of Industrial Relations*, 27/2: 196–213.

Kelly, J. and Heery, E. (1994) *Working for the Union: British trade union officers*, Cambridge University Press, Cambridge.

Kelsey, J. (2005) *The New Zealand Experiment: a world model for structural adjustment*, Auckland University Press, Auckland.

Kennett, J. (2006) 'Houston's janitors win contract with civil defiance' available at <bloomberg.com/apps/news?pid=20601103&sid=ahYAZgBalkXQ&refer=us>.

Kersley, B., Alpin, C. Forth, J., Bryson, A., Bewley, H., Dix, G. and Oxenbridge, S. (2006) *Inside the Workplace: findings from the 2004 Workplace Employment Relations Survey*, Routledge, London.

Kiefer, H. (2005) 'Public remains positive about unions' Gallup Poll News Service, <www.gallup.com/poll/18481/Public-Remains-Positive-About-Labor-Unions.aspx>.

Kloosterboer, D. (2007) *Innovative Union Strategies*, FNV, Amsterdam.

Kochan, T. (1979) 'How American workers view labor unions', *Monthly Labor Review*, 104/4: 23–31.

Kochan, T. (1980) *Collective Bargaining and Industrial Relations*, Richard D. Irwin, Homewood, IL.

Kumar, P., Murray, G. and Schetagne, S. (1998) 'Adapting to change: union priorities in the 1990s' in *Directory of Labour Organisations in Canada 1998*, Canada Government Printing, Ottawa, pp.25–56.

Kumar, P. and Murray, G. (2006) 'Innovation in Canadian unions: patterns, causes and consequences' in Kumar, P. and Schenk, C. (eds) *Paths to Union Renewal: Canadian experiences*, Broadview Press, Toronto, pp.79–102.

Kumar, P. and Schenk, C. (2006) 'Union renewal and organisational change: a review of the literature' in Kumar, P. and Schenk, C. (eds) *Paths to Union Renewal: Canadian experiences*, Broadview Press, Toronto, pp.29–60.

Labor Research Review (1985) 'New Tactics for Labor', 7.

Labour Research (2004) 'Union members pay less in UK', 98/4: 22–23.

Laclau, E. and Mouffe, C. (1985) *Hegemony and Socialist Strategy: towards a radical democratic politics*, Verso, London.

Lancaster House (2007) 'Analysis: Supreme Court reverses direction, extends *Charter* protection to collective bargaining', *Labour Law On-Line*, June 11, pp.1–7.

Leach, D. (2005) 'The iron law of *what* again? Conceptualizing oligarchy across organizational forms', *Sociological Theory*, 23/3: 312–337.

Lerner, S. (2003) 'An immodest proposal', *New Labor Forum*, 12/2: 7–30.

Lerner, S. (2007) 'Global corporations, global unions', *Contexts*, 6/3: 16–22.

Lévesque, C., Murray, G. and Le Queux, S. (2005) 'Union disaffection and social identity', democracy as a source of union revitalization', *Work and Occupations*, 32/4: 400–422.

Lipset, S. and Meltz, N. (2004) *The Paradox of American Unionism*, Cornell/ILR Press, Ithaca.

Lipset, S. and Schneider, W. (1983) *The Confidence Gap: business, labor, and government in the public mind*, Free Press, New York.

Locke, R. and Thelen, K. (1995) 'Apples and oranges revisited: contextualized comparisons and the study of labor politics', *Politics and Society*, 23/3: 337–367.

Logan, J. (2002) 'Consultants, lawyers, and the 'union free' movement in the USA since the 1970s', *Industrial Relations*, 33/3: 197–214.

Logan, J. (2008) *U.S. Anti-Union Consultants: a threat to the rights of British workers*, TUC, London.

Lopez, S. (2004a) *Reorganizing the Rustbelt*, University of California Press, Berkeley.

Lopez, S. (2004b) 'Looking in the wrong place: a reply to Clawson', *New Labor Forum*, 13/1: 4–7.

Luce, S. (2004) *Fighting for a Living Wage*, Cornell University Press, Ithaca.

Luce, S. (2005) 'Lessons from living wage campaigns', *Work and Occupations*, 32/4: 423–440.

McCammon, H. (2001) 'Labor's legal mobilization: why and when do workers file unfair labor practices?', *Work and Occupations*, 28/2: 143–175.

McIlroy, J. (1995) *Trade Unions in Britain Today*, Manchester University Press, Manchester.

McIlroy, J. (2008) 'Ten years of new Labour: workplace learning, social partnership and union revitalization in Britain', *British Journal of Industrial Relations*, 46/2: 283–313.

Martin, A. (2007) 'Organizational structure, authority, and protest: the case of union organizing in the United States, 1990–2001', *Social Forces* 85/3: 1413–1435.

Martin, A. (2008) 'The institutional logic of union organizing and the effectiveness of social movement repertoires', *American Journal of Sociology*, 113/4: 1067–1103.

Martin, A. and Dixon, M. (2007) 'Changing to win? Unions and strikes in the US, 1984–2002', paper presented at the *American Sociological Association Meetings*, New York.

Martinello, F. (2000) 'Mr. Harris, Mr. Rae and union activity in Ontario', *Canadian Public Policy*, 26/1: 1–17.

Martinez Lucio, M. and Stuart, M. (2004) 'Swimming against the tide: social partnership, mutual gains and the revival of "tired" HRM', *International Journal of Human Resource Management*, 15/2: 410–424.

Martinez Lucio, M. and Stuart, M. (2005) '"Partnership" and the new industrial relations in a risk society: an age of shotgun weddings and marriages of convenience?', *Work, Employment and Society*, 19/4: 797–817.

Martínez Lucio, M. and Perrett, R. (2006) *Linking up? The different realities of community unionism*, Bradford University School of Management, Working Paper Series 06/26.

Martinez Lucio, M., Perrett, R., McBride, J. and Craig, S. (2007) *Migrant Workers in the Labour Market: the role of unions in the recognition of skills and qualifications*, Research Series, No. 7, TUC unionlearn, London.

Marx, K. (1992) *Karl Marx. Early Writings*, Penguin Group, London.

Marx. K. (2007) *Dispatches for the New York Tribune: selected journalism of Karl Marx*, Penguin, London.

Masters, M. (1997) *Unions at the Crossroads*, Quorum Books, Westport.

Masters, M. and Delaney, J. (2005) 'Organized labor's political scorecard', *Journal of Labor Research* 26/3: 365–392.

May, R., Walsh, P., Harbridge, R. and Thickett, G. (2002) 'Unions and union membership in New Zealand: annual review for 2001', *New Zealand Journal of Industrial Relations*, 27/3: 307–321.

May, R. and Walsh, P. (2002) 'Union organising in New Zealand: making the most of the new environment?', *International Journal of Employment Studies*, 10/2: 157–180.

Members for Democracy Archive (2008) 'Why the SEIU's Andy Stern is full of shit' <www.m-f-d.org/article/general/mahz0qy2j1m.php>.

Mercer, S. and Notley, R. (2008) *Trade Union Membership 2007*, Department of Business, Enterprise and Regulatory Reform/National Statistics, London.

Metcalf, D. (2003) 'Trade unions' in Dickens, R., Gregg, P. and Wadsworth, J. (eds) *The Labour Market under New Labour: the state of working Britain*, Palgrave, Basingstoke, pp.170–190.

Metcalf, D. (2005) *British Unions: resurgence or perdition?* Provocation Series 1/1, Work Foundation, London.

Milkman, R. (2006) *L.A. Story: immigrant workers and the future of the US labor movement*, Russell Sage Foundation, New York.

Milkman, R. and Voss, K. (2004) 'Introduction' in Milkman, R. and Voss, K. (eds) *Rebuilding Labor: organising and organisers in the new union movement*, ILP Press, Ithaca, NY, pp.1–16.

Moody, K. (2007) *US Labor in Trouble and Transition: the failure of reform from above and the promise of revival from below*, Verso, New York.

Nelligan O'Brien, P. (2007) 'Supreme Court of Canada rules on constitutional rights of union members', *Labour Law*, 16/7: 156–159.

Nissen, B. (1998) 'Utilizing the membership to organize the unorganized' in Bronfenbrenner, K., Freidman, S., Hurd, R., Oswald, R. and Seeber, R. (eds) *Organizing to Win: new research on union strategies*, Cornell University, Ithaca, NY, pp.135–149.

Nissen, B. (2002) 'The role of education in transforming a union toward organizing immigrants: a case study', *Labor Studies Journal*, 27/1: 109–127.

Nissen, B. (2003) 'Alternative strategic directions for the US labor movement: recent scholarship', *Labor Studies Journal*, 28/1: 133–155.

Nissen, B. (2004) 'The effectiveness and limits of labor-community coalitions: evidence from south Florida', *Labor Studies Journal*, 29/1: 67–89.

Nissen, B. and Rosen, S. (1999) 'The CWA model of membership based organizing', *Labor Studies Journal*, 24/1: 73–88.

Ontario Labour Relations Board (1992–2006) *Annual Report*, Queen's Printer, Toronto.

Powell, N. (2008) 'United Steelworkers abandon Dofasco in-house campaign', *The Hamilton Spectator* <thespec.com/printArticle/342333>.

Oxenbridge, S. (1998) *Running to Stand Still: New Zealand service sector labour union responses to the Employment Contracts Act 1991*, PhD thesis, Victoria University of Wellington, New Zealand.

Oxenbridge, S. and Brown, W. (2004) 'A poisoned chalice? Trade union representatives in partnerships and co-operative union-employer relationships' in Healy, G., Heery, E., Taylor, P. and Brown, W. (eds) *The Future of Worker Representation*, Palgrave, Basingstoke, pp.187–206.

Oxenbridge, S. and Brown, W. (2005) 'Developing partnership relationships: a case of leveraging power' in Stuart, M. and Martinez Lucio, M. (eds) *Partnership and the Modernisation of Employment Relations*, Routledge, London, pp.83–100.

PCS (2008) *National Organising Strategy 2008*, PCS, London.

Peetz, D. (1998) *Unions in a Contrary World: the future of the Australian labour union movement*, Cambridge University Press, Melbourne.

Perrett, R. (2007) 'Worker voice in the context of the re-regulation of employment: employer tactics and statutory union recognition in the UK', *Work, Employment and Society*, 21/4: 617–634.

Piven, F. and Cloward, R. (1977) *Poor People's Movements: why they succeed, how they fail*, Pantheon Books, New York.

Rachleff, P. (2003) 'Is the strike dead?', *New Labor Forum*, 12/2: 86–95.

Riddell, C. (2001) 'Union suppression and certification success', *Canadian Journal of Economics*, 34/2: 396–410.

Riddell, C. (2004) 'Union certification success under voting versus card-check procedures: evidence from British Columbia, 1978–1998', *Industrial and Labor Relations Review*, 57/4: 493–517.

Rooks, D. (2004) 'Sticking it out or packing it in? Organizer retention in the new labor movement' in Milkman, R. and Voss, K. (eds) *Rebuilding Labor: organizing and organizing in the new union movement*, Cornell University Press, Ithaca, pp.195–224.

Rose, J. (1995) 'The evolution of public sector unionism' in Swimmer, G. and Thompson, M. (eds) *Public Sector Collective Bargaining in Canada: beginning of the end or end of the beginning?* IRC Press, Queen's University, Kingston, pp.20–52.

Rose, J. (2000) 'From softball to hardball: the transition in labour-management relations in the Ontario public service' in Swimmer, G. (ed.) *Public-sector Labour Relations in an Era of Restraint and Restructuring*, Oxford University Press, Don Mills, pp.66–95.

Rose, J. (2006) 'Collective bargaining performance of newly certified unions in Canada' in Gall G. (ed.) *Union Recognition: organising and bargaining outcomes*, Routledge, London, pp.198–214.

Rose, J. and Chaison, G. (1995) 'Canadian labor policy as a model for legislative reform in the US', *Labor Law Journal*, 46/5: 259–272.

Rose, J. and Chaison, G. (1996) 'Linking union density and union effectiveness: the North American experience', *Industrial Relations*, 35/1: 78–105.

Rose, J. and Chaison, G. (2001) 'Unionism in Canada and the US in the 21st century: the prospects for revival', *Relations Industrielles*, 56/1: 34–65.

Rosenfeld, J. (2006) 'Desperate measures: strikes and wages in post-Accord America', *Social Forces*, 85/1: 235–266.

Rubin, B. (1986) 'Class struggle American-style: unions, strikes, and wages', *American Sociological Review*, 51/5: 618–631.

Samuel, P. (2007) 'Partnership consultation and employer domination in two British life and pensions firms', *Work, Employment and Society*, 21/3: 459–477.

Schenk, C. (2003) 'Social movement unionism: beyond the organising model' in Fairbrother, P. and Yates, C. (eds) *Trade Unions in Renewal: a comparative study*, Routledge, London, pp.244–262.

Silver, B. (2003) *Forces of Labor*, Cambridge University Press, Cambridge.

Simms, M. (2003) 'Union organizing in a not-for-profit organization' in Gall, G. (ed.) *Union Organizing: campaigning for trade union recognition*, Routledge, London, pp.97–113.

Simms, M. (2007a) 'Interest formation in greenfield union organising campaigns', *Industrial Relations Journal*, 38/5: 439–454.

Simms, M. (2007b) '"What are we organising for?" The influence of trade union tactics on Greenfield organising campaign effectiveness', paper presented to the 8th European Congress of the International Industrial Relations Association, University of Manchester.

Simms, M. and J. Holgate (2008) 'Is there an organising "model"? An empirical critique', paper presented British Universities' Industrial Relations Association Conference, University of West of England, Bristol.

Slinn, S. (2003) 'The effect of compulsory certification votes on certification applications in Ontario: an empirical analysis', *Canadian Labour and Employment Law Journal*, 10/3: 367–397.

Smeaton, D. and Bryson, A. (2008) 'Union organising – taking the first steps', Unpublished report for the TUC, London.

Smith, P. and Morton, G. (2001) '"New" Labour's reform of Britain's employment law: the devil is not only in the detail but in the values and policy too', *British Journal of Industrial Relations*, 39/1: 119–138.

Statistics Canada (2007) 'Unionization', *Perspectives on Labour and Income*, 8/8: 18–42.

Stinson, J. and Ballantyne, M. (2006) 'Union renewal and CUPE' in Kumar, P. and Schenk, C. (eds) *Paths to Union Renewal: Canadian experiences*, Broadview Press, Toronto, pp.145–160.

Stirling, J. (2005) 'There's a new world somewhere: the rediscovery of trade unionism', *Capital and Class*, 87: 43–63.

Stuart, M. (2005) *Learning in Partnership: responding to the restructuring of the European steel and metal sector*, Final Report for Fifth Framework Socio-Economic Key Action Award, European Commission DG Research, Brussels.

Stuart, M. (2007) 'The industrial relations of learning and training: a new consensus or a new politics', *European Journal of Industrial Relations*, 13/3: 269–280.

Stuart, M, (2009, forthcoming) 'The United Kingdom: the sound of one hand clapping?' in Winterton, J. (ed.) *Trade Union Strategies for Competence Development*, Routledge, London.

Stuart, M. and Martinez Lucio, M. (2005a) 'Partnership and the modernization of employment relations: an introduction' in Stuart, M. and Martinez Lucio, M. (eds) *Partnership and the Modernisation of Employment Relations*, Routledge, London, pp.1–22.

Stuart, M. and Martinez Lucio, M. (2005b) 'Assessing the principles, risks and gains of partnership: a survey analysis of trade union representatives' in Stuart, M. and Martinez Lucio, M. (eds) *Partnership and Modernisation in Employment Relations*, Routledge, London, pp.101–119.

Stuart, M. and Martinez Lucio, M. (2008) 'The new benchmarking and advisory state: the role of the British advisory, conciliation and arbitration service in facilitating labour – management consultation in public sector transformation', *Journal of Industrial Relations*, 50: 736–751.

Stuart, M., Charlwood, A., Martinez Lucio, M. and Wallis, E. (2006) *Union Modernisation Fund: interim evaluation of first round*, DTI Employment Relation Research Series No. 68, DTI, London.

Sullivan, R. (2007) 'Labor market or labor movement? The union density bias as barrier to labor movement revitalisation', paper presented to *Work, Employment and Society conference*, Aberdeen.

Taira, K. (1980–1981) 'Labor and business in a new international economic order: will workers of the world unite?', *Hokudai Economic Papers*, 10: 68–87.

Tailby, S., Richardson, M., Upchurch, M., Danford, A. and Stewart, P. (2007) 'Partnership with and without trade unions in the UK financial services: filling or fuelling the representation gap?', *Industrial Relations Journal*, 38/3: 210–228.

Tattersall, A. (2006) 'There is power in coalition: a framework for analysing the practice of union-community coalitions' <comm-org.wisc.edu/chapters2006/tattersall.htm>.

Taylor, P. and Bain, P. (2003) 'Call centre organising in adversity: from Excell to Vertex' in Gall, G. (ed.) *Union Organising: campaigning for trade union recognition*, Routledge, London, pp.153–172.

Taylor, R. (1999) '"What are we here for?" George Woodcock and trade union reform' in McIlroy, J., Fishman, N. and Campbell, A. (eds) *British Trade Unions and industrial politics volume two: the high tide of trade unionism, 1964–79*, Ashgate, Aldershot, pp.187–216.

Terry, M. (2003) 'Can "partnership" reverse the decline of British trade unions?', *Work, Employment and Society*, 17/3: 459–472.

Thompson, M. and Bemmels, B. (2000) 'British Columbia: the parties match the mountains' in Swimmer, G. (ed.) *Public-sector Labour Relations in an Era of Restraint and Restructuring*, Oxford University Press, Don Mills, pp.97–127.

Thompson, P. and Bannon, E. (1985) *Working the System: the shop floor and new technology*, Pluto Press, London.

Thompson, P., Warhurst, C. and Findlay, P. (2007) 'Organizing to learn and learning to organize: three case studies on the effects of union-led workplace learning', Research Series, No. 2, TUC unionlearn, London.

Tilly, C. (1978) *From Mobilization to Revolution*, McGraw-Hill, New York.

Towers, B. (2003) 'Comparisons and prospects: industrial relations and trade unions in North America and Britain' in Gall, G. (ed.) *Union Organising: campaigning for trade union recognition*, Routledge, London, pp.173–190.

Trades Union Congress (1999) *Partners for Progress: 'New Unionism' at the workplace*, TUC, London.

Trades Union Congress (2001) *Reaching the Mission Millions*, TUC, London.

Trades Union Congress (2003) *A Perfect Union? What Workers Want from Unions*, TUC, London.

Trades Union Congress (2005) *Supporting Union Reps*, TUC, London.

Trades Union Congress (2006) 'Review of TSSA Travel Trade Campaign', unpublished report, TUC, London.

Trades Union Congress (2007a) *General Council Report 2007*, TUC, London.

Trades Union Congress (2007b), *Workplace representatives: a review of their facilities and facility time – TUC response to the DTI consultation document*, London.

Trades Union Congress (2008) *TUC Activist Academy: organizing at work*, TUC, London.

Turner, L. (2005) 'From transformation to revitalization: a new research agenda for a contested global economy', *Work and Occupations*, 32/4: 383–399.

Turner, L. and Hurd, R. (2001) 'Building social movement unionism: the transformation of the American labor movement' in Turner, L., Katz, H. and Hurd, R. (eds) *Rekindling the Movement: labor's quest for relevance in the 21st Century*, ILR Press, Ithaca, NY, pp.9–26.

unionlearn (2006) *Making a Real Difference – union learning reps: a survey*, unionlearn, London.

unionlearn (2008) *Organising for Learning – building union organisation through learning*, unionlearn, London.

Unison (2007) *Learning and Organising Services – Annual Review 2007*, Unison, London.

United Steelworkers' Union (2008) 'Steelworkers' door remains open to Dofasco employees: USW steps back from process that would have led to bargaining with Arcelormittal' <www.usw.ca/program/content/4935.php?lan=en>.

Upchurch, M., Danford, A., Richardson, M. and Tailby, S. (2008) *The Realities of Workplace Partnership*, Palgrave, Basingstoke.

Urquhart, I. (2007) 'Stinging letters from a labour house divided', *Hamilton Spectator*, 18 September.

US Census Bureau (2006 and earlier issues) *Statistical Abstract of the United States*, <www.census.gov/statab/www/>.

USDAW (2007a) 'Academy reps help boost membership' USDAW website, <www.usdaw.org.uk/getactive/successful_organising/1197975170_26501.html>.

USDAW (2007b) 'Stand-down reps – the way forward in 2008', USDAW website <www.usdaw.org.uk/getactive/news/1197899313_396.html>.

US Department of Labor, Bureau of Labor Statistics (2006) 'Major Work Stoppages in 2005' <www.bls.gov>.

US Department of Labor, Bureau of Labor Statistics. (2008a) 'Union Members in 2007' USDL News Release 08–0092 <www.bls.gov/news.release/pdf/union2.pdf>.

US Department of Labor (2008b) <erds.dol-esa.gov/query/getOrgQryResult.do>.

US National Labor Relations Board (2006) *Seventieth Annual Report of the National Labor Relations Board* <www.nlrb.gov/nlrb/shared_files/brochures/Annual %20 Reports/Entire2005Annual.pdf>.

Van Alphen, T. (2007) 'CAW shelves right to strike', *Toronto Star*, 16 October.

Van Dyke, N., Dixon, M. and Carlon, H. (2007) 'Manufacturing Dissent: labor revitalisation, union summer, and student protest', *Social Forces*, 86/1: 193–214.

Visser, J. (2006) 'Union membership statistics in 24 Countries', *Monthly Labor Review*, 129/1: 38–49.

Voss, K. and Sherman, R. (2000) 'Breaking the iron law of oligarchy: union revitalization in the American labor movement', *American Journal of Sociology*, 106/2: 303–349.

Waddington, J. (2003) 'Trade union organization' in Edwards, P. (ed.) *Industrial Relations: theory and practice*, Blackwell, Oxford, pp.214–256.

Waddington, J. and Kerr, A. (2000) 'Towards an organising model in Unison? A trade union membership strategy in transition' in M. Terry (ed.) *Redefining Public Sector Unionism*, Routledge, London, pp.231–263.

Wallihan, J. (1985) *Union Government and Organization*, BNA Books, Washington.

Wallis, E., Stuart, M. and Greenwood, I. (2005) 'Learners of the workplace unite!' An empirical examination of the UK trade union learning representative initiative', *Work, Employment and Society*, 19/2: 283–304.

Waterman, P. (1998) *Globalization, Social Movements and the New Internationalism*, Mansell, London.

Weir, J. (2006) 'Increasing inter-union co-operation and co-ordination: the B.C. Federation of Labour Organising Institute' in Kumar, P. and Schenk, C. (eds) *Paths to Union Renewal: Canadian experiences*, Broadview Press, Toronto, pp.295–305.

Western, B. (1997) *Between Class and Market: postwar unionization in capitalist democracies*, Princeton University Press, Princeton.

Whitehall College (n.d.) <www.poptel.org.uk/whitehall-college/whitehall/pdf/diduno.pdf>.

Willman, P. and Bryson, A. (2006) 'Accounting for collective action: resource acquisition and mobilisation in British Unions', CEP Discussion Paper No 768, LSE, London.

Willman, P. and Bryson, A. (2007) 'Union organization in Great Britain', *Journal of Labor Research*, 28/1: 93–115.

Willman, P., Morris, T. and Aston, B. (1993) *Union Business – trade union organisation and financial reform in the Thatcher years*, Cambridge University Press, Cambridge.

Wills, J. (2003) 'Organizing in transport and travel: learning lessons from the TSSA's Seacat campaign' in Gall, G. (ed.) *Union Organising: campaigning for trade union recognition*, Routledge, London, pp.133–152.

Wills, J. (2004a) 'Campaigning for low paid workers: The East London Communities Organisation (TELCO) Living Wage Campaign' in Healy, G., Heery, E. and Taylor, P. and Brown, W. (eds) *The Future of Worker Representation*, Palgrave, Basingstoke, pp.264–282.

Wills, J. (2004b) 'Trade unionism and partnership: evidence from the Barclays-Unifi agreement', *Industrial Relations Journal*, 35/4: 329–343.

Wills, J and Simms, M. (2004) 'Building reciprocal trade unionism in the UK', *Capital and Class*, 82: 59–84.

Wilson, T. (2007) *The Future for Unions*, Unions 21, London. Available online at: http://www.unions21.org.uk/pubs/ffu.pdf.

Wojtczak, H. (2005) *Railwaywomen: exploitation, betrayal and triumph in the workplace*, The Hastings Press, Hastings.

Wood, H. and Moore, S. (2007) *Union Learning, Union Recruitment and Organising*, Unionlearn with TUC, London.

Workers Uniting (2008) 'About the merger' <www.workersuniting.org/default.aspx?page=281>.

Workplace Information Directorate (2008) 'Union membership in Canada – January 1, 2007' <www.hrsdc.gc.ca/en/lp/wid/union_membership.shmtl>.

Yates, C. (2000) 'Staying the decline in union membership: union organising in Ontario, 1985–1999', *Relations Industrielles*, 55/4: 640–675.

Yates, C. (2006) 'Women are the key to union renewal: lessons from the Canadian labour market' in Kumar, P. and Schenk, C. (eds) *Paths to Union Renewal: Canadian experiences*, Broadview Press, Toronto, pp.103–112.

Index

Lightning Source UK Ltd.
Milton Keynes UK
UKOW01n0622130416

272151UK00011B/123/P

Also edited by Gregor Gall

UNION ORGANISING
Campaigning for Trade Union Recognition

UNION RECOGNITION
Organising and Bargaining Outcomes

THE FUTURE OF UNION ORGANISING
Building for Tomorrow

Also written by Gregor Gall

THE MEANING OF MILITANCY?
Postal Workers and Industrial Relations

THE POLITICAL ECONOMY OF SCOTLAND
Red Scotland? Radical Scotland?

SEX WORKER UNION ORGANIZING
An International Study

LABOUR UNIONISM IN THE FINANCIAL SERVICES SECTOR
Struggling for Rights and Representation

Union Revitalisation in Advanced E

St Helens College